Deviance and Social Control in Chinese Society

edited by
**Amy Auerbacher Wilson
Sidney Leonard Greenblatt
Richard Whittingham Wilson**

The Praeger Special Studies program—utilizing the most modern and efficient book production techniques and a selective worldwide distribution network—makes available to the academic, government, and business communities significant, timely research in U.S. and international economic, social, and political development.

Deviance and Social Control in Chinese Society

Praeger Publishers   New York   London

Library of Congress Cataloging in Publication Data
Main entry under title:

Deviance and social control in Chinese society.

    (Praeger special studies in international politics
and government)
    Includes index.
    1. China—Social conditions—Congresses.
2. Deviant behavior—Congresses. 3. Social control—
Congresses. I. Wilson, Amy Auerbacher, 1934-
II. Greenblatt, Sidney L. III. Wilson, Richard W.,
1933-
HN672.D48   301.6'2'0951   76-12886
ISBN 0-275-56470-3
ISBN 0-275-89650-1 student ed.

PRAEGER PUBLISHERS
200 Park Avenue, New York, N.Y. 10017, U.S.A.

Published in the United States of America in 1977
by Praeger Publishers, Inc.

Printed in the United States of America

Within the disciplines of the social sciences there is a large and growing interest about China. Too often, however, the complaint is heard from within the disciplines that articles or books about China are esoteric or out of step with social science paradigms. Many China scholars, on the other hand, have voiced the feeling that their materials ought to be better known to their colleagues in the disciplines—a goal that can best be achieved through the application of social science techniques to the analysis of Chinese data. The convergence of the disciplines and the China field is as yet incomplete. This book, an exploration of the problem of deviance and social control in Chinese society, attempts to further this convergence.

It is clearly not possible for one volume to cover all aspects of this subject. Our effort has been to present a series of essays, closely related by a common theme, that can elucidate the general question of deviance and social control in such a way as to benefit both China scholars and discipline-oriented social scientists.

In keeping with the goal of convergence, the scholars whose works are represented here are drawn from a variety of disciplines, and they address deviance and social control from the unique perspectives of those disciplines. The role of the editors has been to define the general parameters of this topic, to select appropriate participants for a preliminary conference on the topic that was held at the International Center of Rutgers University on November 29 and 30, 1975, and to serve as an editorial board for the proceedings. The conference was attended by virtually all of those whose work appears in this volume (two people, who were not able to attend, sent their papers). There were others who did not contribute papers to the publication but whose participation made a notable impact on the proceedings. From this latter group we would expecially like to mention John Philip Emerson, Rensselear Lee, Ta-ling Lee, Miriam and Ivan London, Janet, Salaff, and Ralph Thaxton.

We added one paper that had previously been published elsewhere, that of Professor Victor H. Li of the Stanford University Law School, because although we were unable to secure a representative of the legal field at the conference, conference participants agreed unanimously that an essay in the area of criminality and law would be an essential ingredient in any publication addressing the topic of deviance and social control.

Just as we have sought to stimulate authors in the China field to peruse their materials with a new set of lenses, so we ourselves have been stimulated to approach the business of conference organization with a fresh and highly self-conscious viewpoint. In fact, we think our approach sufficiently novel to be of value to colleagues who might, in keeping with the legacy of C. Wright Mills, conceive of their mission in a similarly self-conscious way. As the essential first step of the project we formulated the general parameters of the conference. We then wrote to a number of scholars whom we felt might have an interest in pursuing this topic from the vantage point of their own scholarly perspectives. We were aware that these individuals had never done work in the area of deviance and social control as such. We were also conscious that by failing to address the topic of deviance as sociologists usually do—in terms of "nuts, sluts, and perverts," or a "hoods, junkies, queers, hookers, and crazies" approach—we might well earn the opprobrium of fellows in the disciplines most concerned with this area. Yet we opted for an approach which acknowledges that any meeting ground between the discipline and the China field must be located where expertise really is. There are few China specialists who are experts on deviance and social control; there are many students of China who know their specific intellectual terrains exceedingly well and for whom the topic of deviance and social control serves as a fresh impetus to research. Our attempt, therefore, was to convince them that a paper focused on this topic would not only help reveal the possibilities of a new approach but could also add another dimension to their work. From our initial letters we were gratified to receive enthusiastic support; we were also encouraged by the positive response of Praeger editors with regard to publishing the conference papers. Since the budget for the conference was quite small, we asked the participants to assume the costs for paper preparation, to find funding for their travel expenses to and from the conference, and to help defray some of the food costs at the conference. This they most cheerfully did. A small conference budget provided by Rutgers University helped to cover some of the overhead costs. The major lesson learned from this procedure was that a conference with a topic that appeals to a number of scholars can attract them without major funding and can be as stimulating as some of the undertakings that characterized a past period of greater affluence.

Perhaps in response to a developing awareness of the relative isolation of those in Asian studies from their discipline-oriented social science colleagues, there has been a growing trend in the China field for conference frameworks to be structured around a set of interlocking hypotheses or, at least, around a series of questions that participants are expected to use as the bases for the development of their own contributions. As social scientists, we feel this method of exploring a new field of inquiry is premature and very possibly counterproductive in terms of stimulating future work. In the initial stages of exploration of a new approach, we believe that a set of predetermined hypotheses or guidelines places restrictions upon data that inhibit the capacity of succeeding scholars to develop more fruitful hypotheses. Although we set forth, for those scholars who were invited to the conference, some definitions of deviance and social control derived from social science literature, we asked them to explore the implications of this approach in terms of the work they knew best, drawing them out in a flow of correspondence that preceded the conference and organizing the conference intself in such a way as to maximize their thoughtful and critical involvement. No attempt was made to cover every aspect of deviance and social control in Chinese society. Rather, the conference attempted to examine this issue from a perspective sufficiently different as to make the utility of the approach itself a subject of debate. As a result, the conference was an exceptionally lively one in which a good part of the effort went into a refinement of those definitions of deviance and social control that yield fruit when applied to Chinese materials. A number of broad themes also emerged, such as the questions of moral entrepreneurship by political authority and of the salience of political deviance. These now appear as prominent features around which future work might usefully concentrate and about which useful hypotheses could be generated.

In this volume we have presented the material in a manner that we hope will most clearly reveal for the readers the goals as they were initially formulated. Following an introduction where some basic theoretical issues are raised and some general themes of the conference discussed, the essays are presented in an order such that those addressing broad underlying cultural or social factors precede more specific analyses of deviance and social control in various social settings.

We hope this volume will stimulate others to further research. For our own part, it is our intention to organize additional conferences to explore other approaches or areas of interest to social scientists that are still underemphasized within the China field. Currently we are in the process of organizing a conference on "Values and Value Change in Chinese Society." We expect to follow this conference with one that will focus on organizational behavior. In preparing these conferences, each of the editors has volunteered to write the introduction for one particular volume, although all three of the editors have helped in the general selection of conference topics, the preparation of guidelines, the selection of participants, and the editing of the proceedings.

The editors wish to give special thanks to the Rutgers Research Council for providing partial funding for the conference. We are happy to acknowledge our debt to Yü Chün-fang, Assistant Professor of Religion at Rutgers University, for graciously providing the calligraphy that decorates the glossary of this volume. In addition, we extend our gratitude to Kay Tranfo, Grace Kurkowski, and Helen Nourse of the Rutgers International Center for helping to organize the conference and for assistance in the preparation of the manuscript. Thanks are also due to Joyce Viscardi, a student in Asian Studies at Princeton University, who serve as rapporteur for the conference, made a number of stimulating comments, and gave us invaluable aid in preparing the index to this volume.

The Chinese terms used throughout this volume have been transliterated into the new pinyin system, which is now the official romanization adopted in the People's Republic of China. For the benefit of readers familiar with common proper names spelled according to the Wade-Giles system, the following representative list is offered:

Chen Boda	(Ch'en Po-ta)
Cheng Yi	(Ch'eng I)
Ding Ling	(Ting Ling)
Hao Ran	(Hao Jan)
Jiang Qing	(Chiang Ch'ing)
Lin Biao	(Lin Piao)
Liu Shaoqi	(Liu Shao-ch'i)
Mao Zedong	(Mao Tse-tung)
Wang Yangming	(Wang Yang-ming)
Zhou Enlai	(Chou En-lai)
Zhu Xi	(Chu Hsi)

CONTENTS

DEVIANCE AND SOCIAL CONTROL IN CHINESE SOCIETY: AN INTRODUCTORY ESSAY
Amy Auerbacher Wilson

American Sociologists

Social deviance has been a rich research area for American scholars over the past ten to fifteen years, with an outpouring of exciting, often controversial, writing. Yet the lack of comparative perspective in this field remains glaring. In the literature minimal attention has been given to deviance and social control in alternative social settings, either temporally or geographically, and the field is the poorer for this omission. Interestingly enough, scholars who have restricted themselves to examining a single social system—contemporary American society—have not even achieved consensus on the nature of deviance within that system. Rather than being a source of gloom, however, the current open-ended state of the field of deviance may actually be fortuitous. Since there is no one firmly entrenched paradigm, a deviance theory with broad explanatory power can be constructed without requiring a virtual scientific revolution.[1]

In parallel fashion, social science literature on modern Chinese society has been growing apace, from modest beginnings a decade or two ago. Today Chinese studies encompass an eclectic array of models for analyzing that society. Within this fluid and disparate field, much room exists for exploration and innovation. Among the possibilities for lively and imaginative research by China specialists are analyses of deviance and its control. Empirical research on these topics not only can enlighten us in general by providing a cross-cultural dimension to these vital social processes, but also can further refine and corroborate our armchair theorizing. In both a substantive and theoretical sense, then, the collective efforts that have produced this volume represent ground-breaking work.

A first step toward rectification of the parochialism found in the study of deviance is to take a critical inventory of existing approaches. This means asking to what extent major models of deviance, derived inductively from observations of American society, can be generalized to other societies. It means specifying approaches that seem to offer promise for more "ecumenical" theorizing about deviance and social control. The current state of the field is such that concepts, propositions, and theoretical models comprise a tantalizing but unwieldy assortment of prospective explanatory tools. Here the canon of parsimony—attempting to explain the most with the least—could use a goodly share of reaffirmation. In short, in the quest for ecumenicism, the basic concepts of social deviance need to be approach with a critical eye toward both efficiency and universality.

THE THEORETICAL BOUNDARIES OF DEVIANCE

Social deviance has two dimensions, according to a leading student of the subject. It is action that fails to conform to a particular rule, or action that is regarded by other people as deviant.[2] This definition combines older formulations that have regarded deviance simply as rule-breaking behavior with more recent conceptions stressing societal reaction to deviance, the latter known also as the "labelling" approach to deviance. At present this synthesis of normative (i.e., rule-breaking) and social control (societal reaction) aspects of deviance offers the most theoretical promise.

Rejection of a strictly normative, or rule-breaking, definition of deviance has stemmed in part from methodological problems encountered in using norms as the criterion for distinguishing nonconformity from conformity. The fit between norms as abstract standards for behavior and specific concrete acts is difficult to ascertain, especially so in complex, pluralistic societies where, for example, a given act may conform to one norm yet deviate from another. Moreover, as a number of scholars have pointed out, in modern societies such as the United States, where the differentiation of deviants is increasingly contingent upon circumstances of situation, place, social and personal biography, and bureaucratically organized activities of agencies of control, the relation between deviance and norms becomes tenuous indeed.[3] However, despite the fact that behavior may be erroneously identified as rule-breaking, departure from some normative standard is at least alleged whenever behavior is labelled as deviant. For this reason, a general theory of deviance requires reference to the normative order.

If social control is broadly conceptualized to include perception of and reaction to deviance, any general analysis of deviance, by virtue of our two-dimensional definition, must also include social control variables. In addition to the normative order and social control, both of which are definitionally linked to deviance, a third minimal element in a parsimonious theory of deviance is the characteristics of those individuals who objectively break rules and/or are regarded as doing so.[4] Writings on deviance have come a long way from the untenable position that deviants are necessarily a different breed and that the cause of deviance is the deviant's distinctiveness. Nonetheless, since it is individuals who experience the social phenomenon we know as deviance, individual variables remain integral to a general theory.

The following discussion by no means presumes to be definitive. Rather, by highlighting a few conceptual issues that seem crucial and juxtaposing the abstract with some concrete illustrations from the American and Chinese cases with which we are most familiar, we hope to set the stage for the subsequent chapters on contemporary Chinese society and suggest other fruitful areas for comparative research.

NORMS

Generally, norms are conceptualized as ideals of behavior—what behavior ought to be rather than actual patterns of social action. A conceptual distinction is usually made between norms and values. The latter, Smelser suggests, set forth in general terms the desirable end states that act as guides to human endeavor, whereas the former are more specific in nature, designating certain regulatory principles necessary if values are to be realized.[5]

Norms vary in content, and an important aspect of normative content is the reflection of the dominant value orientation of the society in which the norms occur. As Erikson has ably demonstrated in his study of early Massachusetts, the predominantly religious value orientation of the Puritans affected the content of Puritan norms and hence the types of deviance occurring within the community. Witches and religious heretics were, therefore, peculiarly Puritan problems.[6] On the other hand, as Becker for one has indicated, laws or other norms may reflect the interest of their specific creators—what he calls the "moral entrepreneurs" of a society—rather than broadly shared societal values.[7] So long as one maintains the possibility of an independent variation of societal values and norms, investigating the degree of congruence between the two in terms of content can then be a fascinating and promising subject for the social scientist interested in the comparative approach.

Today in the People's Republic of China (PRC) the high degree of congruence between values and norms from the standpoint of political content is readily apparent. Parenthetically, we might mention that political deviance has commanded relatively little attention in the United States—at least prior to Watergate. Historically, the American people have been more tolerant of political nonconformity than of other forms of social nonconformity.[8] Moreover, the fact that sociological analyses of deviant behavior have characteristically concentrated upon such substantive topics as mental illness, juvenile delinquency, alcoholism, and sexual aberrations says something about the dominant values and norms of Americans—or of American sociologists, who may be loathe to reveal the less savory side of politics.

Analysts of Chinese society would agree that, to a striking degree, it is the state that plays the role of moral entrepreneur, injecting approved ideological substance into the social rules that are to guide the Chinese masses.[9] In the PRC, therefore, a relatively large proportion of social deviance is regarded as political deviance. The mapping of political vs. nonpolitical normative terrains can disclose much about the current functioning of Chinese society. As Huang documents in his essay for this volume, bad women in Chinese socialist literature typically manifest sexual misbehavior, action that violates traditional Confucian ethics even more than present-day ideological norms. That these rural women in particular are not portrayed as engaging in political deviance seems, in our opinion, in keeping with the relatively subordinate position they still occupy in the countryside.

Normative content may be fruitfully analyzed from the standpoint of salience, or social significance, as well as that of values. Whereas some norms cluster about basic societal requirements, others refer in content to relatively unimportant aspects of social life. By comparing norms in terms of salience, we can draw reasonable inferences about changing social priorities. Hoffmann's chapter on Chinese work incentives convincingly demonstrates how ideological criteria are meant to take precedence in determining worker deviance, yet in fact revolutionary norms continue to conflict not only with stubborn prerevolutionary norms but also with certain economic policy stances of the Chinese Communist Party (CCP) itself. For instance, a perennial problem in Chinese factories involves the use of material incentives rather than preferred nonmaterial means for motivating workers. Similarly, the contributions to this book by Bennett and Greenblatt, both of whom treat the mass campaign phenomenon in the PRC, attest to the complex, contradictory nature of the official party line in China and reveal intricate oscillations in the significance of particular norms from one campaign period to another. We suggest that the very unpredictability of the orthodox normative order has been beneficial for a regime that aspires to being a perpetually revolutionary social system rather than a routinized one. In general, a reasonable degree of normative flexibility is positively functional during periods of rapid social change.

Other promising areas for comparative research on norms include investigation of their range or extent of coverage, their modes of origination and of transmission, and their degree of acceptance.[10] In terms of normative range, it is possible to examine for any given norm or set of normative prescriptions first, the forms of behavior (i.e., range of activities) governed by these norms, and second, the social statuses to which they refer. Relevant to the first type of normative coverage, Munro's chapter probes one distinctive feature of Chinese thinking from imperial times to the present communist era: a tendency to see subjective and objective events as a continuum, a view quite in contrast with the Western (Cartesian) philosophical premise of a mind/body dichotomy. Consequently, the Chinese have defined conformity and nonconformity broadly, to include ideational as well as overtly behavioral components, and the state thus sees itself as legitimately concerned with controlling deviant thought as well as deviant action. With respect to the second type of normative coverage, an impressive collection of research conducted in the United States bears witness to different definitions of conformity and nonconformity according to social status. Similarly, ample evidence from the PRC indicates, for example, that social rules spelling out correct behavior for CCP members or for cadres are frequently at variance with those for individuals with nonelite status. Since party members and cadres are expected to serve as role models for the masses, the more stringent guidelines to which they are subject tend to lessen the desirability of elite positions.[11]

As for modes of origin for norms, crucial questions for comparative research include whether norms are formally enacted, as in the case of law as we know it, or informally derived. In his chapter comparing criminal law in China and the United States, Li notes, as do other Chinese legal scholars, that the Chinese have shown little propensity, historically or contemporaneously, for codifying law. The resultant normative indeterminacy of law, we propose, has potentially significant social consequences. We would concur with Greenblatt that the "elasticity" of Chinese normative precriptions in general is such that the discretionary powers of responsible social control agents in the PRC become awesome indeed.

Closely related to questions of normative origin are those concerning the means for transmission of norms to relevant populations and the socialization processes by which specified societal rules are learned. Abundant—but scattered—information from China is available on such topics as mass communication practices, formal and informal socialization procedures, positive and negative role models, and so forth, all germane to the issue of normative transmission. Li stresses the degree to which educational efforts enhance the accessibility of law for the masses and thus appear to counteract the indeterminacy of legal norms. In China laws are not buried away in law books, Li argues, but rather are rules that are publicized for the benefit of the general public. (To be sure, publicized prescriptions must have clear concrete referents in order for ordinary individuals to comprehend their relationship to actual situations.)

Finally, comparativists might well address the question of normative adherence and acceptance—asking not only whether and to what extent various rules have credibility, but also the degree to which behavior is actually oriented toward adherence. Recognition of the fact that normative adherence has both attitudinal and behavioral components, which vary independently, alerts us to the conceptual complexity of this topic. Normative acceptance is difficult to measure with precision even under the best of circumstances, as observers of American life would admit. Methodological problems are compounded for students of Chinese society, where it is patently not possible at this time to draw up an adequate sample and then conduct intensive questioning. Nonetheless, in a good number of instances we do have disparate pieces of direct evidence from the PRC that, taken together, reinforce scholarly conjectures about the extent of nonconformity, in thought or in action, in China today. As a minor case in point, accounts by the large—and growing—number of foreign visitors often express surprise at the honesty encountered: although hotel rooms are not locked, belongings are rarely stolen. To be sure, visitors' observations are limited in time and space. Yet the high degree of congruence among travelers' experiences and the corroboration with academic opinions do bespeak a new morality with regard at least to common theft.

SOCIAL CONTROL

There exists in every society not only a normative order, or "symbolic universe," but also a system for the control of normative transgressions, an institutionalized structure for maintaining that symbolic universe.[12] Although both deviance and social control are universal facts of social life, each society exercises what Erikson terms a cultural option when it develops a characteristic way of looking at deviant behavior and a characteristic machinery for controlling it.[13] Cultural options are an especially appropriate subject matter for the comparativist. In the current sociological literature on deviance, for example, social control is customarily discussed from the standpoint of specialized, formal agencies: the police, mental institutions, and the like. In the context of a modern society with high degrees of bureaucratization, more informal means of social control, quite understandably, tend to be overlooked. Understating or ignoring the more informal aspects of social control, however, may produce biased results. Such would certainly be the case for Chinese society today, for imbedded within complex organizations are small groups established to perform control, mobilization, and other important functions. The institution of the small group is illuminating as an empirical example of social control whereby the potential contradiction between formal and informal means of social control is decreased.

Social control is used here as the generic term for response to nonconformity and, as such, comprises both perception of and reaction to rule breaking.[14] Although the usual definition of social control is conceptually distinct from norms, we note that norms are, nevertheless, intimately related to perceptive and reactive characteristics of social control. Whether behavior that objectively runs counter to a norm is subjectively deemed deviant depends, in part, on such normative features as salience and degree of acceptance. Acts of judgment may also be affected by the particular normative framework of the judges. To use an illustration from Chinese society, we would expect to find variations among the responses to aberrant behavior made by a family member or a stranger, a functionary of the public security force or the leader of one's small study group (each of whom probably subscribes to a different normative configuration). We should also point out that the normative framework associated with the perception of a given type of deviance does not necessarily coincide with the norms associated with reaction to that deviance. Thomas Szasz, for one, bitingly comments on the fact that "mental illness" is behavior that, in our particular sociocultural terms, is seen as violating psychosocial and ethical norms, yet is treated as a medical issue.[15] Similar kinds of conflict—and the ensuing repercussions—could undoubtedly be brought to light for other forms of deviant behavior.

As social phenomena, responses to deviance have the following intrinsic normative characteristic: there are both prescribed and proscribed (i.e., acceptable and nonacceptable) modes of social control. Normatively prescribed reactions to deviance form a continuum from, say, positive acquiescence to indifference to severe punishment. Although it is conceivably possible to locate any social system along this continuum in accordance with its predominant form of prescribed sanctions, within any given system there is often significant variation among acceptable sanctions. In traditional Chinese society, as an example, we know that legal sanctions were repressive in nature—ideally and actually—but were rarely invoked. The far more prevalent family and clan sanctions tended to be restitutive in nature.

The normative character of social control also raises the obvious question of "deviant"—or proscribed—responses to supposed normative transgressions. Often for reasons of expedience rather than malevolence, social control falls short of desired standards. Given the climate of authority and covertness within which social control agents tend to operate, however, deliberately improper social control activities are not uncommon. Deviant social control, by nature, is difficult to detect. Nonetheless, exposes of official improprieties occuring within the bounds of our own society do emerge periodically. In the contemporary Chinese case, the Cultural Revolution stands out among campaigns aimed at deviance in high places: countless accusations were leveled at responsible persons as revelations of official crime and chicanery came to light.

Furthermore, in any given society the prescribed forms of social control may vary over time. David Rothman has demonstrated in his study of the asylum in the United States how, in theory and practice, perception of and reaction to deviancy and dependency altered with economic, intellectual, and demographic developments. Whereas in the colonial period the customary means for control of these social problems had been informal in nature (with the problem individuals retained within the community), in the Jacksonian era Americans became enamored with asylums. Formal, regularized institutions, generally situated outside the community, consequently became the first rather than last resort for handling the same set of social problems. Rothman also describes the ironic process whereby the initial humanitarian hopes for reform of individuals in asylums succumbed to institutional constraints and pressures that resulted in mere custody of inmates rather than genuine rehabilitation.[16]

In a similar vein, Patricia Griffin, in her work on prision management in the Kiangsi and Yenan periods, deftly documents how Chinese Communist precepts concerning prisons as mechanisms of social control shifted markedly in response to societal exigencies. During these pre-1949 periods party policies regarding release and leniency were tempered by the most pragmatic of considerations: critical food and labor shortages. Griffin found that the scarcer the resources, the more emphasis there was in prison organization on production and education rather than control per se.[17] How social constraints influence modes of control is echoed in Lynn White's detailed case study of China's urban household registration system. In particular, White's chapter specifies the manner in which fundamental economic factors appear to be crucial determinants of the efficacy with which household registration procedures have been carried out in cities since liberation. White concludes that when China's economic climate has been one either of plentitude or of scarcity, control through registration has been less effective than in less dramatic, more moderate economic phases.

As with norms, social control responses can also be compared and contrasted in terms of their content. In concrete terms, typical reactions to rule breaking in the PRC, for instance, include struggle, criticism, and self-criticism, rather unique modes of social control developed and refined by the Chinese Communists. Greenblatt discusses these methods in some detail. The content of social control should be examined analytically as well as in concrete terms. One commonly used set of sociological concepts (already employed with some success to analyze cycles of change in the Chinese countryside since 1949) differentiates normative, coercive, and remunerative modes of obtaining compliance.[18] Hoffmann's chapter, an exposition of social control in the industrial sector of the PRC, traces a long-term transformation from economic (remunerative) to political (generally normative rather than coercive) sanctions. Social control content appears in another context in Greenblatt's chapter on the "manufacture" of deviance. Greenblatt pays special attention to the issue of repressive vs. restrained (i.e., coercive vs. noncoercive) social control procedures when he compares the Soviet purges of the 1930s with the Cultural Revolution and other Chinese mass campaigns.

Predictability and a temporal dimension are other important features, we believe, of social control responses. With regard to the former feature, for the contemporary Chinese case the relative indeterminacy of the normative order, referred to earlier, is mirrored in typical control processes. Both Bennett and Greenblatt comment on the general lack of institutionalization of or regularity in social control. Consequently, the Chinese masses cannot readily anticipate official reactions to wide, vaguely defined areas of potentially deviant behavior. With regard to the latter feature, social control responses may be classified, temporally, as proactive or reactive, to borrow two social science terms.[19]

Reactive responses are those that occur after the fact, once rule breaking has been reported to appropriate social control agents, whereas proactive social control is that in which agents actually search out possible normative transgressions. In contrast to the formal control systems of the United States, which are largely reactive in nature, the Chinese system embraces both types of social control: social control agents expend considerable energy uncovering and treating potential deviance.

We have made several references, both explicit and implicit, to social control agents—the locus from which social control responses emerge, or, more simply, the social audiences that oversee control of deviance. It is our conviction that a pivotal question concerning social control functions in any given social system is the degree of specialization with which they are performed. The field of social deviance would benefit from comparative research on variation among or within social systems in the degree to which social control procedures are performed by those in specialized roles and organizations. Ultimately, theoretical propositions need to be derived concerning the determinants and/or consequences of different degrees of bureaucratization of social control.

A pervasive theme—indeed, probably the dominant one—of this volume (certainly of the lively conference proceedings that shaped our final written product) is the extensive role of the Chinese state as moral entrepreneur. Whether it is justifiable to conclude that the formal state apparatus in China has maintained a virtual monopoly over the defining and enforcing of norms remains, thus far, however, an open empirical question. Li offers one cogent argument against this view in his chapter: criminal laws in the PRC are often enforced informally by small groups rather than by more formal mechanisms. Moreover, Hoffmann provides well-supported evidence that the social control of worker deviance has become increasingly informal in nature, has concomitantly been exercised more often within rather than outside of the work group, and has come to be exercised more frequently at local level base units than at the center.

Whenever social control is performed in the context of a specialized, formal organization, however, its organizational environment becomes a strategic research problem. Comments made above about Griffin's article on communist prison management, published elsewhere, and about White's chapter on household registration in this volume are germane in this regard. In both cases, a number of factors, both intrinsic and extrinsic to the particular agencies responsible—especially macroeconomic factors—significantly affected organizational operation. Greenblatt, too, in his study of deviant recruitment campaigns in the PRC, pinpoints a number of institutional opportunities and constraints that have, alternately, fostered or hindered the success of these campaigns from a social control standpoint. And finally, we draw attention to Bennett's chapter, a more general treatment of mass campaigns, in which several propositions are set forth specifying the conditions that determine the degree to which social control functions are performed by campaigns.

A FUNCTIONAL APPROACH

A crucial juncture between norms and social control concerns the func-tions of deviance in a social system. Following Durkheim's and Mead's earlier and promising contributions, a number of scholars in recent years have adopted a functional approach to deviance. Contrary to common sense (or utopian-functionalist) observations, breaches of norms do not necessarily have negative consequences for a given system. Indeed, deviance may actually operate to strengthen norms and values—what Erikson terms the "symbolic boundaries" of a community—because norms retain their validity only if they are regularly used as a basis for judgment.[20] "Each time the community moves to censure some act of deviation, then, and convenes a formal ceremony to deal with the responsible offender, it sharpens the authority of the violated norm and restates where the boundaries of the group are located."[21]

Using the illustration of political corruption in the PRC, we hope to demonstrate in abbreviated form the general utility of functional analysis by deriving for this specific form of deviance and its control some apparent positive and negative consequences. Opportunities for cadres to engage in corruption, for example, may well increase willingness to take on somewhat risky and hence undesirable positions. In this sense, corruption functions as a positive recruit-ment inducement. Attacks on corruption have, on occasion, functioned as scapegoat mechanisms. In particular, efforts to root out this evil during the Socialist Education Movement of the early 1960s, a period of serious dislocation after the debacle of the Great Leap Forward, seem to have diverted attention from economic hardships and masked the real reasons for deprivations. The normal, ongoing flurries of attention by official control agents to the problem of corruption, on the other hand, no doubt reassured the masses that something was indeed being done about the situation and probably further legitimized the regime in their eyes. Overall, the detection of corruption and punishment of officials' misbehavior have probably served to reaffirm bureaucratic norms and to maintain the symbolic boundaries of the community of officialdom.[22] Despite the number of positive functions political corruption fulfills in the PRC, its negative functions should not be minimized, especially the deleterious effects experienced by individuals and local units most intimately associated with con-crete acts of embezzlement, bribery, graft, and so forth. We would conclude, however, that by keeping the perennial problem of corruption relatively con-tained, the CCP—unlike its Guomindang or Qing predecessors—has been able to avert a good many of its potentially negative repercussions.

DEVIANCE AND INDIVIDUAL ATTRIBUTES

We conclude our discussion of concepts fundamental to the study of deviance and social control with the notion of individual attributes, characteristics of individuals deviant within a given social system. In order to increase the explanatory and predictive power of a general theory of deviance, propositions must include individual attributes both as independent and as dependent variables. From an empirical standpoint, if research is aimed at the microlevel—i.e., individual level—of social analysis, including individual variables becomes mandatory. In microlevel analysis of deviance the following broad kinds of questions pertain: What social characteristics determine whether or not individuals engage in and/or are regarded as engaging in rule-breaking behavior? What are the different consequences for individuals of experience with deviant activities and/or social control measures? The contributors to this volume have tended to eschew microlevel analysis in favor of a more collective focus. That these writers examine deviance and social control in Chinese society from a basically macrolevel perspective is in part perhaps a methodological artifact, related to the kinds of data available and to the kinds of paradigms generally employed in Chinese studies.

Data problems notwithstanding, certain of the research efforts reported upon in this book do successfully incorporate individual attributes. The work of both Bloom and Wilson is social-psychological in nature, explicitly concerned with behavioral and attitudinal patterns characteristic of Chinese individuals. Bloom has, in the course of his comparative research, tested the cognitive style of individuals from a Chinese sociocultural setting, and he contends that the typically low rank of Chinese respondents on a cognitive dimension that he calls "social principledness" has an important bearing on the manner in which they characteristically react to social control and moral authority. Wilson emphasizes the strong group orientation he found among individuals socialized within several Chinese social environments and suggests some of the implications of such an orientation for deviance and its control. Finally, Bennett's chapter, the result of intensive interviewing of refugees from the PRC, specifies at length a cluster of variables that determines individual vulnerability to the social control effects of campaigns.

CONCLUDING REMARKS

In our necessarily brief discussion of the fundamental concepts of deviance, we have suggested several possible routes comparative research might take. The particular normative, social control, and individual variables singled out in our essay—some of which are also analyzed in subsequent chapters on present-day Chinese society—are but a sampling of ones that could and should be more fully explored in future cross-cultural research.

In addition to conceptual questions, the field of social deviance currently harbors a number of other problems and difficulties that tend to complicate or even jeopardize empirical analysis and theory building. A considerable amount of criticism has been voiced, for instance, about the overly descriptive nature of the field of deviance. Frustrations also arise from the extremely relativistic nature of deviant phenomena, for which there appear to be no absolute standards or guidelines. Rather, each social system establishes its own norms governing behavior and its own limits of tolerance for violations of those norms. What a comparative perspective can clarify is the continuum that distinguishes purely unique from more general features of deviance and its control.

As a further example of a problem area in studying deviance, methodological difficulties appear unusually irksome, compounded in part by the innate secrecy of much rule-breaking activity and by the selectivity of social control responses. Finally, accepting official definitions of deviance as given is a common practice that, unfortunately, exposes scholars in the field of deviance to the serious risk of a bias that works against the relatively powerless and in favor of the powerful.

Although a comparative approach to deviance can offer answers to certain of these problems—as demonstrated, we believe, by our own comparative work in this volume—it is by no means a final solution. We have mentioned a few trouble spots in hopes that awareness of them will benefit further pioneering work on deviance and, ultimately, resolve some of the issues.

NOTES

1. For the relation between these concepts, see Thomas S. Kuhn, *The Structure of Scientific Revolutions* (Chicago: University of Chicago Press, 1962).

2. Howard S. Becker, *Outsiders: Studies in the Sociology of Deviance* (New York: The Free Press, 1963), p. 14.

3. See especially John I. Kitsuse, "Societal Reaction to Deviant Behavior," *Social Problems* 9 (1962): 256.

4. These three elements have also been singled out by Stanton Wheeler, "Deviant Behavior," in *Sociology: An Introduction*, ed. Neil J. Smelser (New York: John Wiley, 1967), pp. 608-10.

5. Neil J. Smelser, *Theory of Collective Behavior* (New York: The Free Press, 1962), pp. 24-27.

6. Kai Erikson, *Wayward Puritans: A Study in the Sociology of Deviance* (New York: John Wiley, 1966).

7. Howard S. Becker, op. cit., pp. 146-73.

8. Irving Louis Horowitz and Martin Liebowitz, "Social Deviance and Political Marginality: Toward a Redefinition of the Relation between Sociology and Politics," *Social Problems* 15 (1968): 280-96.

9. For a discussion of this topic see Richard W. Wilson, "Political Authority as Moral Entrepreneur in China," *Issues and Studies* 12 (1976):1-15.

10. These normative categories are among those listed by Judith Blake and Kingsley Davis, "Norms, Values, and Sanctions," in *Handbook of Modern Sociology*, ed. Robert E. L. Faris (Chicago: Rand McNally, 1964), pp. 464-65.

11. For a discussion of career choices facing cadres, see Michel Oksenberg, "Getting Ahead and Along in Communist China: The Ladder of Success on the Eve of the Cultural

Revolution," in *Party Leadership and Revolutionary Power in China*, ed. John Wilson Lewis (Cambridge: Cambridge University Press, 1970), pp. 304-47.

12. The concept "symbolic universe" is that of Peter L. Berger and Thomas Luckmann, *The Social Construction of Reality* (Garden City, New York: Doubleday, 1966).

13. Kai Erikson, op. cit.

14. Recently the even broader rubric "collective definition" has been suggested as a convenient shorthand expression that bridges norms and social control by incorporating rule creation and rule enforcement. In particular, see F. James Davis and Richard Stivers, eds., *The Collective Definition of Deviance* (New York: The Free Press, 1975).

15. Several of Szasz's works address this question. See especially Thomas S. Szasz, *The Myth of Mental Illness: Foundations of a Theory of Personal Conduct* (New York: Harper and Row, 1961).

16. David J. Rothman, *The Discovery of the Asylum: Social Control and Disorder in the New Republic* (Boston: Little, Brown, 1971).

17. Patricia Griffin, "Prison Management in the Kiangsi and Yenan Periods," *The China Quarterly* 58 (1974): 310-31.

18. G. William Skinner and Edwin A. Winckler, "Compliance Succession in Rural Communist China: A Cyclical Theory," in *A Sociological Reader in Complex Organizations*, ed. Amitai Etzioni (New York: Holt, Rinehart, and Winston, 1969), pp. 410-38.

19. Albert J. Reiss, Jr. and David J. Bordua, "Environment and Organization: A Perspective on the Police," in *The Police: Six Sociological Essays*, ed. David J. Bordua (New York: John Wiley, 1967), pp. 25-55.

20. Kai Erikson, op. cit.

21. Ibid., p. 13.

22. Ibid.

BELIEF CONTROL: THE PSYCHOLOGICAL AND ETHICAL FOUNDATIONS

Donald J. Munro

INTRODUCTION

A major target of official Chinese social control policy is the beliefs or opinions held by ordinary Chinese people on nontrivial topics. Above all other characteristics of life in the People's Republic, this generates the strongest negative response from citizens in a liberal democracy like the United States. Our own perspective is informed by a legacy manifest in the old English legal maxim: "The thoughts of man are not tryable; the devil alone knows the thoughts of man." One writer has summarized this legacy as follows:

> It is no accident that in America we find this persistent inclination to focus on the externals of behavior. . . . Historically it has been one of the tasks of liberalism to defend the distinction between a man's mind and his actions, his intentions and his deeds; otherwise there seemed a danger of the individual not being able to defend himself against state action.[1]

The liberal democratic attitude toward opinion control is associated with certain assumptions about the human mind. These are that, as individuals, people possess a private realm (that of consciousness, beliefs, or thought) that normally does not affect others and that should remain immune from tampering by external agents. In other words, the human personality is divided into a social

This chapter is drawn from the author's forthcoming book, *The Concept of Man in Contemporary China.*

and a private realm, and society should have no control over the latter. In *On Liberty*, Mill wrote:

> How much of human life should be assigned to individuality and how much to society? Each will receive its proper share if each has that which more particularly concerns it. To individuality should belong the part of life in which it is chiefly the individual that is interested; to society, the part which chiefly interests society.[2]

One component of individuality is what Mill calls "the inward domain of consciousness, demanding liberty of conscience." Normally, two distinct claims are mixed together in this kind of doctrine. One is the psychological claim that matters of belief usually do not affect other people. The other is the normative contention that they should remain the sole concern of the believer and be immune from manipulation.

Chinese justifications for the control of beliefs also rest on certain assumptions about the nature of the mind. The key psychological assumption is that such mental events as knowing and believing are usually accompanied by covert promptings to act, likely to emerge as open conduct. Because such acts may affect others, the existence of the promptings brings private beliefs and opinions into the public realm. This is a normative claim, namely that opinions are justifiably subject to direction by agents (the rulers) representing those who might be affected by the promptings. The position on the nature of the mind is shared by Confucian and Chinese Marxist thinkers. It is important to underscore this continuity with the past as a means of stressing the strength of the position in China. Otherwise, one might be tempted to regard it as ephemeral and treat it less than seriously. In the analysis that follows, my intent is to explain rather than advocate the Chinese position.

Although the existence of promptings supposedly justifies control of beliefs, the Chines view of the mind does not support claims about individual "responsibility" for acts, as we normally understand that term. Thus, although a prompting may be identified as an act of "will" (*zhi*), this should not be confused with "free will." The present study will conclude with an examination of this matter and its implications for the interpretation of deviant behavior.

CONFUCIAN VIEWS

In speaking of the association of promptings to act with knowing and believing, we are talking about subjective beginnings of action that in some instances were regarded as having their own power to emanate from the mind into overt behavioral form unless impeded by something else, such as a competing thought. Thus we are not discussing specifically the doctrine of the unity of knowledge and action, in which action more frequently refers to publically observable acts. The presumption that these internal events will have outer manifestations may have roots in a general belief during the Zhou period, cited in the *Great Learning*, that "What truly is within will be manifested without."[3] Therein the maxim is cited as a warning to those who do not work to rid themselves of their evil tendencies but vainly seek to disguise them in the presence of virtuous individuals.

In Confucian works, the Chinese terms that I will render with the English "promptings to act" are most frequently *yi* or *zhi*, translated respectively as "intention" and "will." There is considerable evidence that these mental phenomena (and sometimes *si* or "thought" as well)[4] were regarded as emanating forth, such that they potentially leave the person's subjective realm. The language used to describe them reveals that this is the case. For example. Zhu Xi stated that *yi* is an "operation" (*yunyong*) of the mind that "emerges" (*fa*) from it,[5] and that "*yi* is the out-thrust of the mind" (*yi zhe xin zhi suo fa*).[6] He spoke of *zhi* spatially, as the straightforward emanation of the mind (*zhi shi xin zhi suo zhi yi zhi qu di*);[7] *yi* is also spoken of as the activity of the *zhi*. Wang Yangming said that "*yi* is what brings knowledge into operation" (*zhi zhi fa dong shi yi*),[8] and "*yi* is what issues forth (*fa bian*) from the mind. Its original essence is knowledge. What it settles on is a thing."[9] The fact that *yi* was regarded by Wang Yangming as a prompting to act explains why he could say, "The mental phenomenon consisting of a desire to eat is *yi*; it is the beginning of action."[10] (None of this is to suggest that Zhu Xi and Wang Yangming overlapped completely in their interpretations of these terms. Zhu Xi tended to speak of *yi* as prompting to act that followed upon the observation of a host of options, and as often eventuating in selfish acts, whereas the "will" (*zhi*) was more often associated with acts of social service. No such distinction is evident in Wang's usage.)

Because *yi* suggested an emanation whereby a private mental occurrence has a high probability of becoming a publically manifested act, much of neo-Confucian self-cultivation centered on "making the *yi* sincere" (*cheng yi*). In practice, the effort might involve following up a thought to hate evil intentions with a commitment to regenerate that hate every time a new evil intention appeared.* But of course the will (*zhi*) and the thoughts were also to be watched

---

*It may also include meditative practices, such as concentration on one object so as to train the mind not to be distracted by anything to which it is not committed. There is a recurrent term used to describe this state of conscious awareness of the good and bad possibilities within the mind; this is *xing jue*, which we can translate as "being consciously alert." Some Buddhist discussions of "seeds" (*yin*) in consciousness that come to fruition (*guo*) in action dovetail with Confucian references to inhibiting the growth of evil intentions. The Buddhist accounts stem from the notion of karma and concern ways of preventing the fruition from occurring.

for the same reason. Thus Zhu Xi said that "There must be sincerity in thought (*si*) and watchfulness in action."[11]

There are several explanations for the association of prompting to act with knowing (especially moral knowing) in Confucianism. The first lies in the conception of the moral sense (*yi*) with roots in Zhou thought. *Yi* carries the idea not only of discriminating the proper and the improper but also an awareness of an obligation to abide by the judgment in action. The early Confucians developed a sense of the mind as an internal lawgiver, or commander, that commands obedience to the moral judgments it itself makes. The emergence of this dimension of the mind resulted from the internalization of sovereignty. It involved the transition from an original view of the sovereign as heaven, *shang di* (lord on high) or the king, existing external to the individual and sending down decrees (*ming*) to him, to the eventual view of a sovereign as also existing within the individual himself, issuing decrees to the individual.* When the internal ruler determined something to be right and a duty, that duty was like a command issued to the self. Thus there was a correlation between the dictates of the internal moral sense (*yi*) and the external heavenly injunction (*ming*). The heavenly injunctions were to practice certain acts, which were identical with the things that man, in the new conception, would command himself to do.[12]

Yi continued to convey the sense of "command to the self" in neo-Confucian texts. The command makes action in accordance with the judgment as to what is proper more likely than it would be if there were no such injunction. It does not have a motive force of its own. But neo-Confucians frequently linked action of some kind (covert or overt) with it. Thus Cheng Yi (1033-1108) said that "*yi* is knowing the right and wrong and following principle in action; this is *yi*."[13]

The second and related source of the association of prompting to act with knowledge can be found in the doctrine that there are degrees of knowledge, and that "real knowledge" demands manifestation. The knowledge in question is of duties incumbent on the person studying, and the promptings to act in accordance with that knowledge. Cheng Yi spoke of knowledge as deep (*shen*) and shallow (*qian*).[14] The deeper the knowledge, the more possibility that the promptings will thrust forth to manifest themselves in public conduct:

> When knowing is deep, then action in accord with it will necessarily
> be perfect. There is no such thing as knowing what should be done

---

*Mencius described the internalized ruler when he spoke of a heavenly "nobility" (*tianjue*), referring to certain innate moral tendencies that should be valued above human nobility (*renjue*) or the actual occupation of a position of great rank. Xun Zi spoke of the mind as the heavenly ruler (*tianjun*), a label that had been used exclusively to designate the reigning king during during the West Zhou.

and not being able to do it. Knowing and not being able to act is only a sign that the knowing does not go deep.[15]

The probability of overt action is a function of the degree of knowledge of *li*, and feeling once more enters the picture in that the transition into action in accordance with *li* is invariably accompanied by joy.

The Chinese position here is somewhat reminiscent of the Socratic doctrine that "he who knows the good does the good." The difference lies in the Socratic claim that ignorance is the source of evil, in contrast to the neo-Confucian argument that it is selfish desires that cloud the mind. In any case, the Chinese speak of degrees of knowledge, varying in accordance with the amount of clouding.

Third, the association of promptings to act with the mind's private knowing and thinking operations derives some strength from a general principle in Confucian cosmology. This is that there is an inherent dynamism in all entities that permits them to run a course from imperceptible beginnings to publically observable full development. This was then applied to the mind's operations as well. The term used to refer to the imperceptible beginnings with their inherent dynamism was *ji*, which can be translated as "springs of action." Thus Cheng Yi said, "The man of wisdom knows the springs of things; therefore, he tries to be true to himself at the earliest stir of thought."[16] The assumption is that the thoughts share this probability of issuing forth publically. One had best be wary of evil thoughts and repress them before the manifestation in conduct occurs.

This theory can be textually traced back to the *Book of Changes*, wherein the "springs of things" were also clues to good or bad fortune associated with the full development of the entity in question. Neo-Confucian writers were fond of quoting the following passage from the *Book of Changes*:

> The Master said, to know the springs of action [*ji*] is something spiritual. In his interrelations with superiors, the superior man does not flatter, and in those with subordinates, he is not rude. This is knowing the springs. The springs are the minute origins of movement. They are the first signs one sees of impending good fortune. The superior man acts as soon as he perceives the spring.[17]

Cheng Yi's comments on the above passage are broad enough to make *ji* applicable to any incipient action and not just to happenings in the mind:

> The gentleman sees the possibility of such abuses [as flattery and rudeness] in their minute beginnings; that is why he is able not to go beyond the mean. The words "springs of things" mean minute beginnings of movement, which again are the earliest indications of good and bad fortunes which have not become fully manifested. Only "good fortune" is here mentioned, because if one sees the earliest indications of things, how can he let them develop into bad

fortune? . . . The "hidden" and the "revealed," the "weak" and the
"strong" are complementary pairs. When the gentleman sees the
hidden he knows also the strong. A person who is able to see the
springs of things in such a way, is looked up to by all. Therefore, the
Master praises him saying, "He is a model to the thousand."[18]

Normally, when Chinese and Western commentators, past and present,
have discussed Wang Yangming's doctrine of the unity of knowledge and action,
they have examined it in terms of the enduring juxtaposition in Chinese intellectual history between what David Nivison called knowers and doers.[19] The
distinction goes back to the *Book of History*, which says "It is not knowing but
acting which is difficult." Thus the Chinese term action (*xing*) in Wang's theory
has been understood in the sense of public deed. He certainly did use the term
with that sense very often. And he took note of the fact that few of his con-
temporaries shared the thesis about the unity of knowledge and action.

However, having analytically extracted the general association of a private
prompting to act with knowing, we are in a better position to explain why Wang
put forth his doctrine. He was pointing to a fact about the private realm with
which many philosophers could agree but which ordinary citizens were prone to
forget. Thus the behavioral implication of his position gives the ultimate
explanation. In Wang's view, the danger of theoretically isolating the concepts of
knowledge and action is that people will think only of public, manifest action.
They will forget the likelihood that promptings to act tend to manifest themselves, and they will not take the remedial course of being "watchful over themselves when they are alone."

> The Teacher said, "You need to understand the basic purpose of my
> doctrine. In their learning people of today separate knowledge and
> action into two different things. Therefore when a thought is
> aroused, although it is evil, they do not stop it because it has not
> been translated into action. I advocate the unity of knowledge and
> action precisely because I want people to understand that when a
> thought is aroused, it is already action."[20]

In this passage, "action" is used in two different senses. In the line "has not been
translated into action," it is used in the popular sense of overt behavior. In the
line "when a thought is aroused, it is already action," it is the private prompting.
The association of private promptings with knowing and thinking was present in
the doctrines of all neo-Confucians. Wang was reminding those philosophers in
their writings to take note of the two senses of action, lest ordinary people fail
to repress evil thoughts as they arose.

The Confucian account of the detailed components of the psychological
events involved in clustering believing or knowing and acting differs from that of
the Chinese Marxists. But the assumption that such mental events as knowing
and having promptings are closely associated is common to both.

CHINESE MARXIST VIEWS

There are three ways to approach the association of knowing with prompt-ings to act as revealed in contemporary Chinese accounts. One way is through a consideration of the meaning of *renshi* itself. A second is through a study of the relation between statements about knowing and about having covert motives. A third emerges in a consideration of the concept of *sixiang* or thought.

Contextual analysis of statements employing the term *renshi* for some aspect of knowing reveal that it often carries the sense both of to understand or recognize, and to accept.[21] I use the term "accept" in the sense of having a commitment to act in accordance with what is known and approved or disap-proved. In the statement, "Most cadres have already known (*renshi*) the great meaning (*yiyi*) of participating in physical labor and molding themselves in basic units," knowing involves accepting for themselves. "What is your opinion regarding his marriage?" (*Dui ta di hun shi ni di yisi ru he?*) "What is your inten-tion in doing this?" (*Ni zheyang zuo daodi you shenmo yisi?*)

Even in those cases where no explicit reference is made to meaning (*yiyi*) in the sense of value or significance, the notion of acceptance or approval is often still associated with knowing.

"Once having *renshi* [recognized and accepted] simply the quality of thought of the proletariat, one can then educate the common people."[22] And: "Helped by the branch of the association, I *renshi* [recognize and accept] that I must first have revolutionary thought; this is very important."[23] The same applies to another frequently encountered term meaning "to understand." "Only if we truly work for the masses will they finally *liaojie* [understand or accept] us."[24] And: ". . . in order to *liaojie* [understand, appreciate, or accept] the people deeply, we must integrate ourselves with them forming one body, so that one's work will be done well."[25]

Let us consider the second kind of evidence that suggests a clustering of knowing and having promptings to act. Philosophers and psychologists generally repeat Mao's statement in *On Practice* that rational knowledge (*li xing renshi*) is the reflection of the essence (*ben shen* or *benzhi*) and laws of a thing. Their discussions of the object that is known begin to depart from these Marxist views when at other times they refer to conceptual knowledge as involving knowing the meaning (*yiyi*) of something. Knowing the meaning often refers to understanding the value or significance (or lack of value and threat) of the thing for human beings.[26] Furthermore, knowing the meaning is normally accom-panied by an internal prompting to make one's conduct in some way consistent with the value reflected in the meaning. Chinese analytical studies have adopted the Western term "motive" (*dongji*) as a tool for attempting to understand this prompting. The Chinese terms for meaning are unusual in so often and so clearly having the sense of value or significance:* "He feels that there is no value (*yisi*) in being a common accountant who will not be famous."[27] "There is no value (*yisi*) in talking about the past all the time."[28] "Materialist philosophy, expecially Marxism, has an extremely important guiding significance (*yiyi*) vis-a-vis modern natural science."[29]

Statements that refer to meaning (value or significance) as the object of knowledge (*renshi*) typically take this form: "The students understand (*renshi*) the significance (*yiyi*) of working-points. . . ."[30] "They always organize cadres and the masses to learn Chairman Mao's criticism and related teachings . . . to improve everyone's understanding (*renshi*) of the significance (*yiyi*) of women participating in working."[31] "Fully understanding (*renshi*) the significance (*yiyi*) of carrying out the mission, the cadre-fighters were not afraid of hardship, fatigue . . . and gained good results in planting and improving lands."[32] To know the meaning (*yiyi*) of something in this particular sense is to know two things. One is how the thing in question affects some other thing. This is revealed in the common pattern that takes the form, "X, vis-a-vis Y, as an important meaning." The "meaning" informs us that X works in a certain way

---

*In contemporary Western philosophy, many philosophers influenced by the logical positivist school make a distinction between cognitive and noncognitive meaning or factual and emotive meaning. Cognitive meaning is present only where verification or falsification are in fact possible, or, in the case of "operationalism," where the operations needed to confirm or deny can be set forth. Values are considered to be factually meaningless, in that they are not subject to any possible verification steps. Sentences referring to them do not describe a state of any object or subject or a relation. Statements of value are expressions of feelings of the speaker, and, therefore, called "emotive" statements. This theory makes a sharp differentiation between two senses of meaning that is absent in the Chinese case. When the Chinese speak of knowing (*renshi*) the meaning or significance (*yiyi*) of something, they are speaking of factual, verifiable information that may be partially about values. Recently, some American philosophers have sharply rejected the strict separation of emotive and factual meaning. Examples would include Richard Brandt and William Frankena. The same could be said for most American pragmatists.

Occasionally, when we use the word "meaning" or "meaningful" in English, we are saying that something is valuable or significant, as in the statement, "He regards her as having made a meaningful contribution to the cause." But most often, the terms are value-neutral. Similarly, there are exceptions in the Chinese case. The Chinese term *yisi* can denote "opinion" and "intention." In addition, the Chinese terms for meaning can be used in the sense of an "explanation," that may be provided by a list of various acts suggested by a word, by reference to the idea that produced the word or that it produces itself in hearers or readers, or to the use to which it is put. Thus both *yisi* and *yiyi* can be used in a request for the explanation of a word ("What is meant by this word?"—*Zhege zi you shenmo yiyi/yisi?*).

to induce some change in Y or in people's perception of Y. The other thing that the meaning tells us is that this change is of some value or disvalue. Thus we find such contrasting qualifications of meaning as "X can be of completely positive meaning, or it can be of completely negative meaning" (. . . *ju you jiji yiyi ye keneng ju you xiaoji yiyi*).[33]

All of this is background for pointing to the first type of evidence that knowing the meaning of something also includes the idea of having a resolve to act. The evidence can be found in Chinese studies of "motives." The term used for motive (*dongji*) is a Japanese import (Jap. *doki*).[34] It is not used in Chinese psychological studies with the precision that it has in Western texts. But the confusion in usage is itself revealing: when it is used it calls attention explicitly to the existence in Chinese of an idea that would be understood but never clearly articulated were it not for the new availability of the term *dongji* from Japanese sources. The idea concerns an element of consciousness that incites one to act. And that element is normally present whenever one knows (*renshi*) the meaning of something, if meaning contains the sense of value.

It is possible to examine the interrelations between knowing, meaning, and motive. The most explicit studies of the matter by Chinese themselves pertain to the grasp of moral rules by primary school children. They are said to be able to know the social meanings of their acts, and at the same time to be able to take the social meanings as their own motives. Their motives are then depicted as "moral motives belonging to their knowledge" (*renshi shang di daode dongji*).[35] Elements of consciousness that prompt one to act ("motives") are associated with knowledge rather than with desire, will, or feeling. The implication is that when one knows right and wrong or good and bad, one will also have a prompting to act consistent with that knowledge. There is no guarantee that a particular prompting to act will be successfully realized in overt behavior, in view of the fact that competing promptings also occur. Probability of success is a product of the existence of something called "internal moral experience" (*neixin di daode tiyan*), in which knowledge of moral rules derives more from personal comprehension of the reason for them than from recognizing rules as injunctions laid down by other individuals like parents; this comes with age and training.

Statements about having correct knowledge of a purpose or meaning are also used interchangeably with statements about having a correct motive. For example, in another study, the authors use statements about children having a correct knowledge of the purpose or meaning of study (*dui dushu mudi di renshi zhengque di you X%*)[36] as though they have the same content as statements about children having a correct motive for study (*zhengque di dushu dongji*).[37] Knowing a purpose and having a motive are not distinguished.

Thirdly, evidence for the clustering of knowing and action emerges from a consideration of the term "thought" (*sixiang*). The term has a strict and a loose sense, and the former overlaps in meaning with several other terms that pertain to cognition, thereby serving as the focus for our consideration of clustering. In the strict sense, thoughts are beliefs about the nature of the material world (including human society) or about values that are used by the individual to learn more about the world. They are like hypotheses based on factual evidence, with one exception. They normally entail the prompting to act. Like other cognitive aspects of consciousness in Leninist epistemology, thought is described as "a reflection of objective social, political, and economic reality."[38] This points to the origin and possibility of its conveying accurate information about nature and society. Further, it is the outcome of a deliberative process in which other beliefs about the world play a role. The Leninist view of all knowledge as incremental until absolute knowledge is achieved is maintained. Thus, although *sixiang* has the tentative nature of any hypothesis, it denies a conclusion that all the facts seem to indicate at the moment. One Chinese philosophical analysis distinguishes as follows between the two terms most often translated as thought:

> *Siwei* refers to the process of abstractly summarizing when people reflect on things in the material world through their brain. So it is the process of thinking how to do something. *Sixiang* is the end result of reflection, the outcome of abstract summarization, i.e., after a procedure has already been thought through.[39]

The thoughts or beliefs that emerge from such deliberations serve as instruments for gaining further knowledge (*renshi*) of the world in the same way that hypotheses do: "What kind of thought (*sixiang*) should we use to know and grasp the laws of this objective world?"[40] And: "Marxism is the world view of the proletariat, and it is also their thought-weapon (*sixiang wuqi*) for scientifically knowing and revolutionarily reforming the world."[41]

When used loosely, *sixiang* refers to mental phenomena that are not innate but that are also not the result of any deliberative process and normally have no effectiveness in eliciting additional knowledge about the world. As such, the Chinese characters are best translated as "desire" or "attitude" or "habit." For example, in one source we find that lack of desire to learn some theory is described as having incorrect thoughts (not as having its origin in the thoughts but as being the having of incorrect thoughts). Elsewhere we learn that thoughts, especially those bad ones that have their origin in the old society, become habits; this is another indication of the nondeliberative character of "thoughts" in the loose sense.[42]

There is considerable overlap in the meaning of *sixiang* in the strict sense and rational knowledge or theory.* Both are "reflections" of the objective

---

*In *On Practice*, Mao describes rational knowledge as theory (*lilun*). *Sixiang* in turn often doubles for theory, in that a series of beliefs that in one place is called theory will in

world, contain conclusions that available facts indicate, serve to gain further information about the world, and originate through practice. This overlap permits us to apply any conclusion about the association of thought with the beginnings of action also to knowing, as evidence of the knowing-action cluster.

In both its strict and loose senses, thought is often understood as activating and then directing behavior. Not all thought eventuates in action, but there is a strong tendency for it to do so. To this extent, there is congruence in the content of "knowing a meaning" and "having a thought." Both expressions (when "thought" is understood in the strict sense) refer to kinds of knowledge that are intimately associated with action. In the case of *sixiang*, the explicit statements referring to the role of thought in action are of the following type: "All human acts are directed by thought consciousness."[43] "Thought consciousness is that which directs us in our acting."[44] "Thought is the director of action. Whatever kind of thought there is initially determines what kind of action will follow."[45] This conception of the relation of thought and action differs most immediately from that of our own culture in that we do not regard all actions as having a mental counterpart involving conscious awareness.

Our examination of "knowing a meaning" indicated that such knowing was often associated with having a motive (*dongji*) to act. There is evidence that having thoughts is also linked with having motives. For example, the terms "motive" and "thought" are often used interchangeably: "They can only see that some people who are motivated by individual fame and profit (*geren mingli dongji*) can achieve a successful result, but they do not see that those people would work even more, faster, and better and save more money or material if they had less thoughts of individual fame and profit (*geren mingli sixiang*).[46] Or, we may be told that "gratitude is the kind of thought [*sixiang*] that can be the motive [*dongji*] for positively taking part in revolutionary struggle."[47] Elsewhere the context of statements reveals the goal orientation in *sixiang* that is an integral part of having a motive: "They emphasize democracy but neglect centralism; they stress freedom but neglect discipline. They lack the goal/motive/thought [*sixiang*] of really serving people."[48] Finally, as was shown

---

another be called *sixiang*. Now it is incorrect to state that there is a complete overlap between *sixiang* and theory. Sometimes *lilun* includes explanations that are not as much subject to doubt or in need of further modification or testing as are those included in *sixiang*. But this is by no means true of all "theories." Also, the subject matter of *sixiang* is more restricted in scope than that of *lilun*. The former is most often directly concerned with hypotheses regarding rules of behavior or standards for evaluating, or with methods of solving problems ("after a procedure has already been thought through") likely to be encountered in daily personal or job-related work. *Lilun* can encompass this kind of matter and also explanations or hypotheses that refer to matters of universal concern or that are more comprehensive than "thoughts" of immediate application that can be deduced from them.

above, there can be either correct or incorrect motives. Similarly, thoughts are subject to the same judgments. "All actions based on correct thoughts are correct actions."[49] And the close relation between correct thought and correct acts is evident in the common use of the expression "the virtue of one's thought" (*sixiang pinzhi*) to be used where the context calls simply for the idea "virtue."[50] The former expression is used because any observable virtuous act is the manifestation of a correct thought.

The knowing-acting link provides an argument for control by external agencies over what people learn and how they learn it—that is, over the process whereby they come to know and have beliefs. The rulers can claim a need to ensure that facts learned will be associated with appropriate prompting to act, because those incipient acts can affect others. Knowing or believing never remains the exclusive preserve of a private self. However, it would be erroneous to infer from the Chinese emphasis on the beginnings of action that are clustered with knowing or believing a theory of individual responsibility for his acts by the person who has the promptings. In clarifying this issue, we will be able to point to a significant difference between Chinese and Russian views on the interpretation of deviant behavior.

RESPONSIBILITY

Our examination of terms used in Confucian works to denote what we have called "promptings to act" included *zhi*, usually translated as "will." The modern term is *yizhi*. A Westerner who considers the covert mental beginnings of action is likely to think that the process of freely willing (choosing) to act is often involved somewhere in those beginnings. These two facts constitute sufficient grounds for us to investigate whether or not the notion of "freely choosing" is involved in these promptings. The question has significant policy implications. Traditionally in the West the doctrine of "free will" has been tied to the placement of responsibility for acts primarily on the individual actor, with consequent influences on the interpretation of deviant behavior (criminal justice systems) and the role of education. Our conclusion will be that because China lacks the Western philosophical (Cartesian) and religious heritage that we possess, no conception of free will has been consistently bound up with the modern Chinese view of the mind.

We are not saying that all Chinese Marxists deny the ability of men freely to choose. Nor are we saying that there has not been periodic fluctuation in the degree to which the origin of deviant acts is traced beyond the individual to social practice or prior societal influence. We are saying that there has been no formal and explicit introduction of the concept of individual responsibility in a philosophic sense as was done in Soviet thought in the 1930s. And we are saying that there are historical reasons for this phenomenon on both sides. If Russia is party to the Cartesian legacy, China is heir to a different endowment. For example, there was little room for a concept of personal autonomy in Zhu Xi's contention that all people are so preprogrammed to certain kinds of action that monks cannot help but reestablish shadow family networks in their temples, in spite of their best efforts to avoid the lay world. As a result, the Chinese state in its fosterage capacity is held far more responsible for proper and improper acts of people than it is in other societies. This conclusion emerges most dramatically from a study of the Chinese selective drawing on the new concept of man as a conscious activist that emerged in the Soviet Union in the 1930s.

The new Soviet conception of mind included a distinction between an inner realm of consciousness and an external realm of matter. The Cartesian flavor that pervades this conception of mind stems primarily from the "copy theory" of perception, initiated by Engels and developed by Lenin in *Materialism and Empirio-Criticism*. Crucial to the copy theory is the notion of a distinct external world that is cognized or mirrored in the mind, and that remains separate from it. Lenin also had turned the Marxist observation that the proletariat increases its knowledge of its historic role as it becomes more revolutionary into the very different thesis that consciousness (in the sense of understanding of actual conditions of one's time) can be a major factor in one's ability rapidly and succesfully to achieve revolutionary goals.[51] Writers ever since have been fond of quoting Lenin's remark, "The consciousness of man not only reflects but creates the world."[52] Another pillar of the new view of man was Engel's *Dialectics of Nature*, published in 1925.

The Soviet attempt to make room for a view of free will (*svoboda-voli*) is rooted religiously in some aspects of the Judeo-Christian tradition and philosophically also in Cartesianism. "The world is determined, but at modal points in the chains, the individual has free choice (*svoboda-vybora*)." "Social factors play a role, but individuals can make choices." Such is the philosophical context in which the desire to retain free will is discussed. A place is made for individual responsibility, and that is more important to the Soviets than philosophical clarity. The ontological basis for the reintroduction of free will and individual responsibility is the "reflecting" consciousness that mirrors the objective world. The realm of free will is coterminous with that realm of consciousness. It was not prominent in the reflexology discussions of the 1920s.

Soviet philosophers apply to this distinction between matter and the reflecting consciousness the additional distinction between "internal" and "external" conditions, both of which must be accounted for in any explanation of human action. External (material, environmental) factors, on which the determinist would focus, must be mediated through internal, covert ones. The internal conditions are the locus of free will.

Certain philosophical arguments are mustered to justify free choice. Each arrangement of matter moves itself (each brain is such an arrangement), and each level of arrangement has some laws of its own, not being totally explainable in terms of a lower level of arrangement. Thus human consciousness cannot be totally explained in terms of the instincts or neurological phenomena of lesser animals. The Soviets have never abandoned the Marxist doctrine of the social conditioning of mental events and use it when it serves their purposes. Authority for the reintroduction of free will and individual responsibility, on the other hand, can be found in Lenin's *Materialism and Empirio-Criticism*, where Lenin quoted Engels approvingly:

> Freedom of the will therefore means nothing but the capacity to make decisions with real knowledge of the subject. . . . Freedom therefore consists in the control over ourselves and over external nature which is founded on knowledge of natural necessity.[53]

Lenin then proceeded to comment:

> For until we know a law of nature, it, existing and acting independently and outside our mind, makes us slaves of "blind necessity." . . . The mastery of nature manifested in human practice is a result of an objectively correct reflection within the human head of the phenomena and processes of nature, and its proof of the fact that this reflection (within the limits of what is revealed by practice) is objective, absolute, and eternal truth.[54]

The problems with this concept of mind are twofold. One is the idea that mind is characterized by a will that can be directed to goals of the mind's own choosing and that can be the instrument for changing history. This is not compatible with the other Marxist doctrine that the Soviets also wish to maintain, namely that history creates new men. There is no place for such an individual will in the notion of history as the inexorable force of change. In spite of some suggestion in their writings that the hand of history guides the consciousness that creates, to the outside observer the Soviet position is untenable. Claims about a creative consciousness do not square with Marx's insistence that "it is not the consciousness of men that determines their existence, but, on the contrary, their social existence determines their consciousness." There is no place in this statement for the reverse opinion. Further, the meaning of "create" suggests that individuals, motivated by the desire to put into practice political and philosophical theories, are the initial agents of historical change. It would be a funny kind of "creation" that was manipulated by an unseen hand of history. In short, the Soviet view requires a distortion of the meaning of the notion of creation that removes it from the realm of ordinary usage.

Second, the Cartesian overtones are inconsistent with Marx's own disavowal of dualisms in which one pole is an external, extended separate world and the other pole something that thinks.*

---

*Marx did not reject the dichotomy of consciousness and body or of mind and material objects. But, along with Feuerbach, he put forth a more fundamental category

From a philosophical standpoint, if Soviet (and Chinese) officially approved writings introduce a quasi-Cartesian dualism, they must try to answer the question that dualism raises as to how separate and qualitatively different entities interact. How can we know that copies of objects in our consciousness actually resemble the material objects when the copies belong to something (consciousness) that is qualitatively different from matter? Failing answers, their theories command less attention from thoughtful people than they might.

Problems inherent in the Soviet attempts to cope with the social determination of consciousness are evident if one examines only briefly the shifting official line itself. The zigzag from the behaviorism of the 1920s through the free will voluntarism of the 1930s has been repeated. Beginning about 1948, under Stalin's personal pressure, a strict environmental determinism was reintroduced. Robert Tucker's explanation of the 1948 shift was that Stalin sought a basis for the claim that his own formulae for Russia were not arbitrary but undeniably congenial with natural laws. Furthermore, he was dissatisfied with the rapidity with which Soviet citizens "of their own free choice" were adopting the goals appropriate to the new Soviet man and opted for more intensive environmental manipulation. The theoretical origins of the shift can be traced to Stalin's *Economic Problems of Socialism in the USSR* (1952), where Stalin said that Soviet policy should conform to the "objective processes taking place independently of the will of human beings." See Tucker, *The Soviet Political Mind* (New York: Praeger, 1963), p. 96. Natural laws are immutable, and all events are totally predictable if one grasps the laws. In the realm of human behavior, this orientation led him to champion Pavlovian theories of the conditioned reflex. The laws of conditioning are the counterparts of the inexorable laws in nature and society. The consciousness so important to discussions of autonomous man was minimized in analysis. In the words of the psychologist A. A. Smirnov, "I. P. Pavlov's teachings on temporary connections is a firm basis for understanding all the conscious activity of man." A knowledge of the laws of conditioning coupled with a knowledge of what historical forces were operating through the minds of rulers at any given time theoretically could lead to predictability of behavior. The rulers' minds provide the signals for people to act.

---

that includes both consciousness and material objects, calling it "material nature," "nature," or "material." There was no insistence here that consciousness is the same as matter. The essential claim is that nature is not external to man (Descartes). Rather, man's conceptual tools for understanding nature are a function of his needs and activities, and he uses those tools to produce nature. He produces it in the sense that he acts on objects in such a way as to relate them to his own needs and goals. As he acts on them, he alters them or turns them into social (human) phenomena. Through this process alone does he know them. *Praxis* (practice) is the name for this activity. Discussions with Philip Grier were helpful to me in formulating the above criticism.[55]

Yet even with this return to a "reflexology" having certain echoes of the 1920s, there was still some hedging. Stalin himself spoke of individuals being able to "saddle the laws" of nature and make them serve the interests of the state when they understood the laws. Fair enough as a claim. But it makes nonsense of the other claims in Stalin's so-called Michurinistic determinism. And by the mid-1950s there began another swing back toward the propriety of allowing a place for free choice. In time it became permissible once more regularly to use terms referring to subjective consciousness such as "feelings," "will," and "imagination."*

If anything is clear in the Soviet analysis of man it is that there is an acute muddle on the question of whether or not man is an autonomous actor and what precisely such an actor would be. Out of this muddle the Chinese were able to accept the idea that people consciously pursue goals and that rulers should be concerned with education as it affects the formation of those goals. Thus, the

---

*Commentators on Soviet criminal theory have noticed the inconsistency in the Soviet desire to retain concurrently a doctrine of the social conditioning of mental events and the idea of individual responsibility:

> Taken as a whole, Soviet theory can be designated primarily as "social-determinist." The data that Soviet researchers assemble refer predominantly to social factors—education, occupation, residence, family background, etc.—that "shape" or determine the individual. . . . But for practical purposes, in the Soviet Union as elsewhere, to "explain" (even in a determinist way) is not to excuse. This determinism is "soft" enough to accommodate a voluntarist view of each deviant individual. The criminal and delinquent, corrupted as they may be by unfortunate environments, decide to act—they need not act. Their deviant acts are acts of the "will," for which they bear responsibility.[56]

The idea of free choice is also present in the Soviet arguments for punishment as a deterrent, in that they assume that individuals calculate the utility of performing an act before doing it. The centrality of will and responsibility in Soviet penology departs from the trends of the 1920s, when writers referred to "socially dangerous acts" instead of "crimes" and "measures of social defense" rather than "punishments." The current view is reflected in the words of one Soviet psychologist: "A man takes part in the shaping of his own character and he himself bears a responsibility for that character."[57]

The contrasting social determinism dimension of Soviet criminal theory manifests itself most clearly in generalized explanations of the causes of deviant behavior. I. I. Karpets, Director of the Institute of Criminology in Moscow (1972), put forth three "main general causes of the first order," in which crime is attributed to societal defects caused by past or present capitalism: (1) criminals left over from czarist days, (2) the direct (spies, provocateurs) and indirect (Western radio, films, tourists) subversion by capitalist societies, and (3) "consciousness lag." The last of these accepts the fact that "life" (economic and social organizations) determine consciousness, but not all aspects of a person's consciousness change at the same pace after the transition from capitalism to socialism has been achieved. The roots of those elements of consciousness that lag behind still lie in the czarist period. There are also "second order causes," derived from the first, that include gaps between rural and urban living conditions and between mental and manual laborers.[58]

new Soviet man provided a point of departure for the Chinese concept both in its telescoping of the time period of "human nature" transformation and in its introduction of consciousness as one of the leading foci of transformation efforts.

In their explicit statements, the Chinese would agree with the following claim by Soviet authorities that in attempting to control man the object of one's efforts should be his conscious thoughts:

> Soviet psychology is in contradistinction to bourgeois psychology in this regard—bourgeois psychology takes the "unconscious" as a point of departure, as though it were the central core of man's personality, but Soviet psychology . . . has indicated the dominant role which conscious influences play as compared with unconscious influences. . . . Soviet pedagogy holds the principle that it is the conscious personality of man, his conscious behavior, and his conscious discipline that are to be molded.[59]

But the very inconsistencies in the Soviet theory itself lay little obligation on them to accept the notions of "autonomy," "responsibility," or "free choice." They take seriously the position of the *Preface to a Critique of Political Economy* that in the final analysis, "existence determines reality." (This was reconfirmed for me in discussions with Chinese philosophers in the People's Republic in 1973.) They define "existence" in terms of family, work, and educational organization.

Rather than make room for an idea of free will in their discussions of consciousness,* they trace the immediate origin of acts to thoughts.[61] Thoughts in turn are traced to the educational or other experiential sources. Obviously choice-making is recognized, but the selection is in turn traced to antecedent thoughts. Nothing in the Chinese conception of thought suggests autonomous decision for which the individual is solely responsible.[62] Thoughts are links in a causal chain. There is little overlap conceptually with the notion of free will. The term will (*yichi*) means primarily strength of purpose. The significance of this fact for our study is that it increases greatly the ruler's obligation to undertake fosterage. Human evils or transgressions cannot easily be explained away as a product of misuse of free choice by individuals. Instead the state bears a burden of ensuring through educational arrangements that a preponderance of good thoughts exists in the brains of the citizens.

---

*When the Western philosophical concept of "free will" (a legacy to which the Russians have been subject) entered Chinese philosophic discourse, it was understood in terms of the intuitive moral sense that comes down in the Mencian stream of Confucianism. Its Western significance in the cosmological debate over determinism and the moral debate over abuse of choice, leading to commission of sin, were not prominent in China.[60]

Obviously, none of this is meant to imply that "individual effort" is absent from the Chinese theory of state fosterage. One must have the proper interest in making use of the teachings provided by the state and in examining one's own configuration of positive and negative thoughts. As Feng Youlan once said, "[Ideological remolding] depends on your own efforts, although others can be of help. Chairman Mao has taught, 'External causes become operative through internal causes.' This is indeed the case with ideological remoulding."[63] Internal causes here are normally described by Chinese as wishes, desires, or thoughts involving the goal of transformation. They themselves derive from previous education or practical experience.

In conclusion, we have noted the claim common to Russian and Chinese official ideologies that individual people can introduce changes in their environments and themselves as a result of consciously pursuing goals, and they need not wait for changes to take place on a gradual schedule determined by the inexorable hand of history. In China, this vague claim is significant because of its behavioral implications. It suggests that leadership efforts at state fosterage that provide people with appropriate goals will be effective, and that people can have confidence in the changes that they undergo as a result of remolding. It generates optimism and, thereby, psychic effort in the pursuit of ends. Some of the same points could be made about the idea of man in the Soviet Union as conscious goal-seeker capable of introducing changes in his environment. However, the additional factor of assigning to man a "free will" (a basis for attributing individual responsibility for acts) is present in the Russian view. It stems from a Western philosophical heritage having residual influence but not in China. In a word, one cannot infer from Chinese assumptions about the covert beginnings of action and their use of terms like *zhi* or *yishi* the presence of free will as an aspect of mind midway between knowing and acting.

CONCLUSION

In terms of psychological principles, the state derives the legitimacy of its educational efforts to direct the formation of beliefs both from the assumption of malleability and from the position that promptings to act are associated with what is known or believed. The idea of malleability leads to the claim that positive personality traits and skills are possible if the state directs the learning process rather than leaving it to haphazard societal influence. The other position is: because all beliefs about the world are potentially clustered with promptings to act that can affect other people when manifested, it is not proper for state agencies to concern themselves only with the so-called externals of behavior. They have a duty to foster the development of people's opinions as well, so that beliefs clustered with the right promptings are instilled. Consistent with this approach to belief control, in theory, deviancy is explained in terms of a history of inadequate or wrongly directed educational or societal influences, or in terms of an absence of the proper thought configurations (clusters of motives and beliefs). It is not explained in terms of an individual's violation of individual free will.

Yet, one must remember to differentiate between the theory and the practice. Much of the writing and some of the practice concerning deviancy is consistent with the two psychological principles just mentioned. Significantly, inmates are often required to address each other as "fellow student" (*tongxue*) and to refer to their departure from prison as "graduation" (*piyeh*). However, in other respects individuals are still treated as though they were individually blameworthy. Although the authorities may explain deviancy in terms of bad thoughts caused by conditions originating in the old society, a prisoner himself will not have much success blaming the social environment for his bad deed. Both the works of officially sanctioned theorists and state policy guidelines may emphasize the state's educational responsibilities to the associations of negative motives and beliefs, and they may stress the perfected new person that can emerge from the process. But individual villagers may continue to treat members of certain former classes or former prisoners as though they are incorrigibles.

The state is considered to be acting legitimately toward the people when it directs their belief formation. Maoists call this "education and persuasion"as opposed to coercion. Education is an appropriate means of belief control, coercion is not. Yet herein lies a weakness in the doctrine. The distinction between education and coercion simply will not stand in the Chinese case. Threats constitute a form of coercion, which does not always need jails and pistols as its instrument. Threats are used in the educational process. One of the most frequent instruments is the study of negative exemplars. There is little question concerning the consequences that come to the person who resists belief transformation.

To explain the psychological and philosophical foundations of Chinese belief control does not justify that control. Indeed, a liberal democrat could argue against it on any number of grounds, such as its violation of a "right" to freedom of conscience (the existence of which he would have to demonstrate) or its disutility. However, an awareness of the fact that some aspects of Chinese social control have deeper roots than the transitory orientations of certain rulers can still be healthy. It can make the liberal democrat's own reflections on the pros and cons of social intervention in the realm of conscience more flexible and rational. It does so because he understands that there are other psychological theories than the one to which he has been accustomed, and that they may lead to other ways of regarding the control of beliefs.

NOTES

1. Paul Roazen, *Freud: Political and Social Thought* (New York: Vintage Books, 1968), p. 58.

2. John Stuart Mill, *On Liberty* (Indianapolis: Library of Liberal Arts, 1956), p. 91.

3. James Legge, trans., *The Chinese Classics, The Great Learning*, vol. 1 (Hong Kong: Hong Kong University Press, 1960), p. 367.

4. J. Percy Bruce, *Chu Hsi and His Masters: An Introduction to Chu Hsi and the Sung School of Chinese Philosophy* (London: Probsthain, 1923), pp. 262-63. Textual ref. 45.18b-19a.

5. Zhu Xi quan shu (*The Complete Works of Zhu Xi*), Kang Xi 52 edition, [1714]. Xing li, 45.16a.

6. Ibid., 45.17a.

7. Ibid.

8. Wang Yangming, *Quanxi lu* (*Record of Instruction*), 1.18a.

9. Ibid., 1.14b.

10. Ibid., 2.2a.

11. *Zhu Xi Quan shu (The Complete Works of Zhu Xi)*, Kang Xi 52 edition, [1714]. Xing li, 45.16b and 19b.

12. Donald J. Munro, *The Concept of Man in Early China* (Stanford, Cal.: Stanford University Press, 1969), p. 63. My interpretation of this matter was greatly aided by the work of T'ang Chun-yi of New Asia College, Hong Kong.

13. *Er Cheng quan shu (The Complete Works of the Two Cheng Brothers)*, in *Sibu bei yao (Comprehensive Collection of the Four Categories)*. This collection inclues *Yishu Chuan (Posthumous Works); Yi Chuan xian sheng wenji (Mr. Yi Chuan's Works)*; and *Zhouyi chuan* (The Book of Changes). (Shanghai: Zhunghua shuju, n.d.), p. 18.19a in *Yishu*.

14. Ibid., p. 15.16b.

15. Ibid., p. 15.16b. My attention was drawn to these passages by Ts'ai Yung-ch'un, "The Philosophy of Cheng I: A Selection of Texts from the Complete Works" (Ph.D. diss., Columbia University, 1950). Note also: "Knowledge varies in depth. There is a saying of antiquity, 'He is a gentleman who follows *li* with a glad heart.' If one has to make an effort, it means that he simply knows that he ought to follow *li*, but he is not glad to do it. But when he has reached the stage of being glad, then to follow *li* means joy, and not to follow means no joy. Why should he not follow? There is no need to make any effort. But as regards the sage who 'without an effort hits what is right and apprehends without the exercise of thought,' he belongs to a higher level." *Yishu*, p. 18.4a, quoted in Ts'ai, p. 239.

16. *Er Cheng quan shu*, Yichuan xian sheng wenji, p. 4.4a, quoted in Ts'ai, pp. 234-35.

17. *Shisanjing jushu (Commentaries on the Thirteen Classics)*; Vol. 1, Zhouyi shengyi (*Orthodox Commentary on the Zhouyi*) (Taipei: Qi, ming shuju, 1959), ch. 8, p. 76. The early Taoist texts refer to a related phenomenon. For example, the *Tao Te Ching* says: "It is easy to maintain a situation while it is still secure; it is easy to deal with a situation before symptoms develop; . . . deal with a thing while it is still nothing; keep a thing in order before disorder sets in. . . . D.C. Lau, ed., *Lao Tzu Tao Te Ching* (Baltimore: Penguin Books, 1968), p. 125.

18. *Er Cheng quan shu*, op. cit., *Yi zhuan*, p. 2.6a, quoted in Ts'ai, pp. 201-02.

19. David S. Nivision, "The Problem of 'Knowledge' and 'Action' in Chinese Thought since Wang Yangming," in *Studies in Chinese Thought*, ed. Arthur F. Wright (Chicago: The University of Chicago Press, 1953), pp. 113-14.

20. Chan Wing-tsit, trans., *Instruction for Practical Living and Other Neo-Confucian Writings by Wang Yang-ming* (New York: Columbia University Press, 1953), p. 201.

21. Mao himself makes a distinction between a theory that is good (*hao*) and one that is meaningful (*you yiyi di*). A meaningful theory is a valuable one and a theory that is not put into practice may be good but is not valuable: "If one has a correct theory but can only indulge in empty talk about it or files it away and doesn't implement it, then however good that theory is, it is still not meaningful." (Mao Zedong, "Shijian lun" ("On Practice"), in *Mao Zedong xuan ji (Selected Works of Mao Tse-tung)* (Peking: Renmin chuban she, 1964), p. 281. Not only can one have meaningful theories; one can also know the meaning of theories, just as one can know the meaning of situations.

22. Ai Siqi, *Shenmo shi women di yuanda qiantu (What is Our Promising Future?)* (Peking: Zhungguo qingnian chuban she, 1955), p. 10.

23. Ibid., p. 22.

24. Li Baoheng, "Ziran kexue he zhexue di guanxi" ("The Relationship of Natural Science and Philosophy"), *Zhexue yanjiu (Philosophical Investigations)*, no. 2 (1962).

25. "Dai xuesheng dao shengchandui li qu lianxi suanshu benling" ("Lead Students to Production Teams to Practice Arithmetic Skills"), *Jiangxi jiaoyu (Education in Kiangsi)*, no. 3 (1956): 16.

26. *Guang ming ribao (Brightness Daily)*, March 6, 1972.

27. Wu Yiling and Li Zhomin, "Shaonian ertong xuexi mudi yu dongji di fenxi" ("An Analysis of the Aims and Motives of Learning of Children"), *Xinli xuebao (Acta Psychologica Sinica)*, no. 2 (1966): 144.

28. Li Yu-ning, *The Introduction of Socialism Into China* (New York: Columbia University Press, 1971), p. 105.

29. Li Boshu and Zhou Guansheng, "Shaonian ertong daode xing wei dongji tezheng di xinli fenxi" ("A Psychological Analysis of Motivational Characteristics of the Moral Behavior of Children"), *Xinli suebao (Acta Psychologica Sinica)*, no. 1 (1964): 31.

30. Wu Yiling and Li Zhomin, op. cit., p. 139.

31. Ibid., p. 140.

32. Robert Chin and Ai-li S. Chin, *Psychological Research in Communist China 1949-1966* (Cambridge, Mass.: M.I.T. Press, 1969), p. 15. My interpretation differs somewhat from that of the Chins in being tripartite: it includes knowing, feeling (approval or disapproval), and having a prompting to act in accordance with what is known and accepted.

33. An Ziwen, *Qianchui bailian gaizao ziji (Under Numerous Tests Reform Oneself)* (Tientsin: Tianjing renmin chuban she, 1957), p. 9.

34. Wei Yuping, *Wo hedeliao zhengque di chufadian* (I Obtained the Correct Starting Point) (Peking: Renmin wenxue chuban she, 1952), p. 149.

35. Zhang Manhua, "Bu dang jiushi hao xifu yongyuan yao zuo geming ren" ("Don't Be a Good Old-Style Daughter-in-law: Always be a Revolutionary"), *Zhongguo quingnian* (henceforth: ZGQN), no. 7 (April 1, 1966): 18.

36. "Hongsi xuanchuanyuan' di sixiang guanghui: Chaoxian huaju 'hongsi xuan chuanyuan zuotan hui ("The Bright Thoughts of 'Red Propagandist': a Record of the talk on the Korean Play 'Red Propagandist'"), ZGQN, no. 2 (January 16, 1963): 6.

37. Zhong Jingwen, "Nuli Xuexi laodong renmin di yuyan" ("Strive to Learn Working People's Language"), *Yuwen xuexi (Language Learning)* 8 (August 1952): 8.

38. Shen Zhiyuan, "Lun zhishi fenzi sixiang gaizao" ("On the Thought Reform of Intellectuals"), *Zhanwang zhoukan (Outlook Weekly)* (Shanghai, August, 1952).

39. Huang Enan et al., eds. *Bianzheng weiwu zhuyi mingce jieshi* (Explanation of Terms of Dialectical Materialism) (Peking: Tongju dushu chuban she, 1957), p. 80.

40. Shen Zhiyuan, op. cit., p. 12.

41. Li Baoheng, op. cit., p. 3.

42. Wen Wei, "Jiaoyu zinu chengwei gongchan zhuyi jiebanren" ("Educate Children to Be Successors of Communism"), ZGQN, no. 9-10 (May 7, 1962): 14, *Guo Xingfu jiaoyu fangfa*, p. 22.

43. An Ziwen. op. cit., p. 6.

44. Shen Zhiyuan, op. cit., p. 2.

45. "Zemmayang xue yingxiong" ("How Should we Learn from Heroes?"), ZGQN, no. 1 (1966): 27.

46. Xin Chu, "Bo 'liangzhung dongli yiyang xiaoguo lun'" ("Refute 'The Theory of Identical Results in the Two Kinds of Motive Forces'"), in *Renmin ribao wenxuan (Selected Essays from the People's Daily)* (Peking: Renmin ribao chuban she. 1958), p. 92.

47. Guan Feng, "Shilun Lei Feng di shijieguan di xingcheng" ("Examining the Formation of Lei Feng's World View"), *Zhexue yanjiu (Philosophical Investigations)*, no. 5 (1963): 2.

48. An Ziwen, op. cit., p. 8.

49. Xiao Qian, "Lun tiaojian" ("On Conditions"), *Zhexue yanjiu (Philosophical Investigations)*, no. 4 (1962): 9.

50. Nie Shimao, "Bangyang duibi shaonian xuesheng ziwo pingjia di zuoyong" ("The Function of Examples for Comparison in Self-Criticism by Young Students"), *Xinli xuebao (Acta Psychologica Sinica)*, no. 2 (1966): 152.

51. Alfred G. Meyer, *Leninism* (New York: Praeger, 1957), p. 28.

52. See Raymond A. Bauer, *The New Man in Soviet Psychology* (Cambridge, Mass.: Harvard University Press, 1952), p. 100.

53. V. I. Lenin, *Materialism and Empirio-Criticism: Critical Comments on a Reactionary Philosophy* (Moscow: Foreign Language Publishing House, 1952), p. 190.

54. Ibid., p. 193.

55. Philip T. Grier, "Contemporary Soviet Ethical Theory." Unpublished Ph.D. dissertation, Department of Philosophy, The University of Michigan, 1973.

56. Walter D. Connor, *Deviance in Soviet Society* (New York: Columbia University Press, 1972), pp. 44-45.

57. Raymond A. Bauer, op. cit., p. 90.

58. Walter D. Connor, op. cit., pp. 163-64.

59. Quoted in Bauer, op. cit., p. 13.

60. The muddled understanding is evident in Chang Chun-mai's remarks: "Why do men possess a moral sense of right and wrong, and a sense of responsibility and sometimes wish to repent? The cause of a moral decision is to be found in the inner heart and not externally, and such a mental decision derives from free will and not determinism." Quoted in Charlotte Furth, *Ting Wen-chiang: Science and China's New Culture* (Cambridge, Mass.: Harvard University Press, 1970), p. 103. His colleague Fan Shou-kang spoke of free will as subservient to an inner mind, a social conscience that intuits a priori moral principles. As for the superficial form in which the discussions of free will were articulated, a recent study has this to say about the theories of Chang Chun-mai: "Much of Chang Chun-mai's thesis can be traced to European sources. He relied heavily upon the European philosophers Bergson and Eucken and the biological vitalist Hans Driesch. They all believed in the organic uniqueness of human beings and the impossibility of a mechanistic, quantitative analysis of human will. . . . Chang Chun-mai's argument was entirely derived from the theories of European philosophers." Maynard Chou Min-chih, *Science and Value in May Fourth China: The Case of Hu Shih.* Unpublished Ph.D. dissertation, University of Michigan, 1974, p. 147.

Chang's treatment of free will itself illustrates that he had not understood it in Western terms relating to choice of action and responsibility, but rather in terms of the source of man's intuitive moral sense. In short, he neo-Confucianized the concept. There were some perceptive critics of the treatment of free will in China of the 1930s. Lin Mousheng wrote in 1938: ". . . No philosopher denies the existence of the external reality and no scientist repudiates the existence of the inner mind. The philosopher simply asserts that the mind is free from, and independent of, the external world and determines its own outlook on life, while the scientist believes that the external world determines the state of mind or consciousness. Neither, however, analyzes what mind or matter is." Lin Mou-sheng, "Recent Intellectual Movements in China," *China Institute Bulletin* 3, no. 1 (1958): 9. The quotations from Chang Chun-mai and Lin Mou-sheng were brought to my attention by Fred Grunenwald.

61. Li Shisheng, "Zai laodong zhong piancheng xinren" ("Transform Oneself Into a New Man Through Labor"), *Hong Qi (Red Flag)*, no. 18 (1960): 34.

62. For a good essay on the absence of a doctrine of strict moral responsibility in Confucianism, see Chad Hansen, "Freedom and Moral Responsibility in Confucian Ethics," *Philosophy East and West* 22, no. 2 (April 1972): 169-86.

63. *Foreign Broadcast Information Service*, February 5, 1974, p. 133.

3

IDEOLOGY AND CONFUCIAN ETHICS IN THE CHARACTERIZATION OF BAD WOMEN IN SOCIALIST LITERATURE
Joe C. Huang

A major function of socialist literature in mainland China is social control as shown in the positive model for emulation and the negative type for admonition. But this purpose cannot be attained unless socialist literature also draws on human experience and interests the reader with moving episodes. For this reason, we find post-1949 Chinese literature both prescriptive and descriptive. The relative degree and extent of prescription and description depends largely on the role of characters. Most positive characters exhibit traits required of self-denying heroes and dedicated cadres in the course of revolutionary struggle and socialist construction. The predominant influence of ideology on the characterization of heroes and cadres inevitably as reduced artistic consideration to a secondary level. As early as July 1949, Zhou Yang, representing the party in his address to the conference of writers and artists, contended that the single most important feature of socialist literature was the creation of worker-peasant-soldier heroes and heroines who were not just born, but "steeled in the forge of battle."[1]

During the first decade after the revolution "socialist realism" (*shehui zhuyi xianshi zhuyi*) was the ruling theory guiding the arts and literature. In 1958 it was replaced by a new theory called "the integration of revolutionary realism and revolutionary romanticism" (*geming di xianshi zhuyi he geming di langman zhuyi di jiehe*). Despite the theoretic reformulation, the essence of socialist literature has remained the portrayal of the bright side of society and of heroes as the motivating force in socialist transformation. The behavior patterns of heroes and cadres can only be viewed as deliberately idealized for the purpose of emulation by the masses. They are primarily models rather than recreations of real people. They are ideologically oriented figures whose mission is, in the words of Mao Dun, to "exert a positive influence on reality" so as to "speed today forward faster towards tomorrow."[2]

The emphasis on positive characters results in a comparatively relaxed control over the portrayal of negative characters. It is true that in his "Talks at the Yenan Forum on Literature and Art" Mao Zedong identified "aggressors, exploiters and oppressors" as villains.[3] The question as to how to portray them, however, was never clearly answered, but largely left for novelists to grapple with. Consequently, they portrayed villains by relying on traditional models in classical novels and popular tales as well as on their own observations of people in real life. This being the case, negative characters are usually more vividly and colorfully depicted than heroic characters.

The degree of control has been further slackened when it comes to the description of bad women. This is primarily because the deviant behavior of male villains is political while that of bad women is minor and nonpolitical. There have never been female villains in the novels of the post-1949 period. They are at worst only accomplices or minor deviants whose behavior implies no serious political ramifications.

The inability of women to behave in grave violation of political norms derived from their status in traditional society. In the social structure of old China, a woman's role was dictated by Confucian ethics which stressed the subordination of a wife to her husband as one of the "five relationships."[4] Chastity as one of the corresponding virtues applied only to the female.[5] The subordinate status of women never escaped the attention of Chinese Communist leaders. Mao Zedong pointed out in 1927 that women, apart from being subject as men were to the three types of authority—state authority, clan authority, and religious authority—were further subject to the authority of the husband.[6] The Chinese Communists have always treated the liberation of women as a part of social emancipation. This explains why one of the first laws promulgated by the Central People's Government was the New Marriage Law of May 1, 1950. The feudal marriage system was abolished by Article 1 of this law partly because it legalized the superiority of men over women. A woman's inferior status in pre-revolutionary China precluded her assuming the role of a villain in literary works.

The overall absence of ideological control over nonpolitical deviance and the general agreement between a woman's role in traditional society and the Communist conception of it enabled Chinese novelists to portray bad women using their own observations and imaginations. This naturally led to more accurate description of deviant behavior patterns in Chinese society. In this essay I shall focus on bad women characters in five major best-selling novels. These novels, which reflect rural life at different stages of agricultural collectivization, were written by novelists who took part in the activities they described. All of them earned a national reputation, but some became notorious after their works were denounced. The ideological attacks on some of the novels suggest that they are honest works rather than outright propaganda.

In the instances discussed below the conduct of bad women is an important part of the novelists' plot. An intriguing question confronting the student of post-1949 Chinese literature is the relationship between ideology and Confucian ethics. Through comparative analysis we shall see whether deviant behavior patterns violate ideological criteria or only moral codes of conduct. If they are found to be deviations from both political and social norms, we then shall look for their relative importance in the making of a believable story. In other words, we shall determine whether the novelists relied on conceptions of political or nonpolitical deviance to substantiate the fictional images of bad women.

THE BAD WOMAN AS ABETTOR

If the Chinese revolution has done away with the feudal system, the family as the basic unit in the social fabric remains intact. The husband-wife relationship is often described in prosaic language, but it reflects considerable mutual attachment. As positive characters in stories of land reform, the men are usually activist peasants supporting communist cadres at the risk of retaliation by landlords or Guomindang soldiers amidst a raging civil war. Their women are as a rule patient, helpful partners who not only take care of the household chores but also till the land in order that their men will have more time to work for the revolution. In the novels of mutual aid teams and agricultural cooperatives, the men are depicted as eagerly responding to the call of the party and their wives as doing their part to make the collective effort a success. Such descriptions, when presented without much variation, of course, make poor stories. In their endeavor to create human drama Chinese novelists had to dwell on wicked men and immoral women to show darker desires and private longings. The conduct of villains is more or less that characteristic of ideologically conceived exploiters and oppressors. But in the case of bad women, an author's imagination was allowed a freer rein than generally tolerated by ideology.

The bad woman had always been a fascinating subject in Chinese literature because her activities were unconventional and unpredictable. There is nothing exciting about the well-bred woman of the gentry class whose behavior suggests no more than a model of Confucian ethics. Literature, however, is not tales of routine life; the element of entertainment is crucial, as in any form of art. As a result, amorous scenes, for instance, are always described as between men and women of bad repute or between men and supernatural beings—fairies, ghosts, and foxes.[7] That men are allowed to engage in sexual play which does not stain their good social standing while women are denied this privilege demonstrates the inequality between the sexes.

The inferior status of women in the old society, as reflected in classical novels, is defined in communist society theory. Thus, in depicting bad women during the period of transition from the old society to the socialist society, to be consistent with ideology and true to reality, novelists cannot attribute to them traits generally belonging to villains. Women characters can at worst only be accessories to landlords in the drama of class struggle. As a negative example, a bad woman when successfully delineated by a skillful novelist elicits from readers a response of disdain rather than hate. Her conduct may be blameworthy or shameful, but she is used merely as a tool by a landlord villain.

One favorite plot in which a woman's charm is exploited in a conspiracy is called the ruse of beauty (*meiren ji*). The ruse has gained popularity through the description of Diao Chan in *Romance of the Three Kingdoms*. Her dazzling beauty, used as a lure for both Prime Minister Dong Zhou and his adopted son Lu Bu, evokes jealosy and hatred between the two men and causes Lu Bu to join a plot to slay Dong Zhou. Such a tactic, often employed by the weak against the strong, is described in a variety of ways as a conspiratorial scheme by landlords or rich peasants in contemporary Chinese novels. Once they have been deprived of economic and political power, landlords are reduced to a state of impotence. They can do very little either to retaliate or to mitigate harsh treatment awaiting them in the class struggle organized by communist cadres. One thing they can do is to exploit men's vulnerability to tender assault by the opposite sex. Such a scenario enhances plausibility of the conduct of villains.

Chinese writers posit this popular artifice with varying degrees of imagination and sophistication in stories about rural China undergoing revolutionary transformation. *Sun Over the Sangkan River (Taiyang zhao zai Sanggan he shang)*[8] describes land reform in northern Hopei in 1947. The author, Ding Ling, who spent several months in the area, witnessed the unfolding of class struggle in China's vast countryside. A veteran writer of May Fourth vintage, she earned a reputation as an outspoken critic and acrid novelist in Yenan and was reprimanded during the rectivation campaign of 1942-44. *Sun* is considered an honest work and one of the best in socialist literature.[9]

In this novel, Ding Ling portrays the landlord Qian Wengui as a crafty schemer who has married off his daughter to the village security officer and is encouraging his niece, Heni, to win the love of the chairman of the local peasant association. The tactic is partially successful: the security officer behaves like a good son-in-law to shield the landlord. Heni, on the other hand, shows great reluctance to do her uncle's bidding although she has genuine love and admiration for the chairman. What the landlord Qian does, viewed in the perspective of interpersonal relationships in traditional China, contains nothing immoral and illegal. In fact, according to Confucian ethics, a father had the authority to marry off his daughter, and by extention an uncle could do the same to a fatherless niece. Even the use of kinship with local cadres as a safeguard was an acceptable practice of nepotism in a society that honored familial bonds. But the landlord's conduct is presented as an attempt to corrupt cadres and undermine the party policy of land reform. Thus Heni's refusal to be involved in the landlord's scheme does not make her an unfilial and disobedient niece; on the contrary, she appears as a girl with a certain degree of political consciousness.

A similar plot with different implications is found in *The Hurricane (Baofeng zhouyu)*,[10] a novel about land reform in Manchuria. Zhou Libo, author of this novel, once headed the Editing and Translating Department at the Lu Xun Institute of Arts and Literature in wartime Yenan. He arrived in northern Manchuria in the winter of 1946-47 to take part in the struggle. Only after six months of working closely with village people, sharing their anxieties as well as enthusiasm, did Zhou go to Harbin and decide to tell the story of land reform in a novel. He was a serious writer and was denounced during the Cultural Revolution of 1966-69.[11]

The landlord villain in *The Hurricane* is nicknamed Han Number Six. He takes a number of steps to thwart the cadres' preparation for struggle against him. Aside from planting his men among the masses so that they can spy on the activities of the communist work team, mark down those speaking against him, and put in a word or two in his favor at peasant meetings when opportunities avail themselves, he also uses his daughter as an abettor.

Zhou Libo seems to have attempted a bold description of the incident of trapping an inexperienced peasant. After treating the puzzled peasant to a dinner of roebuck venison and good wine, the landlord invites the young man to the inner chamber two nights later and promptly excuses himself. The incident of seduction, though sketchy in detail, is described with a touch of realism. "She stood there in the light clad in blue silk trousers and a white silk jacket, transparent as a cicada's wing, and a pink vest over her bulging breasts. Her hair was loose over her shoulders as if she had just got up from sleep. . . ."[12]

A quick scene follows. After several cups of wine, the woman feigns drunkenness and unbuttons the jacket to expose her pink vest. The young peasant is invited to cool her with a fragrant sandalwood fan. In his great excitement he waves the fan so virorously that it is broken. Instead of reproaching him, the woman bursts into laughter. Emboldened by the liquor and encouraged by the woman's enticing giggle, he makes an abrupt advance on her. The young peasant is of course not to have his way with the landlord's daughter; rather, he is accused of attempted rape and is forced to put a mark on a prepared confession. From then on he is placed at the landlord's mercy as well as at his service as an agent.

The episode is interesting in veiw of the moral significance of the narrative. The realistic touch in the description remains shallow, for the author never tries to portray the inner feelings of the woman toward her role in the wile. She is treated as a pawn, like Diao Chan in *Romance of the Three Kingdoms*, for the sake of exposing the evil nature of the landlord.

There is, however, logic in Zhou Libo's structure of the subplot. He ignores the woman's fine sensitivities because his overriding concern is to make a political point through the description of her immoral conduct. He portrays the landlord's daughter as a seductress and her father's willing accomplice. In her former role she is shown as an unchaste woman measured by Confucian ethics. Her second role as an accomplice in the plot of sabotage is obvious only to politically conscious and ideologically committed readers. The part the woman plays lends credibility to the vicious character and counterrevolutionary activities of the landlord. Once the ugly act of seduction is over, the author simply ignores the existence of the woman. Her final downfall is assumed rather than explicitly depicted in the story.

LIBERTINE TRAITS AS A RESIDUE OF EARLY LIFE

In the post-1949 period women are no longer treated as inferior to men. The change of class structure as well as of the social status of women resulting from the inauguration of a new economic system inevitably affects the characterization of bad women. If literature still cannot escape the influence of its tradition, it must reflect subtle variations and capture the nuances of the new reality. Success or failure in creative works depends, therefore, to a large extent on the ability of the novelist to use tradition without becoming its captive. If contemporary women are still mainly the product of traditional culture, they have nevertheless lived through considerable changes to become different from the generation of their mothers.

The elimination of the landlord class along with all the vices attributed to it does not mean the disappearance of all vestiges of the feudal system. Residual traits in the personalities of those brought up in the old society frequently manifest themselves. The infeasibility of portraying the most obvious type of women accessories in the age of socialism prompts novelists to explore the psychology of bad women.

No vice in the Chinese social code of conduct, whether in traditional or socialist China, is worse than adultery. Sexual relationships outside formal wedlock have always been considered a threat to the family system, which is central to the social fabric. If the communist leadership is concerned with the emancipation of women, they are just as anxious to preserve the family system to assure the stability of society. Therefore, the characterization of bad women in Chinese fiction of the socialist period often relies on the description of adultery.

Adultery is a rare event in post-1949 novels, but in Liu Qing's *The Builders* (*Chuang ye shi*)[13] it is described with unusual candor and unique psychological insights. The author was a *xian* party secretary in southern Shensi province in the early 1950s. From 1953 to 1956, he helped with the development of mutual aid teams in Huangbu Cun, a small village south of the Wei River. Already an acomplished writer whose *Wall of Bronze* (*Tongqiang tiebi*), portraying a peasant militiaman during the defense of Yenan in 1947, won wide acclaim, Liu Qing tells the story of a pioneer mutual aid team in *The Builders* on the basis of his personal experience. It is in fact an artistic version of his nonfiction report, *Three Years in Huangbu Village*.[14] He was under attack during the Cultural Revolution and has not published since. He seems to have been rehabilitated several years ago, and the English version of *The Builders* once again has become available.

In *The Builders* the woman Sufang commits adultery. As a victim in the old society, she has witnessed her father squander away his inherited fortune on opium and her mother sell her body to support the family. After being made pregnant by a waiter in a restaurant at the age of sixteen, she has been hurriedly married off to an obtuse villager. This background paves the way for Sufang's later seduction by her uncle, a rich peasant.

The narrative of Sufang's dissatisfaction with her marital life, as the cause of her libertine behavior, is reminiscent of Golden Lotus in *Water Margin*. Although in the classical novel the description of the amorous affair is much bolder, Golden Lotus is shown merely as an abandoned woman. The treatment of Sufang's physical relationship with her rich uncle Yao Shijie is more restrained, but the description of her psychology in terms of motivation and ambivalence is deeper.

The scene of Sufang's seduction is introduced by an allusive depiction of a bewitching spring day. As she is sifting flour in the seclusion of the mill shed, she watches two turtle doves at play. Pondering over her own life, she is saddened by the prospect of living with a dull husband who fails to give her tender love and a tyrannical father-in-law who often inflicts corporal punishment on her. At this point her uncle climbs down the back wall to rape her. After her initial feeling of horror, a violent sense of moral sin, her second reaction is great satisfaction. She indulges herself in his beguiling affections and enjoys his powerful caresses.

Sufang's relationship with Yao is far more complicated than mere fulfillment of carnal needs. It bears the imprint of her earlier life as the daughter of a prostitute and a pregnant teenager. Her loose morality, shaped in the old society, resurfaces when given opportunity. But it can also be seen as her way of revenge. Whereas many unhappily married women are allowed divorce after the proclamation of the New Marriage Law, she still has to suffer at the hands of her domineering father-in-law. "As she lay with Yao," the author writes, "she said vengefully in her heart to her blind old father-in-law, 'I'll teach you to tell your son to beat me.'"[15]

Sexual immorality was one of the most serious forms of deviance according to Confucian ethics. It is also an important trait of bad women characters in socialist literature. Rape is of course not the fault of the woman. Nevertheless, adultery committed under force but repeated out of choice turns Sufang into a wretched woman. Consequently, despite the fine description of her inner struggle and of the circumstances leading to the incident, Sufang's transition from a victimized woman to a conscious wrongdoer renders her beyond redemption. With her moral downfall, she becomes the rich peasant's tool to induce the withdrawal of two households from the mutual aid team and thus almost wrecks agricultural cooperation at its inception.

In a sort of literary reincarnation the wanton Sufang reappears as Sun Guiying in *Bright Sunny Days* (*Yanyang tian*), published on the eve of the Cultural Revolution.[16] The author Hao Ran is a gifted novelist with authentic peasant background and a product of the age of socialism. In his middle forties, he is one of a few serious writers with a name still untarnished and a promising future. He gives perhaps the most penetrating portrayal of rural China in *Bright Sunny Days, The Golden Road,* and hundreds of short stories. A rich and colorful picture of agrarian society in the process of metamorphosis clearly emerges from underneath party line theses.[17]

Like Sufang in *The Builders*, Sun Guiying has been raped by her stepfather and again by her stepbrother, has worked in her stepfather's gambling den, and has been later married to a husband against her wish. The treatment of the theme, however, differs significantly: if a woman's urfortunate early life sows the seed of her later misconduct, she nevertheless can be redeemed with her own willpower and a little help from the cadres.

Guiying likes Xiao Changchun, the village party secretary, in a respectful way and would be his friend were she a man. This description of her view of the male-female relationship is a subtle way of depicting both an old-fashioned woman and a woman who is a victim of her past immoral behavior. The party secretary, a widower, works among unmarried girls and married women. Their relations are not limited to those that depend on their formal, official capacities as members of the cooperative, but extend to everyday friendships. To Guiying, an old-fashioned woman, it is inconceivable to have mere friendship between a man and a woman: she can never be Changchun's friend. Since from her past experience she knows only one way to be related to a man, she becomes his secret admirer and harbors irresistible passion toward him.

With this frame of mind Guiying easily becomes the victim of her fancy as well as of a vicious plot. There is little need for help from the wife of the vice-chairman of the cooperative to instigate her craving for an amorous affair with her hero. When the party secretary, learning about her illness but unaware that it is a trick, comes to pay her a visit, he finds himself trapped in the woman's bedroom. But instead of showing his temper or trying to force his way out, Xiao discusses her past in a calm voice. He says that what happened to her in the last thirty years was not her own doing, but what is going to happen in the next thirty years all depends on herself. She can start anrew, take part in productive labor, and live a respectable life.

There is no question that the secretary's talk is loaded with political exhortation. But the sincerity of the man and the likelihood of his attitude need not be doubted. The moral criteria Chinese peasants maintain in judging each other's conduct remain as rigid in communist society as they were in traditional

China. Although Guiying's love for the secretary is illicit from the moral viewpoint, there is an element of genuine feeling, and this fact forms the basis for the author's description of the party secretary's endeavor to rescue a sinking woman.

The story has yet to undergo another twist. Shortly thereafter, the vice-chairman of the cooperative, who has instructed his wife to set up the trap, comes back from town to catch the couple in fornication. When he finds Guiying alone in the room, in his drunken state he is suddenly overcome with desire. Instead of taking the vice-chairman as a substitute to satisfy her unquenched erotic thirst, however, Guiying fights off his assault tooth and nail. She is thus shown not to have totally lost her sense of decency, but to have a capacity for reform. She eventually sees the light and joins with other women in productive activities.

A NEW TYPE OF BAD WOMAN AND HER CAPACITY FOR REDEMPTION

In *The Golden Road* (*Jinguang dadao*),[18] the first novel to appear after the Cultural Revolution, Hao Ran portrays a new type of bad woman, quite different from Sun Guiying of *Bright Sunny Days* and in significant ways a happy break from convention. The redemption of Guiying is constructed primarily to fit a social code of conduct rather than to meet ideological criteria. Her past behavior clearly qualifies her as an indecent woman, but immoral stains, according to Chinese ethical codes, can be cleansed once a woman is determined to live a virtuous, new life. Human capacity for reform, a time-honored notion, regains currency in the form of educability of man under the socialist system. Ideology plays a small part insofar as Guiying's reform is facilitated through her participation in productive work.

A woman can also be judged as bad by ideological criteria. In such a case it is not her craving for illicit sexual relations but her pursuit of selfish goals detrimental to the collective interest that turns her into a negative character. A description of selfish motives by itself is insufficient unless selfishness leads to her complicity in a villain's attempt to undermine agricultural cooperation. This is exactly the role Hao Ran assigns to Qian Caifeng in *The Golden Road*, which depicts the transition from land reform to the establishment of mutual aid teams. What makes this woman fascinating is the novelist's trenchant description of her private longings. While all the other women characters are more or less typical, Caifeng is refreshingly different and bustles with life. Married to a barber at the age of seventeen by her aunt, she has recently obtained a divorce and is determined to arrange her own life this time.

Hao Ran portrays Caifeng as a clever, exceedingly talented woman. A piece of fabric big enough only for making a vest will, in her skillful hands, be cut into a jacket with extra material for a pair of cloth shoes. Unlike Sufang of *The Builders*, who bears grudges against her father-in-law and husband, and Guiying of *Bright Sunny Days*, who is basically a laggard and simple-minded woman, Caifeng appears clear-headed. She is able to make herself attractive in a natural way, and indeed with her pretty face there is little need for wearing cosmetics. The image of this woman painted with Hao Ran's dexterous hand has a certain refined quality, unusual yet by no means unnatural. As an available divorcee, she is approached by many a young man and many a glib matchmaker. Once burned in marriage, however, she is extremely cautious in her pursuit of happiness. She envies those women companions who enjoy happy marriages, and looks for an honest and capable man who will love her, adore her, and always remain faithful.

She is at Sweet Meadow Village as a visitor in her cousin's home to avoid the annoyance of an endless stream of suitors and matchmakers. Even as a guest, she keeps herself busy doing laundry, grinding flour, and helping with other household work. A woman such as Caifeng, even with all her self-centered aspirations, would hardly qualify as a negative type, had she not become an instrument in a ruse of beauty plotted by her cousin's husband, the wealthy peasant Feng Shaohuai. Without her knowledge she is turned into an abettor in the subtle, complex political struggle at Sweet Meadow Village.

After land reform, Feng Shaohuai emerges as the most affluent peasant in the village. He has already bought a mule and is ready to enlarge his land holdings and hire farm hands. He eyes the Gao brothers, his first wife's cousins, as his prospective mule drivers. When the elder brother Gao Daquan, a communist, is determined to organize a number of poor families into a mutual aid team, Fend decides to have Caifeng induce his younger brother Erlin to lead a separate life. This way he can not only gain a mule driver but also undercut Daquan's effort by reducing the manpower in his family. It is thus no longer just a case of developing capitalism but one of sabotaging socialism.

In this story the ruse of beauty is raised to a new level of sophistication. Instead of stressing the scheming plot, the author skillfully avoids any direct description of it but focuses on the psychology of the woman who unwittingly becomes a tool and of the man who falls victim to the stratagem. By this arrangement class struggle is pushed to the background and human struggle suddenly sharpened.

Qian Caifeng is not a bad woman in the traditional sense, but is clearly a negative character. Hao Ran does not treat her as a cheap wench with loose morals. There is nothing improper between her and the villain Feng Shaohuai. The author, it appears, portrays Feng as a worthy enemy, wicked in a respectable way. As a cold, calculating man who is determined to build up his wealth, Feng is unlikely to lose his composure, become irrational, and have a scandalous affair with his wife's cousin. Thus, while staying with the Fengs, Caifeng has not become a prey of the villain.

Feng Shaohuai's scheme is very simple: he merely provides an opportunity for an initial encounter between Caifeng and Erlin in the village recreation club. Even on this occasion he remains unseen; only later references make clear his hand in this arrangement. The scene of the meeting is painted in delightful detail:

> ... He [Erlin] swept the floor, sealed the furnace, and took the lock in his hand. As he was going to turn off the lamp, he unexpectedly heard someone stamp feet outside.
>
> Facing the direction, he asked: "Who is it?"
>
> No response.
>
> He called again, "Who?"
>
> Again, no response.
>
> He walked to the door in one stride and saw a woman standing under the eaves. In the light coming through the papered window he saw the woman wearing a bright red scarf and above it tiny snow flakes flying like a swarm of bees.
>
> He changed into a soft tone, asking: "Why, still here?"
>
> The woman stirred a bit.
>
> Gao Erlin said again: "Please go, I shall turn off the lamp and lock up the door."
>
> The woman suddenly chuckled.
>
> Gao Erlin was puzzled, sheepishly standing there, not knowing what else to do and at the same time feeling embarrassed. A man and a woman all by themselves appeared improper, yet rudely turning off the lamp and locking up the door also seemed inappropriate.
>
> After a moment of silence, the woman stamped her feet again and said: "So cold. Is the fire in the furnace out?"
>
> Gao Erlin answered mechanically, "No."
>
> The woman said: "Let me warm up." As she was saying it, she walked by Geo Erlin into the room. Drawing over a stool, she sat down in front of the fire, unhurriedly pulled off her scarf and put it on the table and warmed her hands.
>
> Erlin cast a sight at the room. He saw a young woman over twenty with two curved eyebrows, a pair of clear, large eyes and raven-black hair cut along the neck; wrapped up in the plain, flower-patterned and cotton-padded clothes was a full-blooming body....[19]

It is a picture of a serene snowy night made lively by the presence of a woman exuding youth and charm. The imagery of a lone woman wearing a bright red scarf amidst minute snow flakes evokes a feeling of purity and candor, impossible to be associated with any wrongdoing. In the subsequent narrative not a word said not a gesture made by the woman hints at indecency. The description is worthy of a beautiful love story. But the episode acquires quite different meaning when it is viewed in ideological perspective. With the subtle class struggle then in progress between the capitalist and socialist forces, the love episode turns into a vicious plot to impair the endeavor of developing socialism. The pure and candid relationship between Erlin and Caifeng is simply a deceptive appearance much more dangerous than Feng Shaohuai's other attempts at sabotaging the mutual aid program.

As the mutual affection between Caifeng and Erling progresses, they naturally begin to talk about marriage. Erlin is actually approvingly encouraged by his sister-in-law and his best friend, a dedicated party man. When Daquan, his elder brother, returns from working at a railway depot in Peking, his initial response toward the marriage is also favorable. The description of such reactions shows a significant change of attitude toward marrying a divorcee; divorce would have been a major obstacle in old China. There is, however, the ideological question posed by Daquan. He wants to know whether Caifeng is the kind of woman who will work with them toward the larger goal of building socialism. A suspicion generated by this consideration is whether Feng Shaohuai has had a hand in the affair.

With or without the involvement of Feng, that larger goal is exactly what Caifeng and Erlin are unwilling to pursue. All they want is a cozy little family. Caifeng is interested only in a good, honest husband who will provide her with a comfortable life so that she will never again have to suffer hardships or mistreatment. Erling wants to be left alone to work on his few *mou*** of land, to be with the woman he loves, and to have children. Such thoughts constitute clear deviance from the new political norms. Their interest in selfish gains leads Erlin to break with his brother. This outcome is all Feng Shaohuai has set out to attain; the ruse of beauty has succeeded.

Instead of portraying Caifeng as a licentious woman who seduces young Gao Erlin purely with her physical charm, the author focuses on their personality traits and describes the goal they share. Feng's ruse is merely a catalyst for effecting the union of two minds. This is how the author describes the mental state of the young couple:

> Gao Erlin fell in love with Qian Caifeng, unable to part with her much less give her up. The drawing power and his mental state were not totally out of loosening passions—mutual attraction between opposite sexes—but also due to another factor. For Gao Erlin, a man with little experience, and Qian Caifeng, a woman who had gone through the bitter taste of an old-fashioned marriage, that "other factor" appeared more important and practical. They fell in love at first sight and rushed into marriage because as a rule, a man would

---

*A mou equals one-sixth of an acre.

get old someday and eventually die. He could not always remain a
bachelor, could not live with his brother, sister-in-law and nephew all
his life, but had to get a life partner. . . . Therefore, he tied up himself and all he had with the fate of Qian Caifeng. He had made up his
mind that he would form a family with her, they would bear
children and grow old together.[20]

The love affair between Erlin and Caifeng, measured by Confucian ethics, is
both proper and natural. Even their pursuit of selfish goals, the focus of the
author's narration, only shows the couple as unenlightened, backward elements.
The moral behind this story seems to be that selfish motives may blind people's
better judgment and allow them to be exploited by a villain attempting to
thwart collective endeavor. Herein, therefore, lies the answer for the potential
redemption of Qian Caifeng as an abettor. Once she realizes that she has been
used by her cousin's husband to advance his own interests, she will become a
new woman to join with others on the road to socialism. This is exactly what
happens in the second volume of *The Golden Road*. After suffering much abuse
at the hands of Feng Shaohuai, Caifeng and Erlin finally part company with the
villain and gain their rebirth as the dialectic of class struggle completes its cycle.

CONCLUDING REMARKS

This essay was inspired by a question concerning the relationship between
ideology and Confucian ethics in socialist literature. The lack of ideological
criteria for judging social deviance prompted novelists to look to the legacy of
Chinese literature for guidance. Traditional Chinese literature in its reflection of
Confucian moral codes describes lechery as the worst of immoral behavior. In
portraying a libertine woman the novelists's purpose was not to convey the
romantic nature of the affair; rather, he wanted to expose a villain's dark
motives and to a lesser extent the woman's loose morality in her role as an
accomplice. The picture of the bad woman was intended to evoke contempt
from the reader. Such an approach appeals to the reader with unfailing effect,
for he has been conditioned to see sexual misconduct as the worst of vices.

Our analysis of the novels preceding the Cultural Revolution leads us to
the conclusion that Confucian ethics share a place with ideology in portraying
bad women. The deviant behavior patterns in these novels are not much different from those in classical works. An ideological message cannot get across to
the reader unless it is sustained by a moral persuasion. A woman becomes bad
first as a result of her moral downfall, a nonpolitical form of deviance, and only
then is she implicated in a plot hindering party policy, a political form of deviance. Her salvation comes in the same fashion. According to Confucian ethics, a
bad woman is capable of reform through lessons she has learned; according to

ideology, she can be enlightened by cadres. The difference is minimal, as cadres can easily be replaced by relatives or friends in plot structure.

In a quarter of a century, from the publication of *Sun* and *The Hurricane* in 1949 to the appearance of the second volume of *The Golden Road* in 1974, a trend seems to have emerged: as ideology takes hold, Confucian ethics become less important as a source of behavioral norms. This, however, may be a superficial phenomenon. Underneath the surface of ideological conformity still rests a deeply entrenched social code ofconduct. If Qian Caifeng of *The Golden Road* had been a lascivious woman, it is unlikely that she would have been redeemed. The image of this character actually borders on that of a good woman. Her dencency and frugality are good qualities judged both by Confucian ethics and by communist standards. Perhaps there is still a shade of overlapping between the two. In the final analysis, the love episode between Caifeng and Erlin is structured on the basis of the Chinese literary tradition. The same system of reward and punishment applies here. Moral exhortation, as shown in the ultimate denouement where the villain receives his punishment and the innocent are properly vindicated, is now dressed in the garb of Marxist dialectics.

NOTES

1. Zhou Yang, "The People's New Literature and Art," *China's New Literature and Art* (Peking: Foreign Languages Press, 1954), p. 58. For the Chinese text, "Xin di renmin di wenyi," see Zhou Yang, *Jianjue guanche Mao Zedong wenyi luxian* (Peking: People's Literature Publishing House, 1952), pp. 1-34.

2. Mao Dun, "Reflect the Age of the Socialist Leap Forward, Promote the Leap Forward of the Socialist Age!" *Chinese Literature* 12 (1960): 20. The Chinese text, "Fanying shehui zhuyi yuejin di shidai, tuidong shehui zhuyi di yuejin," appears in *Renmin wenxue* 8 (1960): 8-36.

3. Mao Zedong, "Talks at the Yenan Forum on Literature and Art," *Selected Works*, Vol. 3 (Peking: Foreign Languages Press, 1967), p. 60.

4. John K. Fairbank, Edwin O. Reischauer, and Albert M. Craig, *East Asia: The Modern Transformation* (Boston: Houghton Mifflin, 1965), p. 82.

5. Ibid., p. 667.

6. Mao Zedong, "Report on an Investigation of the Peasant Movement in Hunan," *Selected Works*, Vol. 1 (Peking: Foreign Languages Press, 1967), p. 44.

7. See, for example, *Miraculous Tales from Liao Studio (Liao Zhai zhihyi), Strange Stories Past and Present (Jin gu quguan)*, and other popular romances.

8. Ding Ling, *Taiyang zhao zai Sanggan he shang* (Peking: New China Book Co., 1949); "Sun over the Sangkan River," *Chinese Literature*, Spring 1953, pp. 26-296

9. Joe C. Huang, *Heroes and Villains in Communist China: The Contemporary Chinese Novel as a Reflection of Life* (London: Hurst; New York: Pica, 1973), pp. 183-85.

10. Zhou Libo, *Baofeng zhouyu* (Tientsin: New China Book Co., 1949); Translated by Xu Mengxiung as *The Hurricane* (Peking: Foreign Languages Press, 1955).

11. For more information about Zhou Libo, see the Introduction to my translation of his short story, "The Guest," in the fortcoming special issue on the development of revolutionary literature in China of *Bulletin of Concerned Asian Scholars*.

12. Zhou Libo, op. cit., pp. 125-26

13. Liu Qing, *Chuang ye shi* (Peking: Chinese Youth Publishing House, 1960); Translated by Gladys Yang as *The Builders* (Peking: Foreign Languages Press, 1964).

14. Liu Qing, *Huangbu cun di san nian* (*Three Years in Huangbu Village*) Peking: Writers Publishing House, 1956).

15. Liu Qing, *The Builders*, p. 383.

16. Hao Ran, *Yanyang tian* (*Bright Sunny Days*), Vol. 1 (Peking: Writers Publishing House, 1964); Vols. 2 and 3 (Peking: People's Literature Publishing House, 1966).

17. For a study of the life and works of Hao Ran, see Joe C. Huang, "Haoran (Hao Jan), the Peasant Novelist" in the forthcoming special issue on Literature and Revolution of *Modern China*.

18. Hao Ran, *Jinguang dadao* (*The Golden Road*) (Peking: People's Literature Publishing House, Vol. 1, 1972, Vol. 2, 1974).

19. Ibid., Vol. 1, pp. 215-16.

20. Ibid., pp. 521-22.

4

PERCEPTIONS OF GROUP STRUCTURE AND LEADERSHIP POSITION AS AN ASPECT OF DEVIANCE AND SOCIAL CONTROL
Richard Whittingham Wilson

INTRODUCTION

Application of the political culture approach to the study of China has been both fruitful and disappointing. A number of works have uncovered fundamental value stances of Chinese people,[1] and have suggested new methods of investigation that have taken characterological examination far beyond the national character analyses of three decades ago. Moreover, for a society where much information concerning the political process is either unknown or difficult to verify, these works have valuably supplemented other approaches. On the negative side, political culture studies have been criticized for research founded on questionable data bases, for lack of methodological rigor, or immature theoretical reasoning, and for a tendency to link political events at the macro level to psychological states at the micro level. Much of the criticism is justified. Still, negative opinions of the approach seem more widely held within the China field than awareness of its achievements.

In an attempt to narrow the possibilities inherent in the political culture approach and to identify a relatively defined data source, some analysts have focused on childhood political socialization. In this subcategory scholars, using survey work, interviews, observation, and content analysis, attempt to discern by investigation of the learning process those salient values that are being transmitted from older to younger generations. This approach has the advantage of grounding findings within a firm empirical context. A major disadvantage is that while investigation may indicate that a child becomes disposed to behave, feel, and think in certain ways, there is no certainty that as an adult in an actual political situation this person will manifest a particular pattern that was observed in the socialization process. Critics of political socialization often note that although it appears to be concerned with many interesting problems, it is not concerned with those that directly relate to politics.

This essay will set forth comparative data on the spatial perceptions of group structure and leadership position of Chinese and American children along with some further findings concerning group behavior. Some broader issues from political philosophy that involve different interpretations of freedom and control will also be presented. The essay will not attempt to establish any strict causal or empirical link between these two sections; rather it will be suggested that the broader issues from political philosophy are given greater coherence by an understanding of socialization patterns.

COMPARATIVE SOCIALIZATION DATA ON GROUP STRUCTURE AND LEADERSHIP POSITION

A political socialization study was undertaken in 1970 involving samples of children in Hong Kong, Taiwan, New York City's Chinatown, and a group of Caucasian and black American children in New Jersey. Among the various methods of inquiry used was a questionnaire which contained, among others, three questions examining children's spatial orientations with regard to leadership position and group structure. To assume knowledge of the ways in which a people conceives of leadership and groups based on three questions alone would of course be presumptuous. Therefore, it is appropriate to note that the results set forth here derive from a much larger data base. These three questions, however, do point up differences among the samples tested in perceptions of ideal group structure and of leadership position. It should also be noted perhaps that one objective of the larger study was to examine three geographically separate Chinese communities living under different political and social circumstances in order to ascertain what degree of attitudinal commonality could be observed among them. Commonality, when noted, was assumed to be linked to the persistence of traditional values. The Caucasian and black sample from New Jersey was used for control purposes.

The three spatial orientation questions that were asked are as follows:

1. Here is a group of people. Who is the leader? Put an X on the one you think is the leader.

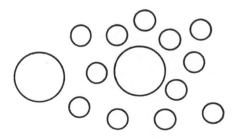

Circles were drawn of unequal size in order to draw the children's attention to the larger ones. The assumption was that the children would tend to select either the large circle outside the group to the left, or the large circle within the group.

2. Here are two groups. Which group would you like to be leader of? Draw a big circle all around the group you pick.

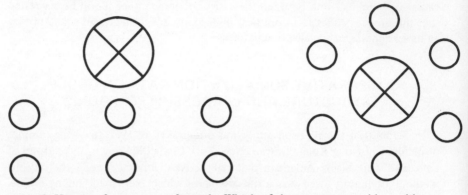

3. Here are four groups of people. Which of these groups would you like to be a member of? Draw a big circle all around the group you pick.

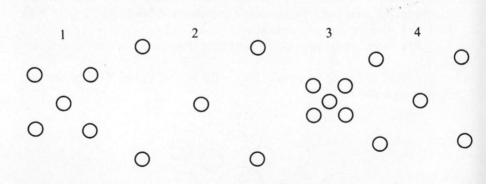

The purpose of this question was to examine the desirability of closeness in group structure. Responses 1 and 3 were grouped together as representing the desirability of a close group structure, and responses 2 and 4 were grouped together as representing the desirability of a loose group structure.

Using an analysis of variance statistical technique, each of these questions was analyzed to study differences among groups (Taiwan, Hong Kong, Chinatown, and New Jersey), between sexes, among grade levels (three, five, and seven), and the interaction among these basic effects. Significance was set at the 0.5 level. For the first two questions the responses were analyzed for whether the children selected a leader outside the group (leadership without) or inside the group (leadership within). For the third question the analysis was in terms of whether the children selected a close group structure or a loose group structure.

For Question 1, for leadership without responses, there was no significant differences among groups or between sexes. There was a significant difference among grade levels and a significant interaction effect between group and sex.*

---

*Differences among groups will be analyzed in the text of this paper. The other differences mentioned in this paragraph are noted below in abbreviated form by question number.

A. Question 1

    1. Differences among grade levels for leadership without (percent)

                Grade 3: 67
                Grade 5: 59
                Grade 7: 45

    2. Group and sex differences for leadership without (percent)

	Male	Female
New Jersey	56	58
Chinatown	44	69
Taiwan	60	50
Hong Kong	59	60

    3. Differences among grade levels for leadership within (percent)

                Grade 3: 23
                Grade 5: 32
                Grade 7: 47

B. Question 2

    1. Group and sex differences for leadership without (percent)

	Male	Female
New Jersey	67	62
Chinatown	51	78
Taiwan	51	77
Hong Kong	51	44

For the leadership within responses there were significant differences only among groups and among grade levels. On Question 2, for the leadership within situation, there was a significant difference among groups but not between sexes or among grade levels, nor were there significant interaction effects. For the leadership without situation there was a significant difference among groups and a significant interaction between group and sex. There were no other significant differences or significant interaction effects. On Question 3 for the close group group structure, there was a significant difference among groups, between sexes, and among grade levels, and a significant interaction between group and grade level. For the loose group structure there was a significant difference among groups, between sexes, and among grade levels, but no significant interaction effects.

Since our major concern here is difference between Chinese and American groups, only tables representing this portion of the data will be presented in the main body of the essay. Our assumption is that certain types of training techniques tend to emphasize highly cohesive groups in which leadership is seen as within and the function of leadership is to create and maintain a sense of exclusiveness, cohesiveness, and hierarchy. Other types of training techniques tend to develop a preference for more loosely organized groups with leadership essentially outside the group and interacting with the group as a whole rather than through internal hierarchic channels with subordinate group members. In

---

C. Question 3
1. Differences between sexes for close groups (percent)
        Male: 71
        Female: 80
2. Differences among grade levels for close group (percent)
        Grade 3: 62
        Grade 5: 82
        Grade 7: 82
3. Group and grade level differences for close group (percent)

	Grade 3	Grade 5	Grade 7
New Jersey	58	83	67
Chinatown	61	91	85
Taiwan	62	84	90
Hong Kong	66	70	88

4. Differences between sexes for loose group (percent)
        Male: 27
        Female: 17
5. Differences among grade levels for loose group (percent)
        Grade 3: 36
        Grade 5: 15
        Grade 7: 16

analyzing the responses from these three questions the responses for each question that fall under the close group/leadership within pattern will be presented first, followed by data for loose group/leadership without responses.

When the four groups were compared for the case of close group/leadership within, the response pattern was as shown in Table 1. Among groups the average of the mean percentage values gives Taiwan 54 percent, Hong Kong 53 percent, New Jersey 46 percent, and Chinatown 43 percent. The average rank orders are Taiwan 1.7, Hong Kong 2.0, Chinatown 3.0, and New Jersey 3.3.*

For the case of loose group/leadership without, the response pattern among groups is as indicated in Table 2. Among groups the average of the mean percentage values gives New Jersey the highest loose group/leadership without response rate with 50 percent, ahead of Chinatown with 45 percent, Hong Kong with 43 percent, and Taiwan with 41 percent. The average rank orders are New Jersey 1.3, Hong Kong 2.0, Chinatown 3.0, and Taiwan 3.7.

TABLE 1

Comparison Among Groups of Close Group/Leadership Within Responses
(percent)

	Taiwan	Hong Kong	Chinatown	New Jersey
Question 1 (leadership within)	37	38	24	36
Question 2 (leadership within)	47	47	27	32
Question 3 (close group)	79	74	79	69
No. responding	335	362	90	297
Question 1: $F = 7.25$				
Question 2: $F = 8.43$				
Question 3: $F = 7.30$				

Source: Richard W. Wilson, *The Moral State: A Study of the Political Socialization of Chinese and American Children* (New York: The Free Press, 1974), p. 95.

---

*Since there are four groups, if one group had been in first place on all questions, its average rank order would have been 1, while if it had been lowest on all questions, its average rank order would have been 4.

TABLE 2

Comparison Among Groups of Loose Group/Leadership
Without Responses
(percent)

	Taiwan	Hong Kong	Chinatown	New Jersey
Question 1 (leadership without)	55	59	56	57
Question 2 (leadership without)	47	48	64	65
Question 3 (loose group)	21	23	15	29
No. responding	335	362	90	297
Question 1: no significant differences				
Question 2: $F = 10.67$				
Question 3: $F = 8.56$				

Source: Richard W. Wilson, *The Moral State: A Study of the Political Socialization of Chinese and American Children* (New York: The Free Press, 1974), p. 97.

While the data presented is not conclusive, it suggests that genuine differences do exist between American children and children from predominantly Chinese societies. On the whole the children from the New Jersey and New York Chinatown placed less emphasis on leadership being within a group than did the children from Taiwan and Hong Kong. All the children tended to see leadership as somewhat without the group context, but this was more marked for the New Jersey and Chinatown groups than for the Taiwan and Hong Kong samples. Children from all four groups tended to prefer membership in closely knit groups. This was more the case, however, for children from Chinatown, Taiwan, and Hong Kong than it was for the black and Caucasian children from New Jersey.

Although the differences were not great, the evidence seems to indicate comparatively greater pressures within Chinese society for close inclusive social relationships, pressures that are reflected in other socialization data in statements concerning the need for unity, cooperation, and suppression of hostility. When one connects the pattern of more highly values group closeness with a greater tendency to see leadership as within the group structure, there emerges a pattern of a highly unitary group structure with a leadership that maintains cohesion through relationships with members that are conceived of at least partially as direct vertical links between the members and the leader rather than as vertical links between the group as a whole and a somewhat separate leader.[2]

GENERAL SOCIALIZATION PATTERNS

These tentative conclusions are given greater validity when placed in the context of other findings derived from studies of Chinese childhood socialization. For children in Taiwan, for instance, the value of the group over the individual is strongly reinforced during socialization. In written, verbal, and visual messages to children the emphasis is constantly upon the primacy of the group and the individual's responsibility to be cooperative with others, obedient to the goals of the group, and, above all, to behave in such a way that credit will be reflected upon the group as a whole. Shaming punishment for deviant behavior, involving the threat of ostracism or ridicule, bring to bear on the individual the full power of the group. In a more positive sense, rewards for appropriate behavior are usually phrased in such a way that the child realizes that his actions have had implications for the status and reputation of the group as a whole. Both of these techniques depend critically upon the child's having internalized the group and its standards as of more importance and validity than the child's own needs or aspirations. As the child develops considerable effort is expended to raise the group level with which the child primarily indentifies from the primary to the secondary level, including, most especially, loyalty to the nation state as a whole.[3]

These data on the development of group spiritedness are given greater breadth if we examine for Chinese and American children the different degrees to which the norms that govern behavior are internalized for various levels of group life. When children from Taiwan, Hong Kong, Chinatown, and New Jersey are compared in this regard it turns out that children from New Jersey generally internalize to a lesser degree at micro, intermediate, and macro levels (family, school, and polity) than Chinese Americans or children from Taiwan and Hong Kong. The major reason for this appears to be that family and school education in the United States is less rigorous about specific and inclusive behavioral codes and less prone to the use of open and consistent shaming when ideals of behavior are violated than is the case in Chinese communities. Moreover, peer group and other subnational identifications appear to be stronger for children from New Jersey and inhibit the development of an unambiguous sense of secondary level membership and a sense of the importance of that membership.[4]

In terms of conformist behavior the data are also revealing. Children from Taiwan especially tend to internalize conformist values more strongly than children from either Chinatown, Hong Kong, or New Jersey, with the children from New Jersey consistently at the lower end of the range.[5] In a test where the children were shown two pictures, one showing a group of people similarly dressed and one showing the same group in varied clothing, the children from Taiwan and Hong Kong responded to the question of which group they would like to be a member of overwhelmingly in favor of those that were similarly dressed (92.5 percent). In contrast only 41 percent of the children from New Jersey and 70 percent of the children from Chinatown selected membership in this group as desirable.[6] In stating why membership in the similarly clothed group would be desirable, Chinese children tended to respond in the following manner: "Because their clothes are the clothes of the group," or "If clothes are orderly then people will have an orderly feeling." American children, on the other hand, tended to respond in the following manner: "I would have more freedom," "Because they show individuality and freedom." or "You don't have to be the same to join a group. You should do what you feel like doing and not be the same."[7]

Chinese children see the leader in group terms, sometimes in the positive sense as someone helpful and loving who helps the group but also as someone who can act in a punitive way upon any given individual without check by intervening or countervailing authority. Criticism of the leader is frequently muted or is permissible only in terms that strengthen the group as a whole. Since followers are expected to model their behavior after that of the leader, criticism of the leader carries the implication of criticism of the group of which he is guide and model; consequently the loss of face which the leader will sustain will also be sustained by other members of that group. Under normal circumstances, therefore, censuring the leader is undertaken carefully both because it may damage an aspect of one's own self identity and also because of the possibility of being subjected to group ostracism for such an act.[8]

One of the factors favoring conformity to group norms in the Chinese context is the belief that opposition to the group and to its leaders is to be avoided whenever possible. During intensive interviews in Taiwan, Hong Kong, Chinatown, and New Jersey, children were asked a number of questions concerning whether one could or could not go against the group. When their responses were summarized and aggregated the pattern in Table 3 emerged.[9] Clearly Table 3 indicates that children from Taiwan and Hong Kong seem especially concerned that the individual not go against the group.

Socialization data tends to support the view that American children have different ideas concerning their role within a group structure than Chinese children; they are far less willing to perceive of conformism and group unity and organization as desirable in and of themselves. The results generally support our contention that for many American children the group is secondary to the individual whereas for many Chinese children group unity and organization appear to be overriding concerns.

TABLE 3

Expressions Regarding Whether One Can Go Against the Group
(percent)

	Taiwan	Hong Kong	Chinatown	New Jersey
Can go against the group	17	33	50	72
Should not go against the group	83	67	50	28
No indication	0	0	0	0
No. interviewed	18	18	6	18

Source: Richard W. Wilson, *The Moral State: A Study of the Political Socialization of Chinese and American Children* (New York: The Free Press, 1974), p. 196.

ISSUE OF FREEDOM AND CONSTRAINT

Perhaps few issues in Western culture have excited as much interest over the centuries as the concept of freedom. One need be only a cursory student of political philosophy to realize that this topic has been a central question since even before the time of the ancient Greeks. In the context of the inquiry into the question of deviance and social control, old questions conderning freedom have particular relevance. Indeed, deviance and social control may be thought of as new terminological handles for some very old questions.

Deviance, in the most general sense, is behavior, opinions, or attributes of an individual or subgroup that transcend some generally accepted standard defined either as a formalized normative code, such as law, or a less formalized standard of widely shared beliefs and attitudes. Inherent in discussions of deviance, where individuals or groups may be defined or labelled as behaving in a manner contrary to accepted norms, is the question of what constitutes permissible forms and types of action.

Social control refers to those social forces that restrain the expression of opinions and behavior or that punish for alleged misdeeds. In this sense group normative structures at both the macro and the micro level delineate appropriate ranges of behavior and opinion expression. Implicit in the notion of social control is an emphasis on the influences and institutions that direct a person's behavior toward a socially accepted pattern. The nature of institutions and social influences is an area of analysis that has preeminently informed works on freedom.

Because of the intimate relationship between questions concerning deviance and social control and other more traditional types of inquiry, it may be desirable to sketch in the briefest possible way some of the relevant issues that have derived from studies of freedom. In setting forth this sketch we are presenting only a few highlights from one of the most voluminous literatures in history. Clearly it is not our intention to contribute to the philosophical dialogue within this literature. Rather we seek to clarify how this literature pertains to deviance and social control. Further, we will suggest how socialization data concerning group structure, leadership position, and the role of the individual within the group may relate to such broader philosophical questions through the linkage between the attitudes that are formed during socialization and the general style and objectives of social control that are deemed appropriate within a culture.

In one of the most famous modern tracts on freedom, Isaiah Berlin pointed out that libertarian political philosophers assume a frontier must be drawn between private life and public authority.[10] As Berlin noted, the consciousness of individual rights is very new. It is a concept held neither by the ancient Greeks or Romans nor by the Jews or the Chinese. It is a concept that arose perhaps during the Renaissance or Reformation and is thus one that has become of peculiar importance only for modern people. The notion of rights is critically related to the function of law, which is to entitle all to a minimum of freedom by denying a little freedom to all. For Berlin, freedom can be defined in two distinct ways. First is the notion of "freedom from," implying the absence of interference beyond some recognizable frontier. Second is the notion of positive freedom, or "freedom to."[11] "Freedom to" derives from the wish to be one's own master, to be autonomous, or to will freely. Berlin believes that there is a profound difference between these two concepts of liberty. In the positive sense of liberty, or "freedom to," men seek to place authority in their own hands. In the negative sense, or "freedom from," the search is to curb authority. Here rights are regarded as absolute within a framework of social norms that have been long and widely held and whose observance has become tantamount within a given social structure to the conception of what it is to be human. Berlin feels, and I agree, that the negative sense of liberty, or "freedom from," is in the end a more humane ideal than the ideal of positive self-mastery by classes or peoples.[12]

Christian Bay, in a later work on freedom, states that in democratic societies freedom of expression is the most important goal.[13] According to Bay, freedom of expression is the crucial freedom because in the long run other freedoms depend on the enlargement and protection of this one.[14] While this would appear to be an espousal of the underlying value of positive freedom, or "freedom to," Bay's formulations take place within a framework that essentially adheres to the overriding good of negative freedom. As he states very early on, no society can give full freedom to all. Social cooperation requires some restraints.[15] Freedom for Bay, therefore, means the expression of individuality or self-expression within the context of some overarching defined limits. Within such a framework of limits Bay seeks to analyze how the individual may maximize his capacity for self-expression by minimizing objective danger, subjective fear, and subjective anxiety. The essential point is that the focus is very much on the individual. Coercion of individuals is seen as the maximum evil and self-expression, within the bounds set by the necessity for social cooperation, as the maximum good.

Attempts have been made by some modern scholars to analyze the origin of these differing concepts of freedom. Given the importance of questions concerning freedom within the Western value framework, it is perhaps not surprising that historical analyses invariably place this question within the context of Western civilization. For Barrington Moore the notion of certain groups and persons having immunity from royal power and the conception of contract as a freely undertaken mutual agreement derived from the feudal relationship of vassalage are crucial legacies from Western medieval society to modern Western conceptions of what constitutes a free society. While notions of freedom may now have worldwide significance, the complex out of which these notions arose occurred only in Western Europe.[16] For Moore the development of modern conceptions of liberty took place very much in the context of positive freedom, or "freedom to," when European peasants sought to get rid of overlords who no longer provided protection but only used their ancient privileges to take away the peasants' land.[17]

While J. L. Talmon does not mention the notions of positive and negative liberty in his monumental work, *The Origins of Totalitarian Democracy*, his analysis is clearly related to them. For Talmon totalitarian or messianic democracy and liberal or empirical democracy had their origins in the eighteenth century, when the prevailing belief in the unity of liberty, virtue, and reason proved false. In the subsequent search to free man from traditional restraints, liberal democrats eschewed the use of force and resorted to trial and error, while totalitarian democrats became exclusivist and justified coercion by elevating themselves to the vanguard of the enlightened.[18] For the totalitarian democrat political ideas are not "a set of pragmatic precepts or a body of devices applicable to a special branch of human behavior" but are "an integral part of an all-embracing and coherent philosophy."[19] While both schools of freedom affirm the supreme value of liberty, the liberal democrat finds the "essence of freedom in spontaneity and the absence of coercion" while the totalitarian democrat believes liberty is "realized only in the pursuit and attainment of an absolute collective purpose."[20] In Isaiah Berlin's terminology the totalitarian democrat adheres to a notion of positive liberty, or "freedom to," in which there is an ideal type of man and in which politics embodies sole and exclusive truth and embraces the whole of human existence. Collective purpose manifested by positive self-mastery by classes or peoples becomes the supreme objective.

In a slightly different manner sociologists and social psychologists have addressed questions of freedom in terms of group structure. For George Simmel the identity of a person is essentially known by his group affiliations. At the subnational level a person can become a member of a number of groups, and each new group membership circumscribes the individual more exactly and more unambiguously, making his particular configuration of group affiliations unique. However, although group affiliation is pervasive, there is no group, according to Simmel, so severe and pervasive in its sanctions that there do not remain some relationships in life that escape it.[21] One of the great achievements of modernity is the shattering of the fetters of the traditional kinship group and the subsequent freeing of the individual to develop his personality through membership in a collection of groups more congenial to his own nature.

Although this review of the literature on freedom is cursory, certain salient features do emerge. Within the liberal Western context it is suggested that a desirable social structure is composed of a number of separate subgroups in which the individual is perceived as the ultimate bedrock. Within an overarching boundary defined in terms of law that sets limitations on individuals, each person is encouraged to seek freedom as a positive value and to achieve greater self-expression and mastery for the self. Within this context the question of social control is how to define the overarching boundary so accurately as to provide for haromonization between an individual's motives and the needs of the social structure as a whole.

In distinction to liberal Western conceptions, the Chinese focus less on the quality of individual human relationships and more on relations between people "as integral parts of social groups."[22] The emphasis is not on the individual and individual self-expression but rather on the integrity and validity of the group as a whole. Individual self-importance is largely defined in terms of the contribution by the individual to the overall functioning of the group. In the modernization process in China the breakdown of identities that traditionally were focused virtually exclusively within the kinship group did not lead, as in the European case, to a bifurcation between identity as defined at the nation state level and identify on the individual level. Rather, identities in modern China continue to be defined predominantly in group terms, although at higher levels of social generalization.[23]

The definition of identity in group terms within Chinese culture is clearly reflected in Chinese socialization practices. Not only is identity in group terms strongly reinforced, but motivation to correct behavior is carried out in terms of rewards and punishments that have their grounding within the group structure. For instance, shaming, which is widely applied in Chinese childhood development, is a technique that demands that the individual perceive himself in group terms. For only by such a perception can threat of group ostracism and group ridicule come to have a highly significant meaning.

For Westerners, with their unique sense of the separateness of groups and of the high value of individual rights, the embracing qualities group life and the submergence of individual identity into a larger group identity are difficult to comprehend. The Western tendency to place a negative value judgment on societies where ideological dissidence is set out as a major category within the deviant area reflects very different conceptions of group organization and individual identity. In China, where the value of the group over the individual has predominance, the most valued norms governing interpersonal relationships stress actions that strengthen group life. Attempts to redefine norms or to test their limits are seen as threatening acts for the group as a whole. As such these acts have political consequences since they reduce the positive freedom, or "freedom to," of the group as a whole. In the Western context, however, group structure is not perceived as inclusive, and the links between the leader and the led are not perceived as tightly bound into a unitary structure. Norms are thought to be an overarching boundary, an ultimate definition of what constitutes appropriate behavior within which the individual is free to structure a relatively personalized life style. In this context the political maverick who tests normative boundaries performs a positive act by more clearly articulating the permissible limits and possibilities of individual behavior. As such, while controversy may swirl about his actions, this individual often assumes an heroic role.

CONCLUSIONS

Socialization data presented here point out that the perceptions of Chinese and American children of leadership position, group structure, and group behavior differ. Although we were not able to test hypotheses strictly, these differing perceptions of structure and behavior appear to be related to two alternate concepts of freedom as they have been set forth in Western political philosophy. The relative stress within Chinese socialization on the maintenance of group unity and the importance of group needs over individual aspirations was noted. Data was presented showing greater pressures in Chinese socialization for conformist behavior and for deference to the dictates of group leadership. The stress of group unity, as in the Chinese case, would appear to make an emphasis upon freedom for the group as a whole, or positive freedom, highly desirable, while the relative stress on individual self-expression, as in the American case, would appear to be congenial to a focus favoring the individual, that is, to sentiments for negative freedom, or freedom from. Differences of emphasis concerning group life and leadership position in Chinese and American socialization provide suggestive clues on how deviance in either society is defined and on what is perceived as appropriate forms and ranges of social control.

While clearly we can make no theoretical claims on the basis of this study, we do feel that the results indicate that socialization studies can provide for a better understanding of larger philosophical issues. The evidence suggests that differing socialization patterns are related to significant and profound differences in the ways in which social behavior is defined in different cultural contexts.

NOTES

1. Two of the most noteworthy examples are Lucian W. Pye, *The Spirit of Chinese Politics: A Psychocultural Study of the Authority Crisis in Political Development* (Cambridge, Mass. and London, England: MIT Press, 1968) and Richard H. Solomon, *Mao's Revolution and the Chinese Political Culture* (Berkeley, Los Angeles, and London, England: University of California Press, 1971).

2. The analysis above was derived, some of it verbatim, from Richard W. Wilson, *The Moral State: A Study of the Political Socialization of Chinese and American Children* (New York and London: The Free Press, 1974), pp. 92-99.

3. Richard W. Wilson, *Learning to be Chinese: The Political Socialization of Children in Taiwan* (Cambridge, Mass., and London, England: MIT Press, 1970), pp. 19-49.

4. Wilson, *Moral State*, pp. 242-47.

5. Ibid., p. 187.

6. Ibid., p. 194.

7. Ibid., pp. 193-95.

8. Wilson, *Learning to be Chinese*, pp. 101, 105-07.

9. Wilson, *Moral State*, p. 196.

10. Isaiah Berlin, *Two Concepts of Liberty* (London: Oxford University Press, 1958), p. 9.

11. Ibid. The material above draws from pp. 11-16.

12. Ibid., pp. 50, 51, 56.

13. Christian Bay, *The Structure of Freedom* (Stanford, Cal.: Stanford University Press, 1958 and 1970), p. 131.

14. Ibid., p. 146.

15. Ibid., p. 15.

16. Barrington Moore, Jr., *Social Origins of Dictatorship and Democracy: Lord and Peasant in the Making of the Modern World* (Boston: Beacon, 1966), p. 415.

17. Ibid., p. 498.

18. J. L. Talmon, *The Origins of Totalitarian Democracy* (London: Secker and Warburg, 1955), p. 5.

19. Ibid., p. 2.

20. Ibid., p. 2.

21. George Simmel, *Conflict* trans. Kurt H. Wolff, and *The Web of Group-Affiliations* trans. Reinhard Bendix, with a foreword by Everett C. Hughes (New York: The Free Press, 1955), p. 166.

22. Etienne Balazs, *Chinese Civilization and Bureaucracy: Variation on a Theme*, trans. H. M. Wright, ed A. F. Wright (New Haven: Yale University Press, 1964), p. 195.

23. Lynn T. White, III, "Corruption Redefined in Liberated Shanghai." Paper presented at the May 18, 1973 Regional Seminar of the Center for Chinese Studies, University of California, Berkeley, pp. 32-38. Cited with the author's permission.

5

A COGNITIVE DIMENSION OF
SOCIAL CONTROL: THE
HONG KONG CHINESE IN
CROSS-CULTURAL PERSPECTIVE
Alfred H. Bloom

The last decade has witnessed a paradigm shift in the fields of linguistics and cognitive psychology.[1] On the one hand, linguists and psychologists have grown increasingly disenchanted with the notion that an individual's behavior might be explained and predicted through exclusive attention to his or her environmental inputs. On the other, there has been a gradual accretion of evidence to support the notion that there exist underlying structural dimensions of human cognition and to suggest that analysis at the level of such dimensions might provide insight into how individuals select among and react to environmental influences—insight, that is, into the psychological connections through which social and cultural experiences become linked to individual behavior.

These structural dimensions are conceived as universal, biologically preprogrammed, developmental paths relating to specific areas of human thought and behavior (e.g., linguistic, logical, moral, and political). It seems universal, for example, that although a child is exposed to grammatical speech from birth, he will not develop the capacity for drawing upon this experience in order to formulate meaningful two-word constructions until around the age of two, that he will not develop the capacity for picking up grammatical endings until approximately a year later, and that he will not "learn" to transform word order to express, for example, the question in English or the *ba* construction in Chinese—a grammatical transformation that places object noun phrases before the verb and marks the preposed object by the particle *ba*—until he has reached a still later stage.[2] Drawing on evidence from the area of general cognitive development, it seems likewise universal that no matter what teaching techniques are used, a child cannot learn to symbolize, to represent one thing by something else, until he or she is around two years old, cannot learn to understand what adults mean when they say that a specific flower is both a flower and a blue flower at the same time until he or she is around seven, and cannot learn to understand what it means to hypothesize until around eleven or twelve.[3] Within the moral realm, Lawrence Kohlberg has provided evidence to suggest that individuals pass through a sequence of developmental stages of increasingly differentiated and integrated moral logic, such that they are at first unable even to understand the abstract notion that a specific behavior can be "morally right" as opposed to merely helpful, enjoyable, or punishable; that at a later stage they master the abstract notion of moral action but equate it with a personal responsibility to comply with the demands of external authority; and that only at an even later stage do they begin to perceive moral action as stemming from and predicated upon a set of personally derived value commitments.[4]

In none of these cases is development from stage to stage understood as necessarily consisting in qualitative leaps rather than in the gradual emergence of qualitatively distinct structures. Nor is growth viewed as a unique function of spontaneous biological maturation. It is seen rather as highly dependent in two important respects on the influence of environmental inputs. In the first place, while development from stage to stage within a specific dimension reflects a loosening of certain qualitative constraints on the individual's formal competence for dealing with a specific class of environmental factors, it is these factors that in every case must provide the context within which the more highly developed capacities can become manifest. Secondly, growth from one formal structure to another is itself viewed as a function of both biological maturation and the availability of sufficiently rich environmental stimuli. Environments that place a functional premium on the development of higher levels act as catalysts to the development of those levels, while environments that reinforce the use of lower level competencies act to inhibit the development of those that lie further along the dimensional continuum.[5]

The present chapter is an effort to apply this conceptual framework to the study of social control in general and social control in Chinese society in particular. It will proceed 1) by defining a structural dimension hypothesized to be active in sociopolitical thinking processes, 2) by providing empirical evidence from three markedly different cultural contexts including that of the Hong Kong Chinese for the cross-cultural reliability and validity of that dimension as defined, 3) by exploring the implications that such a dimension might have for increasing our understanding of the dynamics of social control in any society, and 4) by examining factors within the sociopolitical environment of Hong Kong and the socioculture of Chinese society that might help explain why the Hong Kong Chinese mean response on that dimension is so radically different from that of the Americans and French.

THE SOCIAL PRINCIPLEDNESS DIMENSION

On a fundamental level, the higher stages of Kohlberg's dimension of moral development represent an extension into the moral realm of the higher stages of Piaget's dimension of cognitive development. The attainment of what Piaget calls the concrete operational stage entails the development of the capacity to detach one's self from the perceptual world and encode that world in a system of abstract concepts such as "height," "width," "flowers" and "blue flowers," but is restrictive in that it does not permit hypothesizing by means of these abstract concepts as to how else the world might be constituted. Similarly, the attainment of what Kohlberg refers to as Stage 4 entails a capacity to detach one's self from the pragmatic world of personal costs and benefits and relate to conventional morality as an abstract system consisting in definitions of correct and incorrect behavior. It is restrictive, however, in that it does not permit hypothesizing about how else a moral system might be constituted. By contrast, the attainment of the highest stage along Piaget's dimension, namely formal operations, marks for Piaget the ability to deal with the hypothetical in the cognitive realm—to postulate scientific explanations for events, to envision the empirical implications that such explanations would have if correct, and to proceed methodically to test those implications as the basis for the construction of scientific theory. The attainment of the highest level along Kohlberg's dimension, Stage 6, marks for Kohlberg the ability to deal with the hypothetical in the moral realm—to postulate theories about how moral systems might be constituted, to examine those theories in the light of their implications at the empirical level and to abstract on the basis of that examination a set of personal value commitments for guiding personal behavior and evaluating existing moral systems.[6]

By analogy, the work of Piaget and Kohlberg suggest that one might expect to find a similar dimension relevant to sociopolitical thinking processes, which for purposes of this chapter I will refer to as "social principledness." A low level along such a dimension—low social principledness—would be marked by a capacity for understanding the abstract notion of sociopolitical responsibility at the societal level, but be limited to the view that sociopolitical responsibility consists in unanalytic adherence to the demands of existing political authority, i.e., in placing obedience to that authority above any individual intuition as to what might constitute proper action. By contrast, a high level along such a dimension—high social principledness—would be marked by the development of a personal, analytically derived conception of what values a sociopolitical system should seek to maximize and by a continuing critical evaluation of the degree to which the institutions and policies of the existing system are successful in realizing that goal. An individual who is high on this dimension will then, by contrast to his low-principled counterpart, consistently differentiate between the social and legal definitions of correct action and what he believes to be a morally correct stance. He will consistently reject an unquestioned acceptance of conventionally defined values, an unanalytic response to conventional authority, in favor of becoming his own moral arbiter, responsible for determining whether a demand of the society should or should not be

obeyed, whether a position adopted by the polity should or should not be supported. In those situations in which the value claims for disobedience seem to
him to outweigh the claims for obedience, he will consider it right to disobey.[7]

If this postulated dimension of the sociopolitical thinking process finds
empirical support, it would be likely to prove highly relevant to the issue of
social control, for an individual's position along this dimension would seem
intimately tied to the type of social control to which he would be receptive and
by extension, a society's mean level of social principledness would seem to act as
a crucial variable in the effective management of social control in that society.

AN EMPIRICAL TEST OF THE PROPOSED DIMENSION

In late 1972, I began an investigation to provide cross-cultural evidence for
the reliability and validity of the social principledness dimension as defined.
Since one cannot assume a one-to-one correspondence between a subject's
position on such a dimension and the attitudes he will adopt or the behavioral
responses he will choose in any given situation, it was necessary to construct a
questionnaire that focused on the criteria individuals use in making sociopolitical
judgments rather than on the end products of those judgments. Three months of
initial pretesting in the United States and four months of intensive interviewing
and pretesting in Hong Kong led to the development of an appropriate Chinese
questionnaire. It was distributed to 336 Hong Kong residents, approximately
one-third businessmen and professionals, one-third workers, and one-third students. Eight months later the questionnaire was translated into French, pre-
tested, and distributed to seventy-six students at the Universite de Dijon, Dijon,
France. The translating and pretesting process was repeated for a U.S. sample
three months later, and the questionnaire was then distributed to fifty-two
college students in the New England area. The pretesting served to eliminate
linguistic ambiguities and infelicities and to insure that all questions were not
only meaningful to all subjects in each culture, but were being understood in the
way intended and in a similar manner across cultures. Since in constructing such a
questionnaire one is interested in what subjects feel they ought to do rather than
what they would in fact do, any biasing effects resulting from a subject's
attempt to please the experimenter by responding in the way he thinks he
"should" respond would ironically lead the subject to answer just as one would
like him to.

The questionnaire itself is composed of three sets of intermixed questions
followed by an extensive biographical section. The first set of questions assesses
the subject's position on the social principledness dimension. The second assesses
the subject's level of sensitivity to the human implications of various sociopolitical situations and policy alternatives.* The third is intended as an

---

*As a test in the sociopolitical realm of Kohlberg's assumption of a necessary inter-
relationship between the development of a hypothetico-deductive orientation to morality

exploratory means for providing outside validation for the social principledness dimension.

To lower the risk of the subjective biasing in the coding procedure which seems to plague Kohlberg's purely open-ended work, thirteen of the sixteen social principledness questions are posed in multiple-choice format. Each requires the subject to choose, with reference to either a general statement or a description of a specific situation, between what is hypothesized to constitute (a) a high-principled response, reflecting a readiness to differentiate between the legal standard and a standard of personal political morality and either (b) a low-principled response, reflecting a fusing of the concepts of law and morality and/or (c) an instrumental response, reflecting a lack of any feeling of personal responsibility to the polity other than a desire to avoid its sanctions. To eliminate possible order effects the response alternatives were counterbalanced.

Kohlberg found that subjects often prefer moral reasoning of a higher level than their own even though they are unable to work within the logic of that higher level.[8] To minimize the effect of this potential source of bias, the low-principled alternative is in each case phrased to that it would appear to the unsuspecting eye as the more socially responsible choice, while the explicit reasoning necessary to justify the high-principled alternative is omitted from the statement of that alternative. Thus the high-principled mode of reasoning would have to be prepotent in the subject's mind for him to find that alternative attractive. Subjects were asked, for example, to agree or disagree with the

---

and the development of a humanistic value base for making moral judgments, a set of questions designed to measure the level of subject response to the human implications of sociopolitical situations and policy alternatives was included in the questionnaire, scales of humanism were constructed for each culture on the basis of the responses to those questions, and the scales of social humanism were then compared by correlational and cross-tabulational analysis to social principledness scores. More specifically, the social humanism questions were designed to gauge the subject's readiness to reject statements that attribute personality defects to outgroups for which there is no necessary basis in fact (e.g., "I feel that people who use drugs have less integrity, even before they take up the habit, than those who do not use them"), to reject justifications in various hypothetical situations, ranging from ones involving the threat of invasion to ones involving the usurpation of trade or confiscation of property, and to reject justifications for not intervening in behalf of a victim in an accident situation. Using all of the original twenty-three questions in Hong Kong and France, the scales of social humanism have reliabilities of $r_{tt} = 0.80$ and 0.82 respectively; with fifteeen of the twenty-three, the American social humanism scale has a reliability of 0.83. Comparison within each cultural context of subjects' levels of social principledness with their levels of social humanism refutes the notion that attaining a high level of social principledness would necessarily entail adopting a humanistic value base for sociopolitical judgment. In each culture only 19 to 45 percent of the subjects who scored high on the principledness dimension also scored high on the social humanism scale. There is evidence to support the suggestion, however, that a high principledness score increases the probability that one will score high on the latter scale.

following statement: "Although you might not obey every law, you can at least be sure that if you obey a law, you have done the right thing." To the high-principled subject, who can envision situations in which obeying the law would be the wrong thing to do, a disagree response seems justifiable. By contrast, for the low-principled subject, who cannot envision such situations, a disagree response is likely to seem socially irresponsible.

Alongside the multiple-choice questions, an open-ended question is included within each of the three situationally-specific question paradigms to provide a conext free enough to permit distortions resulting from the constraints imposed gy the multiple-choice format to come to light.

As an example of a situationally-specific question paradigm, subjects were asked to read the description adapted from Kohlberg in which a parent steals medicine for his dying child for lack of any other way of obtaining it. Subjects who agreed that the parent should steal the medicine were asked to differentiate between regarding the stealing as wrong because it was against the law but excusable as an exception, and regarding stealing as the morally correct course of action given the specific circumstances. The low-principled subject may search for excuses to justify the parent's action but cannot bring himself to grant moral legitimacy to his own inclinations when they are in conflict with the conventional moral standard. By contrast, the high-principled thinker, when asked to defend disobedience, will justify such disobedience on the grounds that the moral claims for disobedience in the given situation outweigh those pressuring for obedience, thus making it morally right to disobey. He might regret the necessity of breaking the law, but he would not feel it wrong to have done so. Furthermore, he would consider it morally wrong to punish someone to the full extent of the law for acting similarly in the circumstances.

While responses to the multiple-choice questions were coded such that for each high-principled response the subject received one point and for any other response no points, responses to the open-ended questions were coded by two independent raters on a scale of 0 to 2 of increasingly high principledness. Precise criteria for coding the responses were developed so that the rating task turned out to be quite objective. In the case of disagreement between raters, the average of their ratings was used. All reliabilities are above 0.85 and most ranged from 0.93 to 0.95.

The exploratory validity measures include a nine-question scale assessing the subject's willingness to express opinions in conflict with the official policy of his government; a measure of internationalist orientation focusing on the subject's willingness to posit internationalist principles over national interest, and a paper-and-pencil version of the Milgram obedience-to-authority experimental paradigm, written so as to engage the subject in the actual conflicting pressures of the experimental situation and to force him to make a moral decision as to whether and at what point to end his participation.[9]

Separate unrotated principal component factor analyses were performed on the responses to the social principledness questions in each cultural context as a test of the underlying coherence of the dimension as it manifests itself within that context. The resulting factor solutions were then compared cross-culturally as a test of the cross-cultural uniformity of the dimension.[10]

There is, first of all, strong evidence to indicate that the social principledness questions pick up a dimension of internally consistent reasoning in each of the three cultural contexts. The factor analyses performed on these questions in each culture yield strong one-factor solutions. The drop in latent root from the first to second factor in Hong Kong is from 3.0 to 1.7; in France from 3.2 to 1.4; and in the United States from 4.5 to 1.6. Using as guides the factor loadings on the first factors and the criterion that a question be excluded only if it lowered the coefficient of internal consistency of the scale, scales of social principledness were constructed for each sample. The Hong Kong scale has fourteen of the original sixteen questions, r_{tt} = 0.71; the French, thirteen, r_{tt} = 0.72, and the American twelve of the original questions, r_{tt} = 0.82.

Moreover, striking similarities across the three cultures in the internal patterning of the factor loadings lend strong support to the further contention that the Hong Kong, French, and American scales are capturing a similar dimension of internally consistent reasoning across the three cultural contexts. The question with the lowest factor loading on the first factor of each analysis (and in fact the only question with any loading below 0.1) is the same question across cultures. Spearman Rank Order correlations relating each of the cross-cultural versions of the social principledness scale to the other two all yield significance levels of $p < 0.05$.

Turning to the evidence supporting the validity of the dimension as defined, the one question with the lowest factor loadings across cultures was the only question that was from the start considered to be somewhat tangential to the conceptual core of the dimension. Based on the work of Tapp and Kohlberg,[11] it focuses on the level of abstraction at which the subject views the function of laws in society rather than on the subject's readiness to differentiate between a conventional and an individual standard in assessing personal responsibility to law and political authority. The two questions with the highest loadings are the same across cultures and are perhaps the two which relate most directly to the theoretical nucleus of the dimension as defined, for they focus centrally on whether or not it is necessarily wrong to break a law and whether or not there are exceptions to the rule that all violations are necessarily to be punished. All of the external validity measures correlate in the expected direction with subjects' social principledness scores. Among the strongest and most suggestive relationships, the independent opinion scale correlates positively with social principledness in all three cultures, with $p < 0.001$ (0.378, Hong Kong, 0.622, France; 0.692, United States). The more highly principled the subject the less willing he or she should be to invest external authority with ultimate moral power, whether the authority be that of the nation state or the experimenter in a Milgram obedience-to-authority experimental paradigm. The measure of internationalist orientation, focusing on the subject's willingness to posit internationalist principles over national interest, correlates, as predicted, in a positive direction with social principledness, $p < 0.001$ in Hong Kong and $p < 0.01$ in France and the United States (0.201, Hong Kong; 0.361, France; 0.406, United States). Responses to the paper-and-pencil version of the Milgram experimental paradigm are likewise significantly related to social principledness scores in Hong Kong ($X^2 = 4.114$, $p < 0.05$) and France ($X^2 = 6.775$, $p < 0.01$). There is virtually no variance in the responses to this question in the U.S. sample, suggesting that the subjects might have already been familiar with the experiment.

SOCIAL PRINCIPLEDNESS AND SOCIAL CONTROL

The results of the empirical study can then be interpreted as confirming the operation of the social principledness dimension as an underlying structural dimension of the political thinking process in Hong Kong, France and the United States, thus offering a firm basis for projecting beyond the parameters of the dimension itself to the implications it bears with respect to the issue of social control.

It is undoubtedly true that individuals with very few exceptions are universally responsive to means of social control that rely upon the manipulation of reward and punishment contingencies, especially as those contingencies become of increasing personal significance to the individuals concerned. But if a society is to pass beyond the level of purely pragmatic controls and attain what Weber and Kelman[12] have referred to as "legitimacy" or legitimate control, then that society must begin to depend on higher level types of social control, i.e., types mediated by higher level psychological processes. At this point, the social principledness dimension becomes highly relevant to the study of social control, for an individual's position on that dimension is directly related to his receptivity to these higher types of social control. The low-principled citizen, unlike his high-principled counterpart, readily transfers control over sociopolitical decision-making from himself to the political authority. He should thus be more receptive than the high-principled citizen to prescriptions promulgated by the political authority as to what constitutes meritorious behavior as opposed to subversive activity, as to how a given sociopolitical situation is to be interpreted, as to what attitudinal positions to adopt with respect to the entire range of sociopolitical issues, and as to the appropriate stance to assume (or label to employ) in thinking and taling about various subgroups of the population. (See also Professor Sidney Greenblatt's discussion in this volume.) Motivationally, the low-principled citizen should be most responsive to a flaunting by the system of its symbols of authority and legitimacy, and to appeals made by the system to the sanctity of a specific political tradition, a specific office, or a specific ideology which he has been conditioned to respect. Attempts to gain his support by appeal to the values inherent in the establishment of a specific institution or the adoption of a specific policy alternative, which do not affect him personally and which have not been defined as requiring the support of the "patriotic" citizen, may be met with a disinterested and perhaps even uncomprehending response.

The high-principled individual, on the other hand, would be likely to resist attempts by an authority to impose definitions of correct belief or behavior and to react skeptically to symbolic appeals to the sanctity of a specific political tradition or ideological doctrine. Eliciting his support would require the establishment of institutions and the implementation of policies whose manifest value content is perceived by him to coincide sufficiently with his own value commitments to justify such support.

Just as position on the social principledness dimension can then be seen as highly relevant to the kind of appeal, i.e., means of social control, that is most likely to be effective in eliciting the support of the individual citizen, so can it be seen as related to the level of systemic breakdown that is most likely to induce feelings of dissatisfaction and alienation. The low-principled subject would in this regard presumably be most sensitive to a perceived erosion in the system's ability to continue to provide a reliable authority source upon which the individual can feel securely dependent. This might result, in turn, from a perception that the system is increasingly incapable of maintaining social order, from a perception that the system is acting in such a way as to exclude the individual or his own group from the general climate of security it offers, or from the perception that the system, or the individuals presently running it, are deviating too far from the traditionally accepted symbols and behaviors associated with legitimate authority. By contrast, the high-principled subject would presumably not respond to the erosion of authority per se but rather to a betrayal by the authority of the values to which he feels the system should be committed or to an erosion of authority which would render the system incapable of maintaining such values.

Alienation among low principled individuals would be likely to manifest itself in the form of an undirected general anxiety resulting from a perceived anomic situation in which the symbolic and/or instrumental sources of authority dependence are eroding. By contrast, alienation among high-principled individuals should take a more directed form, in which the concerted aim would be redirecting the system toward its former value commitments or replacing the system with one that would more closely reflect those value objectives.

Summarizing, then, interpreting the evidence for the social principledness dimension in the light of its implications for the issue of social control suggests the need for adopting an analytic framework for the study of social control that focuses not only on a description of the means employed by a specific society for achieving social control, but on the processes at the individual psychological level through which the means in question are expected to produce their effects. Seen within this framework, the success of any specific set of means of social control (other than those which operate at a purely pragmatic level) will depend on a congruence between the psychological processes upon which they have been designed to work and the position along the social principledness dimension of the individuals whom they have been designed to influence. Means that rely on the diffusion of prescriptions of proper behavior, on the imposition of labels of what constitutes subversive activity, or on appeals to the sanctity of an ideology whose underlying assumptions are to be accepted unquestionably, will appeal only to the low-principled citizen. Those that depend on achieving a value congruence rather than imposing a collective value system will appeal to his high-principled counterpart.

The discussion of the relation of social principledness to the issue of social control up to this point has avoided any reference to specific societal contexts; and it may in fact be one of the most important implications of this analysis that once one views the issue of social control as intimately tied to a cognitive dimension such as social principledness, the issue ceases to be susceptible to complete analysis within the confines of any specific cultural or societal context; it comes to rely rather on an understanding of the operation of formal universals in human cognition. In other words, a full understanding of the dynamics of social control in Chinese society as a case in point might be seen as necessarily depending on a prequisite understanding of the universal dynamics of social control at the individual psychological level.

This is not, however, to deny that the specific manifestations of such formal universals do not differ from social context to social context. As discussed earlier, sociocultural experience must provide the context within which these formal universals become manifest—including the specific value bases of the high-principled individuals, and the authority, the symbols, the ideological doctrines, the prescriptions of proper behavior and belief to which the low-principled individuals are responsive. Furthermore, it is the sociocultural environment that seems to play the largest role in determining the actual distribution of a population or segments thereof along the social principledness dimension, although the structure of that dimension as a potential path of development predates the influence of such sociocultural factors.

CHINESE SOCIETY AND THE MANAGEMENT OF LOW SOCIAL PRINCIPLEDNESS

Piaget and Kohlberg have both suggested that continuing individual exposure to conflict that cannot be resolved within one's present level of logical or moral reasoning may, when accompanied by conditions that inspire confidence in one's ability to handle such conflict, encourage a reexamination of the assumptions underlying one's present level of reasoning and thereby motivate movement toward a higher level.[13] By extension it might be hypothesized that a sociocultural environment that tends to increase and intensify individual exposure to conflict between opposing sociopolitical value claims and at the same time inspires the average citizen with confidence in his own ability to resolve such conflict on the basis of his own considered judgment rather than by appeal to established collective standards, would be likely to play a decisive role in fostering the development of high-principled thinking. Conversely, an economic and political climate that limits individual participation in sociopolitical conflicts at the level at which value claims are debated and value hierarchies established, a sociocultural climate that discourages confrontation with such conflict in the interests of maintaining social harmony and rewards the individual for applying established collective standards to its resolution, and an intellectual climate that directs attention way from the cultivation of individual critical faculties would be likely to reinforce low-principled thinking on a societal scale and thereby impede growth along the social principledness dimension.

It is within this explanatory framework that I would interpret the finding that, despite the fact that the social principledness dimension seems to capture a range of reasoning styles that is as inherent to Hong Kong society as it is to American society and French society, the mean level of social principledness of the samples, taken as wholes, differ markedly across cultures. On a range from 0 to 1 of increasingly high social principledness, the mean of the combined Hong Kong population tested is only 0.18, while the population means of the French and American samples are 0.47 and 0.43 respectively, a difference significant in a one-way analysis of variance at the 0.001 level.

The lower level of economic development, reflected in lower levels of education and lower literacy rates, may in Hong Kong tend to restrict the horizons and level of theoretical abstraction of the average citizen's sociopolitical involvements.[14] The political institutions through which Hong Kong is presently governed, which severely limit the number of elected officials and severely circumscribe the domains of policy-making over which these officials exert responsibility,[15] may be acting to reinforce an apathetic response[16] to the sociopolitical sphere and thus to discourage the kind of intense personal participation in sociopolitical value conflicts that seems prerequisite to the growth of high-principled reasoning. To the extent that such factors are typical of lower stages of economic and political development, one might view the level of socioeconomic development of a society as generally related to the distribution of the population of that society along the social principledness dimension.

Predispositions among the Chinese toward assuming deferential attitudes to authority and toward choosing avoidance responses in the face of conflict may also be playing their role.[17] The deferential orientation to authority is reflected in and reinforced by cultivation, during socialization, of unquestioned respect for adult and social authority, in the respect accorded ancestors, in the importance attributed to classical models in art and literature, and in the emphasis placed in education on learning classical texts rather than on developing individual faculties and the confidence to use them. Political regimes have traditionally claimed legitimacy not on the grounds that they are capable of maintaining civil liberties or democratic procedures, but rather on their success in maintaining social harmony—avoidance of conflict on the societal scale. The citizen as a political being was traditionally taught that his responsibility lay in contributing to that harmony by accepting rather than questioning.

Concerning aspects of the Chinese intellectual climate that may be contributing to the stabilization of a low-principled orientation, Donald Munro, in his very exciting paper in the present volume (see Chapter 2), discusses the traditional Chinese view that thoughts exist as promptings to action, that, in other words, no autonomous rational competence exists untied from its action implications. Upon this psychological model of the relationship of thought to action rests, according to Munro, the further implication that if thoughts are inseparable from action consequences, they must be brought under control in order that social behavior itself be effectively brought under control. Implicit in these traditional views seem to be at least two distinct, though interrelated, notions potentially relevant to the maintenance of a low level of social principledness in Chinese society. The first is that if thought is viewed as essentially an internal, unrealized form of behavior and "better" thought is that which leads to specific behavioral consequences considered more socially acceptable, more moral than others, then teaching someone to think quickly becomes equated with imparting proper content (i.e., content that will lead to appropriate behavior) rather than with developing qualitatively higher capacities for organizing experience—a capacity for abstract thinking, for hypothesizing, for individual creative, critical evaluation in the logical, moral, or sociopolitical spheres. The second is that if thoughts are seen as promptings to action and if this view is then taken to justify the right of the social system to impose collective standards of belief throughout the population, then such a view ipso facto justifies the creation and maintenance of a social system whose psychological cement derives from the lower rather than the upper end of the social principledness dimension. Thus, on both the individual and societal levels, the traditional Chinese psychological view of thoughts as promptings to action seems to translate into an apology for a low-principled orientation and reinforces that orientation just as it is reinforced by it.

A second element of the Chinese intellectual climate that might prove relevant to the lower level of social principledness in that society involves the apparently limited importance attributed by the Chinese to the use of the hypothetico-deductive mode of reasoning, so fundamental to the evolution of Western logical and scientific thought. A relatively low emphasis on this mode of reasoning in Chinese culture might be seen as reflected in the lack of development within the Chinese intellectual tradition of scientific theory and formal logics comparable to those of the West. Indeed, in the language itself no distinction is made between the hypothetico-deductive mood (the counterfactual mood—if x were, then y would be, or, in the past, if x had been, then y would have been) and the straight conditional mood (if x, then y).[18]

Piaget and Kohlberg both view the hypothetico-deductive mode of reasoning as crucial to the development of the highest level on their respective dimensions, for it underlies the ability to decenter one's self from a given abstract logical or moral system and to hypothesize about how that system might or should otherwise be constituted. By analogy, one might expect a readiness to employ such reasoning within the sociopolitical realm to be crucial to the development of a high level of social principledness and an intellectual climate that discourages its use to exert a restraining effect on upward movement along that dimension.

My discussion has distinguished a series of society-specific and culture-specific variables which, it is suggested, may be acting in conjunction with each other to help solidify and maintain the low level of social principledness found within the Hong Kong population sampled. Each variable is to be taken as a hypothesis in need of empirical verification.

Turning finally to the relevance of these variables to the issue of social control, one might, on the basis of the analytic framework proposed in this chapter, further speculate that in acting as a group to reinforce the dynamics of low-principled thinking, these variables are in fact acting indirectly to sensitize the population to means of social control that rely on a readiness to transfer the locus of sociopolitical decising-making from the self to the political authority. Whether in Hong Kong or, by analogy, in the PRC, if and when such means become increasingly effective in managing social control, they tend to reinforce the psychological basis upon which they depend, making it increasingly less necessary to back them up with the threat of sanctions, yet at the same time, perhaps, increasingly more difficult to change their psychological basis in the direction of a higher level of social principledness.

NOTES

1. Readers interested in the linguistic aspects of this paradigm shift might consult John Lyons, *Noam Chomsky* (New York: Viking, 1970) and Noam Chomsky, *Reflections on Language* (New York: Pantheon, 1975). Those interested in the psychological aspect might see John H. Flavell, *The Developmental Psychology of Jean Piaget* (New York: Van Nostrand, 1963) and Lawrence Kohlberg, "Stage and Sequence: The Cognitive-Developmental Approach to Socialization," in *Handbook of Socialization Theory and Research*, ed. David A. Goslin (Chicago: Rand McNally, 1969), pp. 347-480.

2. See Roger Brown, *A First Language: The Early Stages* (Cambridge, Mass.: Harvard University Press, 1973.

3. Jean Piaget and Barbel Inhelder, *The Psychology of the Child* (New York: Basic Books, 1969).

4. Lawrence Kohlberg, "From Is to Ought: How to Commit the Naturalistic Fallacy and Get Away with it in the Study of Moral Development," in *Cognitive Development and Epistemology*, ed. Theodore Mischel (New York: Academic Press, 1971), pp. 151-235.

5. See Jerome S. Bruner, Rose R. Olver, and Patricia M. Greenfield, et al., *Studies in Cognitive Growth* (New York: Wiley, 1967); Michael Cole and Sylvia Scribner, *Culture and Thought: A Psychocultural Introduction* (New York: Wiley, 1974); and Lawrence Kohlberg, "Stage and Sequence," pp. 347-71, for a discussion of the role of environmental factors in affecting growth along developmental-structural dimensions.

6. In Kohlberg's treatment of Stage 6, the attainment of a hypothetico-deductive orientation to the question of morality is viewed as necessarily entailing the simultaneous development of a set of humanistic principles which, henceforth, form the value base for personal moral decision-making (see Kohlberg, "From Is to Ought," pp. 204-13). The development of a humanistic base as opposed to any other (e.g., aesthetic, nationalistic, nihilistic) I view as a separate achievement, not necessarily entailed either logically or empirically by the attainment of a hypothetico-deductive orientation towards morality, though rendered more probable by such a development. Such an interpretation brings Kohlberg more in line with Piaget, preserves the structure/content distinction which originally motivated Kohlberg's work and which forms the basis of Kohlberg's defense that his work does not reflect the thinking of any cultural tradition, and finds strong empirical support in an investigation carried out in conjunction with the one discussed in this chapter. See my "Two Dimensions of Moral Reasoning: Social Principledness and Social Humanism in Cross-Cultural Perspective," *Journal of Social Psychology*, February 1977.

7. A dimension of the sociopolitical thinking process such as social principledness would offer an explanation in cognitive-developmental terms for certain of the distinct channels at the individual psychological level through which, as Weber has observed, a political regime can achieve legitimacy, and likewise for the distinct psychological modes through which Kelman, analyzing from the individual rather than the systemic perspective, has noted that individuals attribute legitimacy to political regimes. See Max Weber, *The Theory of Social and Economic Organization* (New York: The Free Press, 1964), pp. 124-32, especially with regard to his distinction between legitimacy based on tradition, affectual ties, and legal contract on the one hand and that based on a rational belief in the absolute value of the system (*Wertrational*) on the other. See also Herbert C. Kelman, "Patterns of Personal Involvement in the National System: A Socio-Psychological Analysis of Political Legitimacy," in *International Politics and Foreign Policy: A Reader in Research and Theory* (rev. ed.), ed. J. N. Rosenau (New York: The Free Press, 1969), pp. 176-88. Kelman draws a distinction among three modes of legitimacy attribution—the normative, characterized by an unquestioned acceptance of the right of a political system to prescribe citizen behavior within specific domains; the identificational—characterized by an emotional identification with the role of "good citizen," defined as one who defends and supports the political system; and the ideological—characterized by a conscious appraisal of the system as one which expresses the values to which the legitimator is himself committed. Since both the normative and identificational modes entail a sense of responsibility to surrender to the political authority the right to determine what constitutes correct action in the socio-political sphere, I would view them as subtypes of low-principled thinking, bearing slightly different etiologies at the emotional level. The ideological corresponds closely to the present notion of high-principled thinking. Kelman's analysis, however, remains tied to the view that such modes exist as a set of alternative processes of sociopolitical reasoning from which any given citizen could presumably select any given one at any given time, rather than viewing such modes as anchored in a developmental dimension of sociopolitical competence. See also Herbert Kelman and Alfred Bloom, "Assumptive Frameworks in International Politics," in *Handbook of Political Psychology*, ed. Jeanne Knutson (San Francisco: Jossey-Bass, 1973), pp. 261-95.

8. Kohlberg, "Stage and Sequence." See also E. Turiel, "Developmental Processes in the Child's Moral Thinking," in *Trends and Issues in Developmental Psychology*, ed. Paul H. Mussen, Jonas Langer, and Martin Covington (New York: Holt, Rinehart & Winston, 1969), pp. 120-33.

9. See S. Milgram, *Obedience to Authority: An Experimental View* (New York: Harper and Row, 1974). The experimental paradigm consists in confronting a naive subject who has volunteered and been promised payment for participation in a psychological experiment with a task involving the delivery of increasingly severe electric shocks to someone whom he assumes also to be a naive subject. The experimental test is the extent to which the subject, under the pressure of the experimental context and the experimenter's personal insistence that he continue, does in fact continue to deliver the shocks. In the running of the experiments, no one is actually exposed to shocks, but a depressingly large percentage of those subjects who think they are in fact delivering shocks continue to do so even beyond the point at which it is presumed that the intensity of the shock might be highly dangerous and at which time the "victim" is presumably no longer capable of response.

10. See A. Przeworski and H. Teune, *Logic of Comparative Social Inquiry* (New York: Wiley-Interscience, 1970) for a discussion of this statistical technique.

11. J. Tapp and L. Kohlberg, "Developing Senses of Law and Legal Justice," *Journal of Social Issues* 27, no. 2 (1971): 65-71.

12. Weber, op. cit., pp. 126-27; Kelman, op. cit., pp. 278-79.

13. See also B. Inhelder and H. Sinclair, "Learning Cognitive Structures," in *Trends and Issues in Developmental Psychology*, op. cit., pp. 2-21; and, in the same volume, J. Langer, "Disequilibrium as a Source of Development," pp. 22-37, and E. Turiel, pp. 120-37.

14. D. Lerner, *The Passing of Traditional Society: Modernizing the Middle East* (New York: The Free Press, 1958).

15. The only governmental body in municipal Hong Kong to which members are elected is the Urban Council, whose powers are restricted to such concerns as sanitation and park maintenance; and even that body is composed of six official members of the government (all British in 1973), ten citizens appointed by the governor, and only ten members elected by the small segment of the population enfranchised to vote (in 1965, according to A. K. Wong, for example, only 200,000 out of a population of 3.4 million). See A. K. Wong, "Political Apathy and the Political System in Hong Kong," *Hong Kong Law Review*, 1972, pp. 1-20; and John Rear, "One Brand of Politics" in *Hong Kong: The Industrial Colony*, ed. Keith Hopkins (Hong Kong: Oxford University Press, 1971), pp. 55-139.

16. Wong, op. cit.

17. R. W. Wilson, *Learning to be Chinese: The Political Socialization of Children in Taiwan* (Cambridge, Mass.: MIT Press, 1970); L. W. Pye, *The Spirit of Chinese Politics: A Psychocultural Study of the Authority Crisis in Political Development* (Cambridge, Mass.: MIT Press, 1968); R. H. Solomon, *Mao's Revolution and the Chinese Political Culture* (Berkeley, Cal.: University of California Press, 1971).

18. A. Bloom, "Linguistic Impediments to Cross-Cultural Communication: Chinese Hassles with the Hypothetical." Unpublished manuscript.

CAMPAIGNS AND THE MANUFACTURE OF DEVIANCE IN CHINESE SOCIETY
Sidney Leonard Greenblatt

EPIDEMICS OF DEVIANCE

This essay stems from the work of Walter D. Connor, specifically from an article published in *American Sociological Review*, entitled "The Manufacture of Deviance: The Case Study of the Soviet Purge, 1936-1938,"[1] where Connor draws upon research by Kai T. Erikson,[2] Hugh Trevor-Roper,[3] and Elliott P. Currie[4] on religious deviance of a special "epidemic" form.

An "epidemic of deviance" is described as event in which 1) large numbers of people are recruited into deviant status, 2) persons so recruited are largely innocent of the acts with which they are charged, and 3) traumatic effects are visited upon the society in which it occurs. Most important, epidemics of deviance are events that are shaped and sustained by the very agencies of social control entrusted with their suppression.[5] By demonstrating that the Soviet purge meets these conditions quite as well as the Inquisition and the "Quaker Invasion" of Massachusetts Bay Colony, Connor extends the study of the manufacture of deviance into two realms where the study of deviance seldom appears at all: the disciplinary realm of area studies and the subtopical realm of political deviance.

Since social control agencies are held to produce the "recruitment of deviants," Connor searches the works of Erikson, Trevor-Roper and Currie for factors that relate to control systems. He groups them into essentially two categories, cultural factors and structural factors. Cultural factors affect, in broad strokes, the kinds of behavior social control agents will be likely to define as deviant. Thus, in the Soviet Union, a highly politicized society, epidemics are defined as political in character; in the societies where the Inquisition functioned, deviance was defined in religious terms.[6]

Structural factors can be subcategorized into two types: factors affecting the "deployment pattern," i.e., the process of recruitment to deviant status; and factors affecting the number of potential deviants a control system can recruit— its capacity. Connor finds the key to factors of the first type in Elliott Currie's distinction between "repressive" and "restrained" control systems.[7] In a repressive control system, agencies of social control, using extraordinary legal powers, operate independently of any other sociopolitical institutions. Such, Currie holds, was largely the case in the continental experience of the Inquisition. In a restrained control system, agencies of social control operate within a framework of institutional checks and balances such as those that operated during a good part of the Inquisition in England.[8] Repression and restraint, as Connor tends to use those terms, refer both to the process of recruitment to deviant status or deployment pattern and to the products of that process. Thus, the Inquisition in England, in contrast to its continental counterpart, was restrained both in terms of the process by which deviants were identified and labelled and in terms of the outcomes, i.e., the number of lives lost and the value of properties confiscated.[9]

In his extension of these observations to the Soviet case, Connor elaborates the NKVD's deployment pattern and classifies the Soviet control system as repressive. The Great Terror or Purge of 1936-38 was an event of epidemic proportions; its epidemic character was largely due to the fact that the agency primarily responsible for its prosecution, the NKVD, was Stalin's personal instrument and thus wholly independent of institutional restraints. Its scope increased when, in August 1937, extraordinary powers were granted the NKVD, legitimizing confessions obtained by the use of physical force.[10] This measure, along with the institution of a quota system for recruitment of deviants, the hiring of *seksots* (toughs) as recruitment agents, the use of "conveyor-belt" (round-the-clock) interrogation methods, and the focus on confession rather than persuasion, served to expand the recruitment process until arrest became virtually synonymous with confession. Ultimately as the logic of the purge closed in on itself, low recruitment rates became indicators of disloyalty, and some NKVD recruitment agents became targets of the very process they had helped to set in motion.

Both the number of people recruited and the capacity to absorb deviants expanded at an enormous rate. It is with regard to this point that Connor makes an important modification in the work that has gone before, particularly in Erikson's treatment of the limits to the manufacture of deviance. In his study of the "Quaker Invasion" of Essex County in Massachusetts Bay Colony, Erikson finds a sharp rise in the rate of recorded offenses without an accompanying rise in the number of convicted deviants. The county's fixed capacity for housing or "absorbing" deviants is held to explain the apparent paradox. Most of the time, Erikson argues, when a community attempts to assess the size of a prospective deviant population, it is actually measuring the capacity of its own control apparatus.[11] The number of deviants a community encounters is thus fairly constant over time. Connor, drawing his fundings from the Soviet case, contrasts this "constancy thesis" to his own "thesis of elasticity."[12] In the Soviet Union, the capacity to absorb deviants was elasticized partly because of the availability of the Siberian wastelands and other frontier zones and partly because of the availability of guards, barbed-wire enclosures, and other paraphernalia of social control at very low cost. The explanation for elasticity also resides in the characteristic ways power was distributed in the Soviet control system and the uses of power manifested in its deployment pattern. When a "radical asymmetry of power" in an already repressive system is coupled with a "snowballing" deployment pattern, even though it is still appropriate to recognize limits to the manufacture of deviance, it is accurate to describe those limits as "elastic."[13]

This essay seeks to retain Connor's emphasis on political deviance in repressive control systems, but to extend his findings for testing to the People's Republic of China. It will introduce the campaign as an epidemic of deviance, compare deployment patterns in pre-Cultural Revolution deviance recruitment campaigns with the Cultural Revolution, attempt to throw some light on changes in the Chinese Communist control system over time, question the symmetry of power in the Chinese case, and test Connor's thesis of "elasticity."

THE CAMPAIGN PHENOMENON IN COMMUNIST CHINA

Campaigns or movements (*yundong*) describe massive mobilizations of manpower, material resources, time, and energy to achieve specified, often multiple goals, sometimes sequentially, sometimes simultaneously.[14] They are processes of planned change usually sponsored by politically superordinate agencies and usually implemented among designated subordinate target populations. They may vary independently by 1) target population (the particular stratum or substratum the campaign is intended to mobilize), 2) size (the number of participants), 3) locus (whether the campaign in question is national, regional, provincial, local, organizational, or some combination of these), 4) goals (redistribution of material resources, redistribution of power and authority, increase in outputs of various kinds, control of deviants, dissemination of information, celebration of persons and events, socialization to new norms, control of the natural environment, introduction of new policies, or some combination of these), 5) duration (the length of time covered by any given campaign), 6) intensity (the amount and kind of participation required of those mobilized to carry out the campaign, 7) scope (the number and types of activities in which participants share), 8) pervasiveness (the degree to which the campaign encompasses the life activities of individuals and groups), and—because campaigns can be treated as continuous or intermittent processes—9) rate of succession (the rate at which campaigns succeed one another for any given chronological period, target, set of goals, or series of locations).[15]

Campaigns are a ubiquitous phenomenon in mainland China. While no complete tally of campaigns has, as far as I am aware, ever been undertaken, over 150 can be identified for a single organization over a twenty-three-year period.[16] Periods of successive campaigning alternate with prolonged lulls in campaign activity. In terms of process, there are campaigns within campaigns—drives that are subdivided to focus either on subtargets or on one or more goals in a set of multiple goals. Some campaigns go through a full cycle from initiation to termination; some are terminated at intermediate stages in the campaign cycle; and some change rubrics, goals, targets, or loci in the course of intermediate stages of mobilization or as part of a revival that occurs long after the completion of an earlier cycle.[17]

Campaigns produce a multifarious array of products: meetings, speeches, technical innovations, new forms of organization and communications, "activists," individual and organizational "models," new party and league members, heroes, heroines—and deviants. Seen as processes of planned change, they tend, for any particular organization or institution in which they occur, to speed innovation of one kind or another by breaching bureaucratic barriers to change, and among the innovations that campaigns effect are those techniques concerned with the identification, location, and sanctioning of deviants.

Although deviants are one product of the campaign process, not all campaigns involve their recruitment. Emulation campaigns and campaigns that are celebrational or informational seldom appear to involve the mobilization of agencies primarily concerned with the surveillance of deviant political behavior. That is not necessarily true of campaigns concerned with production and/or redistribution of power, authority, and material goods and services. Such campaigns often call into operation units entrusted with surveillance of political behavior and public security to aid in the search for recalcitrants, malfeasants, saboteurs, and malcontents or ideological recidivists with privileged access to material goods and services, some of whom are said to be hidden among elites already exercising power and authority.[18] These are, however, sideline activities in support of the main goals of the campaign (though such sidelines can become the mainsprings for a deviance control campaign). For deviance control campaigns in general, defining and managing deviance *are* the principal functions performed.

DEVIANCE CONTROL CAMPAIGNS

Deviance control campaigns have a long history. They can be traced back to the Anti-Rich-Peasant Campaign of the Kiangsi Soviet period.[19] In terms of organizational sophistication, the Rectification Campaign of 1942-44 is acknowledged as the most pertinent predecessor to the modern deviance control campaign, but there were other pre-Liberation campaigns that figure in that legacy, including the campaigns against landlords and rich peasants carried out in the early stages of the Land Reform Movement and the rectification campaigns that succeeded them.[20]

The period after 1949 is marked by a long list of deviance control campaigns. The most exemplary include the Campaign Against Counterrevolutionaries and the Thought Reform Campaign of the early 1950s; the Campaign Against the Worship of America carried out as a part of the Resist America Aid Korea Movement, the Campaign Against Bourgeois Influence in Art and Literature, the Campaign Against Hu Feng, the Campaign Against Counterrevolutionaries, the Three Anti, Five Anti, and Double Anti campaigns bridging the early and mid-1950s; the Rectification Campaign launched in the aftermath of the Movement to Socialize Agriculture in the mid-1950s; the Anti-Rightist Campaign, the Campaign Against the Right-Tending and the rectification campaigns of the late 1950s; the Socialist Education Campaign, the Four Cleanups Campaign, the Great Proletarian Cultural Revolution and its associated campaigns in the 1960s; and most recently the Campaign Against Confucius and Lin Biao.[21]

Like other campaigns, those that focus on deviance control serve to facilitate planned change in the institutions and organizations in which they occur. But their focus on deviance recruitment has distinct consequences for those institutions and organizations. 1) Like other campaigns they breach bureaucratic barriers to change by eliminating barriers to the visibility of behavior.[22] In the case of the deviance control campaign this function is most frequently served by the activation of organizational units concerned with surveillance that normally lie dormant,* by the creation of new units designed to enhance visibility and breach bureaucratic boundaries,[23] and/or by the incorporation of public security "services," rendered by agencies outside the targeted organization, into the campaign process. 2) Deviance control campaigns shift the locus of authority away from routine administrative channels and chains of command to party and league (*qingnian tuan*) chains of command, bringing to bear the "expertise" of leadership cadres trained to identify political and ideological "problems" (*sixiang wenti*). 3) Like other types of campaigns, deviance control control campaigns inflate time budgets beyond those embodied in routine work schedules, reaching, at peak periods of intensity, a continuous twenty-four hour cycle.[24] Deviance control campaigns tend, however, to achieve such high levels of participation by simultaneously reducing the proportion of the time budget allocated to routine tasks in a more concentrated effort to expose political deviance. At

---

*Small groups are always structural elements ready to be mobilized, as are systems of inspection and investigation that function on a routine, scheduled basis but are available for intensification when campaigns arise.

times, routine organizational tasks may performed to a minimal degree or not performed at all.[25] 4) Though very difficult to measure, it would appear that all types of campaigns increase the flow of both instrumental and expressive communications, and it is probable that expressive communications dominate instrumental as campaigns approach peaks of intensity and exhortation assumes an ever greater role. Deviance control campaigns follow suit; communications are heavily dominated by criticisms, self-criticisms, charges and countercharges, debates, evidences, experiences, accounts, etc., as they are conveyed through notes, dossiers (*dangan*), large-character newspapers (*dazi bao*), blackboard newspapers, speeches, testimonies, and other ad hoc means of communication. 5) More than other types of campaigns (with the exception of emulation campaigns) the deviance control type tends to treat norms that govern routinely defined workaday statuses and roles (including those held by party and league personnel) as selectively relevant to political and ideological performances during the campaign.* Thus the fulfullment of such norms is not, in itself, a ground for defense against labeling. The violation of such norms is, however, a relevant ground for the attachment of a negative label. 6) In a congruent way, deviance control campaigns give primacy to role relationships that may be muted during periods between campaigns. This, if class relationships are relatively unimportant during "routine" periods (especially before the Cultural Revolution), class affiliations and relationships are primary during a campaign. 7) Unlike other types of campaigns, deviance control campaigns subtly shift norms that guide political performances away from broad and diffuse commitments to national construction and participation in routine political study toward specifically demonstrated ideological commitment and active participation in "class struggle" (*jiehji douzheng*). 8) Finally, deviance control campaigns tend to reduce diverse measures of performance applied in other types of campaigns to that criterion which presumes to measure ideological commitment: consistency of speech and action in the widest possible variety of concrete situations and over the greatest possible range of concrete relationships.

Insofar as deviance control campaigns include among their goals the redistribution of power, authority, and access to material goods and services,

---

*For students in particular this point is important, as participation in the "struggle for production" and in "class struggle" took precedence in the determination of political activism during the late 1950s over either academic or political study, which had been dominant criteria of participation in the early 1950s. As Gordon Bennett points out in his contribution to this volume, the dilemmas that confronted "experts" during the campaigns of the 1960s are similar to those confronted by students at an earlier date. A narrow interpretation of both their roles was of negative value to judgments concerning campaign performance.

purge tactics will form part of the battery of techniques employed in the management of deviant behavior. But if purges are defined as purposive applications of coercion (not necessarily involving the use of terror) to eliminate ". . . rival authority figures—actual, potential, or imagined—as well as their subelites, disciples, and subordinate bureaucracies . . .",[26] then few Chinese deviance control campaigns are, technically speaking, purges, for few focus solely on elites, subelites, or subordinate bureaucracies. The term "disciples" raises a problem because it implies that purges may extend beyond elites, and Chinese deviance control campaigns do trace erroneous political "lines" (*luxian*) to sources with no personal or organizational affinity to elites and subelites undergoing a purge. "Disciples," however, connotes that the sources to be eliminated are persons rather than ideas; Chinese campaigns aim typically at the eradication of erroneous ideas and the reform of the persons who hold them; reform does not exempt such persons from removal from positions of authority.[27] In this sense, deviance control campaigns incorporating purge tactics are most suitably described as "social prophylaxes."[28]

Such considerations would seem to nullify a comparison between campaigns as a mode of recruitment of deviants and the Great Purge of 1936-38 in the Soviet Union. There are, however, additional considerations that make the comparison possible. First, the Great Purge met at least one condition defining a campaign. It was a broad-based movement mobilizing large numbers of nonelite persons as both participants and targets, and the term "campaign" has been used to denote this condition.[29] Second, though few in number, there are instances of Chinese deviance control campaigns that more nearly resemble the Great Purge in their focus on persons rather than ideas, their epidemic quality, and in the application of terror as a tactic: the Futian Affair of 1930,[30] the anti-subversive campaigns of 1938-39 and again in mid-1943,[31] the extermination of landlords, the Three Anti and Five Anti campaigns, the purge of Gao Gang and Rao Shushi, the Anti-Rightist Campaign, the Four Cleanups Campaign, and the Cultural Revolution. Of these several campaigns, however, only the Cultural Revolution approaches the Great Purge in size and scope. It differed radically from earlier deviance control campaigns (though it was inspired by selected aspects of the Anti-Rightist Campaign) in terms of the size of the purge incorporated in it, the extent to which physical coercion appears to have been employed, and its scope as an epidemic of deviance. It most nearly approaches the Great Purge in its deployment practices. Differences remain, however, in the character of the control systems in these two cases and in size and scope. Indeed, no campaign, the Cultural Revolution included, serves as a perfect analogue to the Soviet purge. Elucidating the differences between them, however, offers useful insights into the dynamics of deviance epidemics. To make the most of such an opportunity we shall first turn to an examination of the deployment patterns of pre-Cultural Revolution campaigns, then attempt a comparison of our findings with the Cultural Revolution, and finally offer some generalizations about the relationship of the Chinese experience to the Great Purge and to deviance epidemics generally.

PRE-CULTURAL REVOLUTION DEVIANCE CONTROL CAMPAIGNS: DEPLOYMENT PATTERNS AND ELASTICITY

A deviance control campaign of the pre-Cultural Revolution variety typically began with the dissemination of prepared documents and speeches defining the goals of the campaign. In most instances this was done by assembling all potential participants in a given organization (either as a sole target or as one unit in a targeted locality) to receive documents and hear speeches, sometimes several hours long, by representatives of the local or national party apparatus and members of the local ad hoc committees established to manage the campaign. Interviewees from the mid- to late 1950s report that opening or inaugural speeches were sometimes several hours long and assiduous note-taking was required. In some cases, inaugural speeches and documents marked the birth of a new campaign; in some cases they signified the onset of a campaign at a new site. In the latter instance, testimonies to the success of the campaign at sites where it was already underway would accompany opening statements. For the audiences, these assemblies were occasions for note-taking, for they were recognized as the preparatory stages in an intensifying chain of events where basic political and ideological knowledge might be subject to detailed on-the-spot testing.

Inaugural assemblies were followed by a mobilization of all those organizational units that would be concerned with functions essential to the prosecution of the campaign: communications, personnel, surveillance, security, and sanctioning. In most cases, these units were new in the early 1950s, implanted by the very campaigns they were designed to serve.* By the mid-1950s they had already been operative for some time; campaigns simply enhanced their roles beyond those performed in noncampaign periods.[32]

The most strategic among such organizational units were the "small groups" (*xiaozu*) that studded almost every organizational chart. Like ongoing or experimental small groups in the West, they tended to derive their fundamental strengths for the socialization and social control functions they pursued from their face-to-face character;[33] they ranged in size from three to thirty, though

---

*In factories and schools the establishment of small groups and like organizational units typically coincided with the reorganization of those institutions immediately after take-over. Communications channels and organizational effectiveness were "tested" in the first nationwide campaigns to follow reorganization: Thought Reform in the schools and the Three Anti Campaign in most industrial and commercial enterprises.

most groups appear to number around fifteen to twenty. Like work groups in the West, small groups were formal organizational units, but unlike work groups they were at the bottom of any given level of an organization's unit hierarchy, and they pursued functions that went beyond the setting of informal work norms. In fact, they were more often scenes for the enforcement of behavioral norms promulgated by organizational authorities than sites for the kind of informal resistance that is said to characterize Western work groups.[34] Communications channels and chains of command intimately linked small group leaders with their superiors, and small group operations were subject during campaigns, to continuous review by superior authorities. Superiors even intervened to assure the proper functioning of a small group, but that was rare, for it made superior authority patently visible and undermined that element of voluntarism in the small group that still is one of the sources of its continued vitality.[35]

In the lulls that separated campaigns, small groups served routine functions of political and ideological socialization and social control. Such functions were summed up in the titles "study" (xuexi xiaozu) and "life examination" (shenghuo diaocha xiaozu) small groups—the two dominant forms of the 1950s.[36] In the aftermath of the speeches inaugurating a campaign, study groups moved to a more frequent meeting schedule and an intensive study and discussion of campaign documents.

The "study" phase and the phase that followed it—"criticism/self-criticism"—were important steps en route to the recruitment of deviants because they served to establish the salience of what were otherwise abstract ideological statements common in inaugural speeches and documents. To be more specific, "study" equipped the members of the group with a common ideological vocabulary for assessing themselves, their relationships with others, and the situations in which those relationships occurred.[37] It served as an occasion for translating abstract "isms" (zhuyi) in campaign documents into identifiable categories of familiar behavioral "problems"—making those "isms" available as labels.[38] The process of labelling advanced a step further as the campaign intensified and small groups moved from the more passive learning stage of study to a more active stage of criticism/self-criticism.

In criticism/self-criticism, group members were asked to search themselves and their fellows for the symptomatic indicators of behavioral problems identified in a more general way in the study phase, and to trace those problems back to the errant thought that gave them birth. This was the last phase in the establishment of salience and the first phase in the actual process of recruitment.

Criticism/self-criticism has often been described as a process of "cleaning out" or "washing away" the "dust" and "dirt" that accumulate in the mind.[39] In another favorite image, it was seen as a "cure" for the "germs" and "infections" that "contaminate" one's thought.[40] These images had their roots in a long-standing tradition that located the sources of error in the effects of an unfavorable environment upon the mind. An evil environment gave substance to evil thoughts. Such thoughts, if left unchecked, entered the realm of action, spread, and contaminated without limit. (See Chapter 2 of this volume.) In modern terms, the vestiges of the old society and the influences of imperialism and revisionism continued to provide an environment for hostile thought.[41] Assuring correct behavior required the continuous presence of counterstimuli produced by disciplined education, political practice, social pressure, and self-conscious self-criticism—or, to borrow from an earlier legacy, "watchfulness even when alone."[42] Otherwise the mind would slip, gather dust and dirt, or become infected. A deviation was never conceived of as segmental and isolated; rather it was a latent change of mind that was cosmic in its consequences, because it would affect the thoughts and actions of others if it was not brought under conscious control. The process for identifying and correcting such errors, criticism/self-criticism, was a corrective process only so long as it was applied continuously and without inhibition; only if one were to "say all one knows without reserve" and was willing to let others "help" identify one's own "problems."[43] The norms of comradeship, by which group members were enjoined to help each other trace errors in action to their sources in thought, buttressed the process of criticism/self-criticism. Withdrawal, passive or active, was unacceptable to the group and grounds for an assumption that a serious problem was at hand.[44]

Criticism/self-criticism could effectively serve to nip deviance in the bud only because checks on the consistency of speech and action were built into the process. Given the fact that thought, the potential source for error, is invisible, inconsistency in the visible aspects of behavior—speech and action—was a sure sign of the existence of a problem for which a comrade required the urgent help of the group.[45] Thus, the organizational mobilization of all those devices that maximize visibility of members' speech and action, including criticism/self-criticism, assured that all feasible sources of evidence would be exploited in the effort to identify and correct a problem

There were several ways in which visibility was maximized, First, small groups were so constructed as to contain overlapping memberships, so that individuals' claims to consistency could be checked against the group members' collective memory. Second, small group leaders had access to superior authorities who actively superintended more than one group. Notes collected and passed up the supervisory chain from the multiple groups of which an individual was a member were likely to contain signals of inconsistency, and if they were sufficiently interesting to note readers or sufficiently related to the principal targets of the campaign, they would be sent back to the groups from which they originated earmarked for concentrated attention.[46] Third, small group leaders, usually through the intercession of higher authorities, could gain access to the dossiers (*dangan*) maintained in the personnel departments of the organization where a campaign was underway, and the dossiers offered access to group members' past performances and associations—useful clues to current behavior.[47]

Finally, organizational incentives were utilized to reward those who demonstrated an ability to discover problems and mobilize others to correct them.

The traditions defining the locus of deviance, the norms of comradeship, and the techniques of organizational mobilization combined to make the small group a repository of specially prepared biographies of potentially sanctionable deviants—biographies jointly constructed by potential deviants and their comrades and woven into a logical history of deviance from bits of isolated data. Whether or not such biographies became official depended in part on their salience for the campaign then underway, the response of individuals to charges preferred against them by group members and drawn from the biographical record in the next phase of recruitment, and demands from superior authorities to target specific individuals or meet established but flexible quotas for recruits.[48] Whether in statistical terms it was the politics of voluntarism or command that determined the character of recruitment in any given campaign for a given group—in other words, whether recruitment developed out of the momentum of a campaign or from prior decisions that fixed cutoff dates and numbers—is still unknown.

As deviance control campaigns reached peaks of intensity, small groups moved from criticism/self-criticism to "struggle"—an intense form of criticism in which individuals were singled out for the attention of the group. Generally, cases singled out combined unfavorable class standing with reticence in response to criticism and outstanding inconsistencies of speech and action. Cases were now given informal labels and sanctioned. But small groups were limited in the permanence of the labels they could affix and the sanctions they could mete out.[49] Shunning was the maximum penalty a small group could apply in its own right. It was no mean penalty, for those subject to it were treated as enemies, and the withdrawal of emotional support of the group could be total.* Sanctions

------

*An interview with a student who bore a "right-tending" label produced the following description of what it meant to be shunned:

No one would smile at me. No matter where I went, comrades would stop their conversations. Their laughter and smiles would cease, and they would step aside until I passed. When I went to the cafeteria, everyone turned away from me. As soon as I sat down at a table, everyone there would move away from me. When comrades in my small group received tickets to the movies, I wasn't given any. If I went to a movie on my own, I stood at the back of the theater to watch because I didn't want to be seen or to be made even more unhappy knowing that people would only move away if I sat down. I didn't have a friend in the world. At night, I would stay in my room and cry. I couldn't even stand to let the sun into my room during the day. I would draw the curtains so that no one would see me. It went on like this for two months.

A young woman who had recently graduated from college and been assigned a new job in a governmental agency described her encounter with shunning:

such as this were not easily weathered, but they were far more humane than the terror applied in the Great Purge or campaigns in which targets were deemed beyond the range of such correctives as criticism/self-criticism and struggle. A recanting by a recruit could lead to the removal of the label and the shunning and a complete readmission into the group. But this would often require repeated confessions of error and reiterations of resolve to turn a new leaf sufficiently "genuine" to lead the groups to cast out the biographical record so painstakingly constructed and to readmit the recruit as if reborn into its fold. If the group's acceptance was not earned by the end of the campaign, a recruit's case was likely to pass beyond the small group for formal labelling and sanctioning.

The application of formal sanctions required the invocation of higher levels of organizational authority in the form of ritualized hearings held, insofar as it was necessary to repeat the process more than once, at each of several successively higher levels in an organizational hierarchy.[50] At such hearings, charges were formally preferred against a recruit, recruits were given a formal opportunity for a reply, and the reply was either accepted or rejected by the "masses" present by formal invitation. Friends and associates could be called in to give testimony, and this was sometimes an opportunity, though generally a limited one, for snowball recruitment. If the reply by a recruit was accepted (which once again might require repeated "confessions"), a deviant label affixed at the small group level might be removed altogether or reaffirmed and recorded as a "minor error" (xiaoguo) in the recruit's dossier. Administrative penalties might or might not be attached, though if they were they were likely to be minor penalties such as deprivation of special allowances, subsidies, or privileges. If the reply was not accepted and hearings at higher levels of authority were convened, then the deviant label affixed was likely to be more pejorative and stigmatic; a "large error" (daguo) would be recorded in the dossier, and administrative penalties ranging from withdrawal of privileges to loss of status, loss of livelihood, expulsion from schools, cooperatives, communes, offices, the party or the league, incarceration, combinations of these penalties, and in rare instances, execution. Where such harsh penalties as expulson, imprisonment, and

---

During my first week on the job, I was told that I need not attend small group meetings because I had to have time to become more familiar with the organization and my work. Then one day, a week later, I was asked to sit in on a group meeting as an observer. The members of the group were criticizing comrade X, who was a fellow worker in my section. He was a nice person, and I liked him. I felt sorry for him. When the meeting was over, he happened to walk right past me, and I smiled at him.

The following day, when I attended the next session of the same small group, I was the one who was criticized. "Comrade Lin lacks class consciousness," someone said. "She cannot draw a clear boundary line between our enemies and our friends." "She is a bourgeois sentimentalist and does not understand that it is right to show hatred toward our class enemies."

execution were involved, public security organs were mobilized to assume primary oversight of the case.

It is important to note that the process of deviance recruitment in pre-Cultural Revolution deviance control campaigns distinguished between relatively temporary, informally sanctioned deviant status and relatively permanent, formally sanctioned deviant statuses. This partial separation of recruitment and sanctioning processes established a structural framework for selecting a small number of institutionally sanctionable deviants from a much larger pool of temporary, informal recruits. While the criteria employed for the definition of the latter could be loose, the formal procedures invoked for the former assured that there would be some congruence between the offense committed, the label applied, and the sanction meted out. Recording errors and notating performances in the dossiers were also sanctions, for dossiers followed their subjects through their entire adult careers and could, if readers of the dossiers were sufficiently motivated to attend to their contents, affect job opportunities, promotions, privileges, opportunities for schooling, travel, housing and, of course, chances for recruitment in subsequent campaigns.[51] Yet at the same time the dossiers helped to assure a minimal degree of congruence among alleged offenses, labels, and sanctions first because they could be drawn upon as sources for systematization of otherwise informal and loose criteria used in the initial phases of small group recruitment in a current campaign or in campaigns yet to some; second because they could serve as post facto rationalizations for such informal criteria; and third because, as entries in the formal record, they were, however rarely in fact, theoretically subject to review and "rectification."[52] Hence cases had to be written as rationally accountable biographies of clearly and inevitably sanctionable deviants. The public hearings— a form of status degradation ceremony—helped in assuring that this function was performed, for they were the scenes at which rationally accountable biographies were officially entered into the dossier as internally consistent records of a recruit's intentions and his or her emergence into deviant status.[53] These ceremonies defined the degrees of ideological error upon which choices from the full range of possible sanctions were presumably based.

Thus, while all of the procedures above facilitated the recruitment of deviants, they also acted to constrain recruitment as loose and indeterminate criteria at the level of the small group took objectified, determinate form at higher levels.[54] Despite this regularization of procedures, there were a number of sources of elasticity in the system. One source lay in the form of logic that linked errors in thought to errors in action with potentially cosmic consequences. This conception coupled with the requirement to search out such errors in oneself and in others produced, whether out of institutional demand, social expectation, or genuine personal commitment, salient (because they were personalized) publically enunciated constructs correlating invisible "erroneous" thought with overtly visible actions and potential but as yet veiled consequences.

Thus, wearing flowered shirts from Hong Kong could be traced to "secret worship of foreign things," with a potential for "undermining China's anti-imperialistic stance." Walking hand-in-hand with a girl friend in the park could point toward "egoism" or "harboring feelings hostile to the collectivity" with a potential for "undermining the unity of the masses." Smiling at a person in "struggle" with the group could be evidence of "bourgeois sentimentalism" with the potential consequence of "confusing the boundary line between the enemy and ourselves." Such charges were usually fuel for criticism/self-criticism, but if coupled with a reticent attitude toward the group and a suspicious class background (counterrevolutionary, landlord, capitalist, backward element), they could also be the fuel for the more potent sanctions a small group could bring to bear. Logic of this kind made virtually any form of nonconformity subject to a deviant label and to some form of sanctioning.

Another source of elasticity in recruitment derived from the snowball effect in formal hearing procedures. Classmates, teammates, comrades, intimate friends, relatives, acquaintances, and neighbors could be called upon as witnesses to offer testimony for or against a recruit facing formal charges. The testimony such people gave was open to question by audiences and authorities with the result that witnesses were themselves drawn in as recruits.[55] In the cases of which I am aware, witnesses were not subject to charges levelled at the same hearing or even at the same level where the principal recruit's case was being heard. They were returned to their own groups to face criticism.

Elasticity in the number of recruits bears a more complicated relationship to elasticity in the capacity to absorb deviants than in the Soviet case. Since most informally labelled deviants and some formall labelled deviants were expected to be absorbed into the very institutions from which they derived and other formally labelled deviants were absorbed into prisons and labor reform camps, one must distinguish between internal and external capacity.

Internal capacity was elasticized by the manipulation of time and space that accompanied the campaign process. As a campaign moved through a succession of stages from its inauguration to termination, the ratio of routine to campaign activities altered.[56] At periods of high intensity, routine activities came to a near if not total halt. Available time and space were monopolized by the campaign, and deviant labels were assigned, managed, and withdrawn—all in the same spatiotemporal arena. Classrooms, workshops, and fields were scenes of small group mobilization. The effects of shunning were most pronounced when recruits were made to confront the weight of group opinion every day, all day on the walks surrounding factories and schools, in dining halls and dormitories.[57] This technique for expanding the capacity to absorb deviants into the very institutions where they are discovered rests on powerful normative claims: that certain kinds of deviants are reabsorbable—the thesis of "educability" dominant in the 1950s—and that the "cure" of political deviance is sufficiently compelling a cause to warrant the risks involved in sometimes prolonged disruptions of productive and administrative routines.[58]

Elasticity of external capacity derived from such innovations as "tiger beating," a technique employed during the Five Anti Campaign.[59] Agitators mobilized worker activists into "tiger beating teams" to seek our and harass errant capitalists until they confessed their crimes and paid their debts to the state and the people. Those targeted by the campaign were marched into their residences or offices and "imprisoned" for prolonged periods of time while tiger beaters drawn up at the entrances shouted accusations against them. This particular form of harassment and humiliation brought on a rash of suicides.[60]

The Anti-Rightist Campaign prompted another innovation—this time of a technique that had been originally designed to serve another purpose. The *Xiafang* Movement, or Movement Down to the Countryside, initially referred to the episodic transfer of cadres into the countryside, partly to educate urbanites in rural values, partly to relieve population pressure on the cities, and partly to reduce the size and complexity of urban bureaucracies.[61] In the aftermath of the Anti-Rightist Campaign, however, large numbers of "rightist" and later "right-tending" cadres and intellectuals were sent down to the countryside to "reform through labor" and "learn from the masses" for terms that averaged about nine months but ranged from three months to three years.[62] Recruits given shorter terms went down to the countryside with their entire departments or sections, established residence in local villages, and worked in the fields alongside the villagers. But they met to continue the processes of criticism/self-criticism and struggle under the auspices of their own units. Surveillance, also at the behest of their own units, was as close as rural conditions made feasible. If recruits' errors were sufficiently severe to warrant it, they did not return to urban workplaces with their units, but remained in the countryside either under the supervision of local public security officers or in labor re-education camps.[63] For brief periods of time, then, the transfer of whole units assured the manpower necessary for surveillance, and the vastness of China's countryside provided unlimited space. Both these conditions facilitated an enormous expansion in the capacity to absorb deviants.[64]

PRE-CULTURAL REVOLUTION EPIDEMICS OF DEVIANCE

The deviance control campaigns of the pre-Cultural Revolution period, taken either singly or as a whole, met at least two of the conditions for deviance epidemics: they recruited large numbers of people into deviant statuses and visited traumatic effects on the society where they occurred. Statistics on recruitment are notoriously unreliable because of the manifest political interest they serve in Peking, Taipei, Moscow, and Washington. Estimates by relatively disinterested observers may, however, give some idea of the size and scope of the recruitment process. James Harrison establishes the number of executions between 1949 and 1961 to have been somewhere between a low of 1.5 and a high of 3 million.[65] By way of contrast, Gordon Bennett cites a figure of approximately 20 million persons who were officially labelled in the course of campaigns that took place over the same period.[66] Statistics on the number mobilized vary sharply from one site to another and from one campaign to another, but judging from figures on the *xiafang* movements, it is probably not far out of line to suggest that as many as 60 million were active participants in the succession of deviance control campaigns that took place between 1949 and 1965.[67] These figures are partial testimony to the traumatic effects deviance control campaigns have had on Chinese society, but they speak perhaps less eloquently in this regard than a more general claim that deviance control campaigns were largely responsible for the change in China's demeanor in the years following Liberation. Deviance control campaigns were a major instrument in the final demise of gentry rule in the countryside. They ushered in an age of socialism in agriculture and industry, paved the way for the introduction of new systems of socialization and social control in every sector of society, and—through the incorporation of purge tactics—they underlay all the most important shifts in elite stratification and mobility. In the wake of the retreat of the early 1960s, deviance control campaigns were a major instrument for the purge and reconsolidation of rural leadership and for the redirection of rural development.

The second qualification for an epidemic of deviance—that the persons recruited be largely innocent of the acts with which they are charged—is more problematic. Few of the criteria adduced to establish the reality of a deviant act were as fictitious as those that marked the proceedings of either the continental or the English Inquisition, and unlike the Great Purge, in only limited instances in the Chinese case was arrest along equivalent to proof of the commission of a deviant act.[68] Yet quotas for recruitment, an emphasis on confession, and snowball recruitment in the formal hearing phase of a campaign were present, and these are features that help to preserve a resemblance between the Chinese and Soviet cases. Even the Inquisition is not as far-fetched a locus of comparison as it might seem, for the sort of logic that linked thought to acts and acts to a complicated web of potentially disastrous consequences was not far from the logic that undergirded charges of witchcraft. Both required fantastic leaps of judgment. But in the Chinese case such logic made an act criticizable, not subject to official sanction. Furthermore, the logic linking thought and action was not the sole determinant of judgments about deviant behavior even where ctiticizability was concerned. The members of the small group called for other criteria, including assessment of the degree to which the class background of a potential recruit might determine a propensity toward serious deviance and the degree to which a potential recruit's attitude toward the group, evidenced in interaction with members and leaders, might propel that person into a permanent state of rebellion. All this means that even from the point of view of the victim of labelling, there was an element of voluntarism that legitimated the decisions made in one's own case. To put it slightly differently, even though decisions cast for or against individuals were outcomes of a process that included the paraphernalia of command (quotas, surveillance, etc.), those decisions were also arrived at through assessments by oneself and one's comrades sitting in judgment as a community and functioning in an accountable way.[69] The personalizing of deviant acts and the objectification of biographies into dossier entries substantiated the belief that decisions concerning deviance were accountable. Connor addresses the dynamics of labelling in the Great Purge, but the role of ideology as a vocabulary, a repository of social and political types, and a source for the construction of deviant biographies receives little attention because it was eclipsed as an element of deployment by arrest, confession, and entrapment. From this point of view, the deployment pattern evident in the Cultural Revolution bears a close resemblance to that which operated in the course of the Great Purge.

THE CULTURAL REVOLUTION: DEPLOYMENT AND ELASTICITY

James Harrison's division of the Cultural Revolution into five stages helps to clarify the vicissitudes in deployment patterns over the period from the end of 1964 to mid-1969.[70] Stage one began with the criticism of Liu Shaoqi's actions during the Socialist Education Movement and the appointment of the Group of Five to develop plans for a new cultural revolution at a work conference convened between December 1964 and January 1965. In this initial stage, the Cultural Revolution most resembled the 1954 purge of Gao Gang and Rao Shushi in both form and process except for the speed at which high-ranking personnel were singled out for attack, the number of such personnel removed from their positions, and the extent of the rift among China's senior leaders that the purge revealed. While an attempt was made to expand the movement in Mao Zedong's now famous endorsement of Peking University rebels in May 1966, the dispatch of work teams to the universities and Mao's own temporary withdrawal kept the first stage in the control of party moderates.[71]

The Eleventh Plenum of August 1966 ushered in stage two and with it a new agency of social control in the form of the Red Guards. Red Guard organizations, spurred on by the sixteen-point decision of August 8 and by the endorsements of the Cultural Revolution Group, demonstrated their acumen in attacks against "the four olds" (old ideas, habits, culture, and customs). With approval for "long marches" to Peking to "exchange revolutionary experiences," the formation of Red Guard units spread nationwide.[72]

As Mao's "little generals" sought an appropriate form and forum for their activities, and middle- and lower-ranking party and state functionaries jockeyed to evade Red Guard participation in a purge aimed against them (a successful maneuver in the Anti-Rightist Campaign), the first signs of factional tension emerged among Red Guards.[73] "Conservatives" were arrayed against "rebels" partly as a reflection of class interests and partly through the machinations of party and state cadres faced with the threat of a purge.[74] To remedy this situation, the Cultural Revolution Group unleashed a more explicit public attack against China's "power holders" and through its leading spokeswoman, Jiang Qing, sought to lend the weight of Mao's personal authority to the revolutionary left in what remained to the end of stage two an indeterminate struggle.[75]

Stage two set the conditions for stage three when, in December 1966, the Cultural Revolution Group expanded Red Guard operations into the realm of the working class. Then in January 1967 an order linking the People's Liberation Army (PLA) and the Red Guards in a "seizure of power" unleashed the "January storm"—a combined movement of the left to take over the reins of government and the urban economy and supplant the provincial and municipal establishment with "three-way alliances." The January storm provided Red Guard rebels with extraordinary powers for the recruitment and management of deviants.

Resistance by targeted groups due to opportunism, genuine fear of the disorder that might ensue in agriculture as preparations for the spring harvest neared, the manipulation of workers by opposing factions that came to be known as "economism," the chaos created by claims and counterclaims to legitimacy from contending Red Guard factions, and the tendency of regional military authorities to prefer order rather than chaos and act on the situation as they saw it (a stance exacerbated by the Cultural Revolution Group's failure to clarify factional disputes) all fed into the making of the February "adverse current"—a forceful intervention against the left. The Cultural Revolution Group responded to the adverse current with a purge of military personnel and an incitement of the left to take up arms. Red Guard groups, now fueled by implicit signals from Peking and by the supply of more potent weapons (sometimes gained by seizure, sometimes handed over), began to engage in full-scale factional war. In mid-1967 deviants were being recruited as captives and subjected to the full panoply of coercive techniques that marks recruitment in a civil war.[76]

Stage four was marked by a "Maoist Thermidor," launched in Jiang Qing's speech of September 5, 1967 denouncing factional chaos and Red Guard clashes with the PLA.[77] By late 1967 a purge of the ultraleft was underway in all circles. Red Guards were ordered to lay down their arms and return to their original units. Now the PLA was given full authority to clean up the left in its own ranks, assume control of the administrative machinery in factories and schools, and take over public security functions.

The fifth and final stage began in March 1968 with the purge of Yang Chengwu as acting military chief of staff and a new round of violent factional clashes in the late spring and summer of 1968.[78] Despite the reversal of March, however, the Cultural Revolution was drawing to a close. Mao Zedong's tearful repudiation of the Red Guards in July, the return to military administration through the dispatch of PLA-supported work teams, and the completion of the formation of provincial revolutionary committees by the fall of 1968 now brought the campaign to its concluding phase. Its repercussions were far-reaching, however, and in numerous ways the Cultural Revolution continues.

Because stage one set some important conditions for subsequent Red Guard involvement in deviance recruitment, and stages four and five were occasions for an exacerbation of violent conflict that had begun earlier, stages two and three are the proper foci for a discussion of deployment patterns in the Cultural Revolution. Between August 1966, the beginning of the second stage, and September 1967, the end of the second, the full array of social control devices had been put to use.

The purge of Lou Ruiqing in stage one (and later the suspicion cast on his successor, Xie Fuzhi) may well have been the most important precondition for the assumption of powers of social control by Red Guards in later stages of the Cultural Revolution. Whether in pursuit of direct orders to keep hands off the student movement of May 1966, out of fear of the purge then threatening to encompass them, or possibly on the assumption that the goals of the Cultural Revolution and the interests of established bureaucracies (police and public security agencies included) could both be met by shunting rebels into subsidiary tasks of social control, university and middle-school administrators, police, and public security personnel acted in such a way as to provide open access to all phases of deviance recruitment first to middle-school and university student rebels and then to the Red Guard organizations they spawned.

The students, encouraged by Mao Zedong's endorsement of the rebels at Peking University, eager to demonstrate their revolutionary purity and guided by their own administrators, assaulted faculty members with little other warrant than personal rancor, faulty class background, "one character mistakes" (*yi zi zhi cuo*), and administrative finger-pointing.[79] "Study" and criticism/self-criticism—prior steps in the gradual intensification of campaigns—were eclipsed by an immediate call to "struggle" errant faculty. This leap into the most intense phase of the recruitment process obviated the need for biographical accounts to legitimate the use of the most pejorative labels and the application of harsh sanctions; to become a target was to be already guilty. Labelling and sanctioning were thus immediate, and the character of the labels and sanctions applied was such as to point up the gap between the revolutionary purity of the labellers and the extreme degeneracy of the labelled. A new vocabulary of deviance, supplied by propaganda concerning the official purge then underway in higher circles, provided the linguistic weaponry of the Cultural Revolution. Abstract ideological terms that stressed the primacy of ideas gave way to highly personalized invective, and shunning that represented the withdrawal of group emotional support in anticipation of a recruit's re-acceptance by the group gave way to direct, often violent, assault. Teachers were unceremoniously anointed with dunce caps marked with such phrases as "poisonous snakes" (*dushe*) and "monsters and freaks" (*niugui sheshen*), sometimes paraded down the streets or forced to kneel to accept the ministrations of the angry masses; beatings were not uncommon.[80] These procedures supplanted formal hearings of the kind evident in earlier campaigns and blurred the distinction between informal and formal labels and sanctions. The application of administrative sanctions, however, continued to remain in the hands of administrative authorities.

The arrival of Cultural Revolution work teams on campuses across the nation marked a brief reversal of the students' role in deviance recruitment. Student labellers were now the targets of tactics they were instrumental in creating.[81] But the withdrawal of the work teams in August 1966 and the endorsement of newly formed Red Guards revived the activities of student rebels and extended their jurisdiction.

When the Red Guards took action against the "four olds," they assumed powers normally in the hands of police and public security cadres, sometimes in concert with them and sometimes on their own. Bands of middle-school and college youth, directed to their targets by local police, raided urban and rural neighborhoods where the "seven kinds of black" (*hei qi lei*) (landlords, rich peasants, counterrevolutionaries, bad elements, monsters and freaks, rightists, and capitalist roaders) were known to reside. They ransacked homes, apartments and stores, confiscated or destroyed "black goods" and singled out occupants for public "struggle." In some areas, one group succeeded another in successive assaults against the same neighborhood on the same day.[82] In the earliest stages of the campaign against the "four olds," targets were more or less randomly selected. Individuals with faulty backgrounds, having a history of negative labels, possessing foreign goods, luxury articles, symbols of the old culture, long hair, tight pants, and colorful clothing were equally subject to "struggle," labelling, and physical assault. Later, Red Guards appear to have developed a more systematic pattern of deployment. Neighborhood raids were undertaken in a search for especially good examples of undesirable behavior, and street trials were staged with residents of favored class background mobilized to serve as denouncers. Confiscated goods and recalcitrant recruits were handed over to public security offices.[83] Such measures as these were, however, parodies of the formalized hearings of earlier vintage, for the determination of what constituted an exemplary case appears to have rested on merely quantitative grounds, i.e., having more foreign goods, more paintings, more antiques, a worse class background, etc.

Despite the twists and turns of the Cultural Revolution, well documented elsewhere, the role of the Red Guards in recruitment of deviants steadily enlarged through the second and third stages. Ever greater access to the instruments of social control and to potential target populations, despite occasional setbacks, was either provided by elite initiative or seized by the Red Guards themselves with the encouragement of the Cultural Revolution Group. By August 1966 Red Guards were already entering factories, though the extension of the Cultural Revolution to factories and mines was not made official until December.[84] By September, Red Guards, encouraged by critiques of regional and local party officials and aware that they had been shunted into subsidiary tasks of social control, turned from the destruction of the "four olds" to an attack on regional and local establishments. This was the first step en route to the mobilization of the Red Guards as principal instruments in the purge of party and state officials. That step was legitimated by the reiteration of the August call to "bombard" the "headquarters" of "capitalist roaders" in the party, the revelation of the crimes of Liu Shaoqi in November, and the incitements of the Cultural Revolution Group's most prominent agitators: Jiang Qing, Chen Boda, and Lin Biao.[85] The scope of Red Guard deployment was made complete when a ten-point directive of December 15 gave Red Guards a free hand in the mobilization of the peasantry and carried the Cultural Revolution into what had been the relatively protected realm of rural agriculture.[86]

Red Guard access to the instruments of social control increased most spectacularly as Mao and his left-wing supporters charged the "little generals" with the principal task of bringing down the party establishment. In the course of the "January storm," Red Guards assaulted urban and regional centers of the Party establishment seizing offices, communications, transport, and publications first in Shanghai and then in other cities around the country. A six-point declaration of January 13 empowered revolutionary rebels to supervise public security and assured public security support of the left.[87] In fact, Red Guard revolutionary rebels had, in many cases, already seized public security offices and materials, including their sacrosanct dossiers. Released from the controls that had been exercised over the use of public records and armed with hair-splitting logic for their interpretation, Red Guards employed the dossiers as weapons both in the seizure and sanctioning of "capitalist roaders" in the Party and in warfare against their own factional opponents. Statements torn out of context were now fuel for the most vicious attacks, and rank, no matter how impressive, no longer served as a bulwark against labels and sanctions formerly used to solve "contradictions between the enemy and ourselves."

The importance of dossiers and like materials in facilitating the recruitment of deviants during the Cultural Revolution cannot be overstated. They held the key to the release of students, workers, and peasants from the constraints that institutions of social control formerly exercised and afforded them more effective access to elite figures than had occurred in any earlier campaign, with the limited exceptions of the Gao Gang, Rao Shushi affairs and the Hundred Flowers Campaign.

To understand how the nonparty masses, students included, were released from constraint requires a brief review of their role in deviance control campaigns prior to the Cultural Revolution. In the early and mid-1950s students were more often witnesses, active or passive, to the recruitment of deviants than they were targets.[88] But the campaigns of the late 1950s, with special emphasis on the Anti-Rightist Campaign, produced in many students and workers with faulty class backgrounds and poor records of political performance the stigmatization that accompanied the more severe political labels applied to nonparty elites and lower-ranking party cadres in earlier campaigns. Since the dossiers were repositories of these already sanctioned and potentially sanctionable labels and records, as was pointed out earlier, and since appeals from judgments contained in them were rarely granted, they were themselves a powerful sanction, a continuous source of anxiety, and thus a constraint on political action. Acute concern about the dossiers was understandable, for few students (or any others for that matter) ever caught a glimpse of anything more than selected excerpts from their own and others' dossiers.

The lessons concerning the dossiers brought home to the student generation of the late 1950s and early 1960s were extended to peasants, workers, and new generations of students by the Socialist Education and the Four Cleanups Campaigns and by the early stages of the Cultural Revolution. Official repudiation of the Socialist Education and Cultural Revolution work teams opened the way for demands by students and rural party cadres that the labels and biographies compiled by the work teams be expunged from the record and that the sanctions be removed.[89]

A decision in the summer of 1966 to establish a "reception station" (later, a Joint Reception Center) for hearing complaints against work team verdicts indicated the leadership's determination to erase erroneous labels and sanctions.[90] Further instructions from the Central Committee in October 1966 to "hand out and burn" materials used in schools and other units to "purge the masses," signaled the desirability of removing constraints on student mobilization.[91]

The decision of the summer of 1966 opened a Pandora's box. Petitioners, whose travel was greatly facilitated by the movement to "link up" and "exchange revolutionary experiences," swamped the Joint Reception Center and reception stations in Peking, and as the movement to reverse verdicts grew in 1967 and 1968, other reception stations across the nation were confronted by a deluge of complaints. Though earlier instructions had made it clear that the "five kinds of elements" (landlord, rich peasants, counterrevolutionaries, rightists, and bad elements) were forbidden to use these facilities and that reversal was intended only for the victims of erroneous work team verdicts, complainants included people of every conceivable status seeking redress for labels and sanctions handed down as far back as the Land Reform Movement.[92] Peasants, workers, Red Guard rebels, and officials exposed to recent Red Guard attacks poured into reception stations, and many refused to leave until their demands were met. Despite the clarity of original rulings on the subject, the unanticipated flood of complainants brought confusion to the reversal of verdicts in most places, and the movement was called to a halt in 1968.[93] While it lasted, it gave testimony to the anxieties the dossiers continued to arouse, and regardless of the difficulties that attended the movement, its effect was such as to release many persons from the fear of recruitment to deviant status and free them for direct political action, including the recruitment of deviants.

The instructions of October 1966 were intended to have the same effect, and to a certain extent they did. But they were equally important in affording the nonparty masses effective access to elite figures—a second important function of the dossiers. Here too, a brief review of the situation prior to October 1966 may help clarify the importance of the dossiers.

Deviance control campaigns prior to the Cultural Revolution were alike in most of the functions they performed for the organizations in which they occurred. They were also alike in deployment patterns and, with some exceptions, in elasticity. But rectification campaigns, which were deviance control campaigns in every other respect differed in one major regard. They were primarily "in-house" affairs in which the nonparty masses participated sometimes as witnesses but rarely, if ever, as executors. Party members, on the other hand, were often executors in deviance control campaigns aimed at the nonparty masses. Criticisms levelled against party members involved in campaigns that targeted nonparty personnel were registered in the files and earmarked for rectification campaigns when party members met in their own small groups for pursuit of campaign goals. This difference had few implications for deployment patterns; deployment functioned as it was described earlier in the essay. It did, however, have implications for elasticity in the number of deviants recruited and in the permanence of labels and sanctions. Quotas on recruits from within party ranks differed from those applied to the nonparty masses. Party members had greater opportunities to appeal labels and sanctions handed down, and further quotas governed the number and character of appeals to be granted.[94]

There were exceptional instances when rectification campaigns were designed to incorporate the mobilization of nonparty masses. The purge of Gao Gang and Rao Shushi and the Hundred Flowers Campaign both involved the mobilization of intellectuals to criticize party personnel. But the Gao Gang-Rao Shushi affair led to the organization of subsidiary and separate movements not directly related to the purge itself. The Hundred Flowers Campaign, by contrast, most resembled the Cultural Revolution, for it unleashed a rebellion of students, faculty, and third-party elites against party authority in a fashion remarkably similar to the early stages of the Cultural Revolution, but failed to provide the instruments of social control necessary to breach party defenses and eliminate the barrier that separated the party from the nonparty masses.[95]

The decision of October 1966 to destroy "black materials" compiled by party work teams went further than decisions in any previous campaign to eliminate one form of defense party authorities might apply to maintain the boundary between party personnel and nonparty people. To many Red Guards it appeared to be an open invitation to put dossiers to effective use on their own behalf. In the winter of 1966, and with greater force in the "January storm" of

1967, Red Guard rebels as well as their factional opponents, rejecting assurances that the dossiers had in fact been destroyed and that no new black materials were being compiled, sealed organizational and public security files to prevent their use as a constraint on their activities and confiscated dossiers for use in the recruitment of party figures and factional opponents to deviant statuses.[96] A powerful instrument of social control, denied to student critics in the Hundred Flowers episode, was now in student hands. Few internal party "secrets" revealed by the dossiers and other materials obtained by seizure escaped attention.[97]

In terms of their place in deployment practices, dossiers were used in ways distinctly different from earlier campaigns. Since students, and for that matter other groups among the nonparty masses, were seldom privy to the events, situations, and occasions that provided the contexts for the contents of the dossiers of ranking party members, these documents were the sole sources of reference for charges made against party personnel. Establishing congruence between labels and the behaviors they presumed to describe was virtually impossible. Instead, Red Guard groups constructed records of sanctionable offenses by broadcasting their own finds in tabloids of their making and incorporating the discoveries of other Red Guard groups using records seized at various times and from various places. One rebel group with its cache of "secret" documents would cull from the publications of another to fill out and elaborate empty spaces in its own a priori record of guilt.[98] In this way, ranking party personnel were made accessible to the nonparty masses as recruits to deviant statuses.

PLURALISTIC RECRUITMENT

The recruitment of deviants during the Cultural Revolution was complicated by the fact that social control had been radically decentralized during stages two and three. In some cases decentralization served the specific intentions of the Cultural Revolution Group, in other cases it emerged by virtue of their default, and in still other instances it derived from initiatives taken from below without reference to central leadership. As a result, a multiplicity of agencies of social control were engaged in the recruitment of deviants, and they often recruited from each other's ranks.

The Cultural Revolution work teams, mentioned earlier, were alternately agents of recruitment and, once repudiated, targets of Red Guard recruitment. Local police and public security agencies, though hampered by purges at the central and regional levels and by ambiguity in instructions from the center, continued to recruit deviants from among "lawless elements" in the Red Guards, particularly during the tumultuous movement to link up and exchange revolutionary experiences.[99] Murder, arson, rape, theft, and embezzlement were still sanctionable offenses, and the massive movement of millions of Red Guards across the country afforded unusual opportunities for the commission of crimes.[100] Yet police and public security cadres were also targets of Red Guard recruitment, particularly during and after the January seizures of power. Fear that police and public security forces were using the prosecution of criminals as pretexts for their more reactionary political intentions led Red Guard rebels to challenge the need for law and order and to attack those charged to uphold it. This occurred in spite of orders from the center condemning illegal acts and threatening perpetrators with the full force of the law.[101]

The entry of the People's Liberation Army (PLA) as the principal partner in three-way alliances forged in the aftermath of the power seizures of January 1967 marked the mobilization of yet another agency of social control. Under a succession of ambiguous orders to assume responsibility for public security, protect the revolutionary left, and restore order, local and regional PLA garrisons resorted to measures of their own making. In some places they arrested, labelled, and sanctioned Red Guard rebels; in others they allied with rebels to take action against counterrevolutionary factions. In some instances they mobilized and armed factions of their own, and in yet others they sat on the fence to await the outcome of factional warfare.[102] Red Guard organizations responded to the PLA in kind. They readily accepted weapons and logistical support for use against factional opponents when PLA units served as their sponsors. When PLA units either sat on the fence or opposed them, they resorted to the seizure of weapons stocks and to armed clashes against PLA troops. In such instances, the PLA served as a source of recruits to deviant statuses.

Factionalism was perhaps the most exasperating source of pluralism in recruitment of deviants. It had been endemic almost from the start of stage two when Red Guards split between "conservatives" and "rebels"—a conflict accelerated by regional party authorities who sought to influence Red Guard mobilization by forming fake Red Guard organizations of their own or bribing those already in existence.[103] With the massive enlargement and proliferation of Red Guard organizations on the eve of the "January storm," the situation grew even more complicated. In an effort to establish a firm basis for deepening the purge, the Cultural Revolution Group sought to cope with the inordinate task of distinguishing between genuine and false contenders for recognition by the center.[104] Few of those contenders had unambiguous credentials. In the absence of other reliable means to assure their recognition and convinced that recognition by the center was essential to their cause, Red Guard factions sought to attain legitimacy by forcefully eliminating their opponents. Thus the very effort to secure control over the burgeoning Red Guard movement succeeded in fanning the flames of factionalism. It also provided an incentive for an escalation in factional violence exacerbated as weapons of war were either voluntarily supplied or seized. The violent clashes between Red Guard factions in mid-1967 and 1968 were fought with every conceivable form of armament, and the casualty rate soared.[105]

The resort to factional warfare and the onset of virtual civil war in armed clashes between Red Guard factions and units of the PLA did much to simplify recruitment and deployment. The "enemy" were simply those who were affiliated with opposing factions and units. They were no longer viewed as potential or even actual recruits but as captives to whom none of the civilities, appropriate to a limited conflict, were due. Brutality occurred on all sides, and torture and summary execution entered the deployment repertoire of PLA units, Red Guard rebels, and counterrevolutionaries.[106] To bring the conflict to an end, unified military force and counterterror were brought to bear on all factions, particularly those belonging to the ultraleft segment of Red Guard forces.[107]

Pluralism in recruitment during the Cultural Revolution obscures many of the details of deployment practices. While it is fairly clear that the standardized procedures of pre-Cultural Revolution deviance control campaigns eroded during the Cultural Revolution, how complete that erosion was, in what specific regards, for which particular agencies of social control, and over what length of time, are difficult questions to answer. At various stages during the Cultural Revolution, to cite an example, Red Guard rebels and public security authorities cooperated. Red Guards seized and labelled recruits and then turned them over to public security for sanctioning. But it remains unclear how, under these conditions, public security cadres chose an appropriate sanction from the battery of options available to them, especially when recruitment was in Red Guard hands and Red Guard judgments were often specious.

There is some evidence that the deployment pattern used by Red Guards leaked into the repertoires of other agencies of social control.[108] The eclipse of criticism/self-criticism in favor of intense "struggle," the resort to beating and humiliation of recruits, the application of torture to extract confessions and to summary executions ultimately became manifest features of deployment among all the varied agencies of social control. Ambiguity in central directions and radical decentralization may have helped to produce this condition, but it is more likely that these nefarious procedures were the outcome of a vicious cycle of violence unleashed when mutually antagonistic agencies of social control were pitted against each other either by intent or by default. If this is an accurate description of what in fact occurred, then pluralism in recruitment was accompanied by a singularity of deployment. A variety of agencies of social control employed the same basic deployment pattern, eschewing the step-by-step progression to deviant status evident in pre-Cultural Revolution deviance control campaigns.

ELASTICITY AND ITS LIMITS

To a certain extent we have already touched upon one source for the expansion of elasticity in the number of recruits. The direct as opposed to the step-by-step approach to the recruitment of deviants, the erosion of stand-ardized procedures, the equivalence of seizure, arrest, and guilt, and the resort to arbitrary construction of deviant biographics, all served to make deviance an infinitely expandable category. While deviance was theoretically open to infinite expansion even in the campaigns of the pre-Cultural Revolution period, in this instance it was practically and effectively so. Red Guards could recruit as many deviants as their number and logistical supplies made feasible. That this was indeed the case is partly substantiated by the fact that differing Red Guard groups set differing quotas of their own on the number or percentage of any given unit's personnel who would be subject to recruitment.[109] Such quotas, arbitrarily arrived at, were probably generalized measures of the Red Guards' capacity to manage deviants.

As in previous deviance control campaigns, capacity was both internal and external. Schools were excellent locations for an expansion of internal capacity since they ceased to function as educational institutions for nearly two years. As the Cultural Revolution deepened, especially after the withdrawal of the work teams, they became Red Guard bastions. Recruits, and later captives, could be incarcerated in classrooms and basements while upper floors served as watch-towers and staging platforms for the bombardment of enemy-occupied buildings nearby.[110] Factories and office buildings seized by contending factions served a similar purpose. To the extent that Red Guards were able to seize transportation facilities for their own use, they could reach deep into suburban territory to recruit, and recruits and captives could be transported over considerable distances. Such facilities added to the range over which recruitment extended, the number of recruits, and the efficiency with which space for their absorption was utilized.

External capacity expanded in both routine and innovative ways. New recruits, Red Guards included, were added to the rosters of labor re-education camp inmates, and assignments to the countryside (*xiafang*) continued through-out the Cultural Revolution. Early Red Guard recruitment, in the course of the movement against the "four olds," was characterized by some of the same tech-niques employed in the Five Anti Campaign. As in the case of "tiger beating," recruits were virtually imprisoned in their own houses and apartments, harassed, humiliated, and often physically assaulted.

One innovation derived from the use of suburban pig pens and enclosures for fowl as "animal exhibits" (*dongwu zhanlan*). Recruits were forced into these cramped enclosures and kept there for days on end. People in the surrounding areas were then mobilized to see the "exhibits" and express, in equally innova-tive ways, their contempt for the "animals" within.[111] How widespread a prac-tice this was or for how long it was maintained is unknown. Other innovations included the erection of stockades and the appropriation of stadiums to hold recruits and captives, a measure to which Red Guard rebels, their factional opponents, and units of the PLA all resorted.[112] Again, how far such innovations went in replacing prisons and labor re-education camps or how far they could have gone had the violence continued is, at this point, a matter of speculation.

Expansions in capacity, particularly internal capacity, bear a price tag. Though schools were sufficiently divorced from the productive sector to permit full-time embroilment in the tumult of the Cultural Revolution, China could not long afford to risk either the spread of violence or the allocation of its youth to unproductive recruitment tasks. Factories, communes, and transport were far more strategic economic sites, and disruptions of their routine functions were threatening both domestic development and foreign trade. Most commentators seem to agree that disruption of transport could not have continued, though disagreements are evident on the extent of damage done to rural agriculture and industry. When unified military force was brought to bear in order to bring the Cultural Revolution to a close, China, by most accounts, was already approaching the limits of elasticity in her capacity to absorb deviants.

THE SHAPE OF POWER

There can be no doubt that the Cultural Revolution, like the Great Purge, qualifies as an epidemic of deviance. Over half the party and state leadership of the pre-1966 era was purged, though rehabilitations have since modified this impact.[113] Untold numbers of nonparty people figured as witnesses, participants, recruits, captives, and casualties. Large numbers of people were recruited to deviant statuses (how many we cannot know), including the Red Guard rebels ultimately repudiated and sent into the countryside to engage in reform. While it is impossible to prove, it is inconceivable that there were not many innocents among the campaign's recruits, captives, and casualties. In terms of its effects on Chinese society, the Cultural Revolution was a revolution in fact as well as in name, though its consequences for China's future shape and direction are still being played out. It created a new and pervasive role for the PLA, shook the foundations of party rule, and in anticipation of succession revealed more than one irreparable fissure among the top contenders for Mao's mantle. It ushered in a new "Maoist" era with a host of innovations to challenge bureaucracy in the polity and the economy and the rule of expertise in education, medicine, and engineering.

In more intangible ways, the Cultural Revolution also undermined the ideological legacy of the Yenan era. The thesis of "educability" so prominent in the deviance control campaigns of the early 1950s, built into the training and sanctioning of succeeding generations of party members, was challenged both from above and from below. From above, despite later rejoinders, radical leaders of the Cultural Revolution Group goaded Red Guard audiences to attack and destroy far-ranging "enemies." In their incitements to violence they rejected the value of reform and regeneration and scoffed at such tactics as "the mild rain" of criticism/self-criticism.[114] From below, Red Guards, eager to demonstrate their total commitment to the revolution and to the charismatic figure of Chairman Mao, drew upon their own sense of what political realities called for in ways that did violence to the ideology of the 1950s. One amendment to the ideological legacy they contributed was the "thesis of the blood line" (*xuetong lun*)—the claim that those are red who are born red and its corollary: those who are black are born black. However dubious a contribution this was, it expressed a sentiment shared by many who did not espouse the thesis but reflected on the cumulative experiences of deviance control. Although the thesis and its corollary were firmly rejected by Mao and his associates, the corollary was, in fact, enacted in recruitment practices.[115] It was enacted, in my view, despite official rejection, because it served as an expedient for mobilizing youth against rivals and "enemies" in the top ranks of the party.

All of this serves to point up differences between the Cultural Revolution and the Great Purge. Though badly eroded, ideology played a greater role in the former than in the latter, and the role it played reflected a lengthy cumulative history of deviance control. From this perspective, the Cultural Revolution was not an historically unique and isolated event, though numerous of its facets were unique.

In other regards, the Cultural Revolution should be grouped not with all other deviance control campaigns but with the Socialist Education and Four Cleanups Campaigns. In part this is because it grew out of the latter campaigns, but it is also appropriate because these campaigns, in particular, bore evidence of the widening rift between Mao Zedong and his opponents.[116] In this regard too, the Cultural Revolution differed markedly from the Great Purge. If the Great Purge was marked by a radical assymetry of power exercised at Stalin's behest under the singularly centralized control of the NKVD, the Cultural Revolution was marked by radical conflict over power, exercised sporadically in Mao's name by a host of decentralized and mutually competitive agencies of social control.

Decentralization of social control was not, in itself, a unique feature of the Cultural Revolution; it was an approach often employed in earlier campaigns to maximize salience and meet local conditions, and while it entailed problems of coordination and articulation, so long as a relatively unified elite exercised power at the top, the recruitment of deviants followed a predictable pattern. But decentralization meant something quite different during the Cultural Revolution. Given the conflicts between moderates and radicals at the top and the speed with which one directive replaced, supplemented, or contradicted another, local agencies of social control often chose to treat central directives with varying degrees of inattention. In the absence of firm decisions, often the intent of an order was, as a context and in the presence of a strong tendency to read between the lines, more important than its content.[117] Despite these conditions, central governance of the campaign did not collapse altogether or want for investments of sometimes heroic leadership efforts. Members of the Cultural Revolution Group, especially Zhou Enlai, attempted to maintain order by advising Red Guards, sending out investigatory personnel, and supporting the integrity of police and public security functionaries against determined attacks.[118] In selected areas of agricultural and industrial production, the Cultural Revolution Group succeeded in protecting laborers from the rampages that accompanied factional warfare and armed clashes with the PLA.[119] Yet ambiguity remained the most pronounced feature of the centrally exercised authority. The desire to quicken the purge took precedence over caveats against destruction. How deep that desire was is partly indicated by the fact that members of the Cultural Revolution Group were willing to risk Red Guard condemnation of their behavior and feed their own subordinates to Red Guard recruiters rather than stem the tide of violence.[120] Even Mao Zedong, who recognized and condemned the excesses of the Red Guards before the most violent phases of the Cultural Revolution began, preferred to deepen the purge than to act on his own discontents with its principal executors.[121]

Despite this fundamental difference in the shape of power, deployment patterns in both the Cultural Revolution and the Great Purge were alike. Both resorted to arrest and seizure, extraction of confessions, torture, and summary executions. In both, incentives to stretch elasticity to its limits were present. Thus deployment in deviance epidemics can assume the same form even where a radical asymmetry of power is not present. Ambiguity in the central exercise of power, coupled with radical decentralization of social control and pluralistic recruitment, produces the same results.

CONCLUSIONS

Besides commending modifications in Connor's observations concerning the shape of power, the data from the Chinese case also suggest modifications in other aspects of Connor's findings.

The thesis of elasticity holds up well in the case of the Chinese deviance control campaigns. But the Chinese case demonstrates that elasticity is created not only by the erection of stockades, barbed-wire enclosures, and other either temporary or permanent spaces for absorbing deviants; it is also created by manipulations of the very environs in which routine, everyday tasks are performed. Full recognition of the phenomenon of elasticity, the range it can assume, and the problems to which it gives rise, requires a consideration of both its internal and its external forms.

Much more can be said concerning the relationship between deployment and elasticity. The characteristic means agents of social control used to identify, label, and sanction deviants—whether in the Inquisition, the Great Purge, or the Chinese deviance control campaign—were crucial determinants of the number of deviants who could be "discovered." In the Chinese case, in particular, given enormous elasticity in the capacity to absorb deviants, the capacity to define them loomed larger than the quantity of available space for their incarceration. In China before the Cultural Revolution, the capacity to define deviants rested on an elaborate ideological superstructure, containing definitions of "correct" and "incorrect" behaviors, buttressed by a unified system of social control. This situation differs from either the European Inquisition or the Great Purge, where specious standards made the capacity to define deviants virtually coterminous with the number of recruiters Inquisitors and NKVD agents could mobilize. If the capacity to absorb deviants in these cases assumed greater weight than the capacity to define them, it is perhaps because the normative order had eroded so completely as to obviate rational standards for the appointment of deviant labels.

In the Chinese case we are able to see both the reign of normative order and its erosion in historical context. The repetitive targeting of the "five elements" in successive deviance control campaigns severely strained the credibility of the thesis of educability at the root of recruitment practices before the Cultural Revolution. Yet repetitive targeting was built into deployment long before the Cultural Revolution began. The commitment of previous errors, recorded in the dossiers during a given campaign, was a signal for re-recruitment in subsequent campaigns. As a result, the same groups constantly returned to the scene of "crimes" already committed. It is not surprising then, that many would come to regard the "five elements" as unregenerate. Yet that determination was itself as much a product of deployment as it was the result of any reticence on the part of recruits. In the early experience of deviance control campaigns, ideological standards served to constrain the capacity to define deviants, but the cumulative repetition of that experience gradually undermined the role of ideology in deployment practices until it reached a state not unlike that in the Inquisition and the Great Purge. Quotas for formal and informal recruitment of deviants and standards for their definition gave way as Red Guards recruited as many deviants as they could reach and defined deviants merely by seizing them.

The logic that underlies the construction of deviance is thus as appropriate a focal point for studies of the manufacture of deviance where deviance takes political form as it is in those instances where it assumes religious garb. The Chinese case points up the importance of historical context for analyses of deployment and the construction of deviance. Furthermore, it suggests that the relationship between deployment and elasticity is highly variable over time and under differing constellations of power and authority.

Whatever the value of these observations, the Chinese experience offers an extremely fruitful field of inquiry into the dynamics of deviant behavior, and as descriptive accounts multiply, more systematic comparisons with deviance epidemics in other settings should become possible.

NOTES

1. Walter D. Connor, "The Manufacture of Deviance: The Case Study of the Soviet Purge, 1936-1938," *American Sociological Review* 32 (1972): 403-13.

2. Kai T. Erikson, *Wayward Puritans: A Study in the Sociology of Deviance* (New York: Wiley, 1966).

3. H. R. Trevor-Roper, *Religion, the Reformation and Social Change* (London: Macmillan, 1967).

4. Elliott P. Currie, "Crime Without Criminals: Witchcraft and Its Control in Renaissance Europe," *Law and Society Review* 3 (1968): 7-32.

5. Connor, op. cit., p. 403.

6. Ibid., p. 404.

7. Currie, op. cit., pp. 16-18.

8. Ibid., p. 20.

9. Connor, op. cit., p. 403.

10. Ibid., p. 407.

11. Erikson, op. cit., p. 25.

12. Connor, op. cit., pp. 404-05.

13. Ibid., pp. 410-12.

14. There is now a considerable literature on individual campaigns, but the treatment of the campaign phenomenon in its own right, as an independent variable, is rare. An early attempt is Frederick T. C. Yu, "Campaigns, Communications and Development in Communist China," *Communications and Change in Developing Countries,* ed. Daniel Lerner and Wilbur Schramm,(Honolulu: East-West Press, 1967), pp. 195-216. A more analytic approach can be found in G. William Skinner and Edwin A. Winkler, "Compliance Succession in Rural Communist China: A Cyclical Theory," *A Sociological Reader on Complex Organizations,* ed. Amitai Etzioni (New York: Holt, Rinehart, and Winston, 1969), pp. 410-38. Gordon Bennett, whose contribution appears in this volume, is the author of a forthcoming monograph on mass campaigns that is likewise analytical in its approach.

15. The concepts of "intensity," "scope," and "pervasiveness" are drawn from Amitai Etzioni, *A Comparative Analysis of Complex Organizations* (New York: The Free Press, 1961), particularly pp. 12-13, 20, 42, 82, 95-96, 129-30, 160-61, 163, 175-78, 203, and 270-74). The concept of "rate of succession" is implicit in Etzioni's discussion of "cyclical" and "successive" compliance.

16. Sidney L. Greenblatt, "System Determinants and Social Construction in Chinese Reality: A Study of the University, Students and the Campaign Cycle During the 1950s," an unpublished paper presented to the panel on student culture at the 25th Annual Meeting of the Association for Asian Studies, Chicago, March 29 to April 1, 1973. The paper contains a list of forty campaigns aimed at faculty, students, and staff of Peking University between 1949 and 1960. The current number derives from amendments to the original list and updating through the Campaign Against Confucius and Lin Biao.

17. The Three Anti Campaign bled into the "New" Three Anti Campaign in January of 1952, changing targets, audiences, and location. The Anti-Rightist Campaign, begun in May 1957, maintained its title until the spring of 1958, but it was extended to new targets in new locations after August 1957. It was given a new burst of life under the auspices of the Double-Anti Campaign in January 1958, and under that title extended into 1959 with the Campaign Against Rightist Tendencies begun in October of that year. These extensions of the Anti-Rightist Campaign drew upon mobilization already undertaken in the spring of 1957; they did not begin anew. See "Women bixu zai chuanguo fanwei nei he geji jiguan jianjue douzheng," *Tianjing da gong bao,* 1952, p. 1. The stages of the Anti-Rightist Campaign are reviewed in Franz Schurmann, *Ideology and Organization in Communist China* (Berkeley: University of California Press, 1968), pp. 61, 195, 215, and 361.

18. A. Doak Barnett, *Cadres, Bureaucracy and Political Power in Communist China* (New York: Columbia University Press, 1967), p. 404.

19. Ilpyong J. Kim, "Mass Mobilization Policies and Techniques Developed in the Period of the Chinese Soviet Republic," in *Chinese Communist Politics in Action*, ed. A. Doak Barnett (Seattle: University of Washington Press, 1969), pp. 78-98.

20. On the Rectification Campaign of 1942-44 see Boyd Compton, *Mao's China: Party Reform Documents, 1942-44* (Seattle: University of Washington Press, 1952) and Mark Selden, *The Yenan Way in Revolutionary China* (Cambridge: Harvard University Press, 1971). On early land reform and rectification campaigns, see John Wong, *Land Reform in the People's Republic of China: Institutional Transformation in Agriculture* (New York: Praeger, 1973), pp. 273-81.

21. Merle Goldman, "China's Anti-Confucian Campaign, 1973-74," *China Quarterly* 63 (1975): 435-62.

22. "Visibility" (or "observability") is one of twenty-six in a provisional list of group properties identified by Robert King Merton. As Merton notes, "This property refers to the extent to which the norms and role-performances within a group are readily open to observation by others (status inferiors, peers, and status superiors)." Robert K. Merton, *Social Theory and Social Structure* (London: The Free Press of Glencoe, 1964), p. 319.

23. One such new unit in the mid-1950s in schools was the "investigative post" (*jiandu gang*) drawn from factory practices. Each school class had four to five "investigators" (*jiandu gangyuan*) to fill "health investigative posts" (*weisheng jiandu gang*), "cultural investigative posts" (*wenming jiandu gang*), "austerity investigative posts" (*jieyue jiandu gang*) and "general investigative posts" (*zong jiandu gang*). These were claimed to be surveillance units and were abolished in 1956. "Xuexiao li buyi jianli jiangang," *Zhongguo qingnian bao*, May 12, 1956, p. 4.

24. One anonymous cadre at the First Machine Industry's Ministry School for Machine Instrument Manufacture in Hankow gave his or her version of an "inflated" time budget for the nights from April 17, 1956 to April 15, 1956:

17th — League members' conference
18th — Criticism-discussion (Had things to do. Didn't attend)
19th — Theoretical Study
20th — Branch convenes young League member mass meeting
23rd — Discussion of feeling toward participation in Youth League
24th — League small group meeting to discuss problems of youth entering the League
25th — Supposed to be theoretical study, but also had to convene meeting of small group leaders and an enlarged meeting of small group leaders.

This budget is based on a daytime schedule of 6 a.m. to 9 p.m., with bedtime at 11 or 12 p.m. The source is "Wei shenmo bu gei wo wenke shijian?" in *Guangming ribao*, May 20, 1956, p. 6.

25. Though, as Richard Baum points out in a modification of Skinner and Winkler's work on campaigns and compliance, in agriculture at least, peak periods of campaigning were typically seasonal. Campaigns were designed to reach their peak periods of intensity during the slack winter months of December through February and thus minimize the disruption of routine productive tasks. Richard Baum, "The Cultural Revolution in the Countryside: Anatomy of a Limited Rebellion," *The Cultural Revolution in China*, ed. Thomas W. Robinson (Berkeley: University of California Press, 1971), p. 385.

26. Alexander Dallin and George W. Breslauer, *Political Terror in Communist Systems* (Stanford: Stanford University Press, 1970), p. 25.

27. Ibid., p. 30. The same sentiment is expressed in James Pinkney Harrison, *The Long March to Power: A History of the Chinese Communist Party, 1921-72* (New York: Praeger, 1972), p. 466.

28. Jerzy Gliksman, "Social Prophylaxis as a Form of Soviet Terror," *Totalitarianism*, ed. Carl J. Friedrich (Cambridge: Harvard University Press, 1954), pp. 68-69.

29. Dallin and Breslauer, op. cit., p. 28.

30. Harrison, op. cit., pp. 212-17.

31. Ibid., pp. 340-42.

32. Martin King Whyte, *Small Group and Political Rituals in China* (Berkeley: University of California Press, 1974), pp. 2-3.

33. Ibid., pp. 8-10.

34. Pressures in informal work groups to set and maintain rates of production in the face of managerial demands are well documented in the Hawthorne studies. F. J. Roethlisberger and W. J. Dickson, *Management and the Worker* (Cambridge: Harvard University Press, 1939) and Henry A. Landsberger, *Hawthorne Revisited* (Ithaca: Cornell University Press, 1958). The "protective role" of small work groups in the West receives special emphasis in Robert Presthus, *The Organizational Society: An Analysis and a Theory* (New York: Knopf, 1962), p. 221.

35. Interviews with persons who served as leaders and members of small groups in the late 1950s and early 1960s make it clear that preserving a balance between the institutional obligations of the small group and "voluntarism" among its members required astute leaders aware of the costs and benefits of the various strategies available to them. Such astuteness was rare. Small group leaders could effect a mobilization of group members on behalf of the larger organization they served by relying on their personal charisma, but excessive attention drawn to oneself could lead to accusations of "individualism" or "commandism." They could rely on superior knowledge of doctrine to attain that end, but this might engender charges of "dogmatism" or "doctrinairism." They might rely on their superior knowledge of group members' behavior, but this might lead to alienation among the members by making obvious the existence of superior authority beyond the group's boundaries. Small group leaders could rely on the support of party and league members, though this strategy might drive a wedge between party and league members and nonparty, nonleague members of the group. Finally, they could rely on intervention from outside, but for reasons noted in the text, this was a measure of last resort. See also Whyte, op. cit., p. 38.

36. Martin Whyte's informants refer to the latter type as "livelihood self-examination meetings" (*shenghuo jiantao hui*), but judging from the frequency with which such meetings took place and the character of the problems they discussed, these were probably different versions of the "life-examination small group" (*shenghuo diaocha xiaozu*). Ibid., p. 66.

37. Study of the functions of ideology as a language and ideological language as a cognitive framework, despite a proliferation of terminological studies, is all too rare in research on China. One source of material on lexical change is the enormous body of role-model literature that emanates from China. It has been put to use in Mary Sheridan, "The Emulation of Heroes," *China Quarterly* 33 (1968): 47-72. See also Sidney Leonard Greenblatt, *The People of Taihang: An Anthology of Family Histories* (White Plains, N.Y.: International Arts and Sciences Press, 1976).

38. On the roots of "isms" and their place in Chinese ideology see David S. Nivison, "Communist Ethics and Chinese Tradition" (Cambridge: MIT Center for International Studies, 1954), pp. 23-29. See also James Chieh Hsiung, *Ideology and Practice: The Evolution of Chinese Communism* (New York: Praeger, 1970), pp. 129-33.

39. Mao Tse-tung, *Quotations from Chairman Mao Tse-tung* (Peking: Foreign Languages Press, 1966), p. 259.

40. Ibid., p. 260.

41. Nivison, op. cit., p. 43.

42. Ibid., pp. 47-48.

43. Mao Tse-tung, op. cit., p. 260.

44. On the necessity of speaking out and implications of "help" in solving ideological problems see Robert J. Lifton, *Thought Reform and the Psychology of Totalism: A Study of "Brainwashing" in China* (New York: Norton, 1961), p. 261.

45. On "helping" see Ezra Vogel, "Voluntarism and Social Control," in *Soviet and Chinese Communism: Similarities and Differences,* ed. Donald W. Treadgold (Seattle: University of Washington Press, 1967), pp. 171-72.

46. Interview at Hong Kong's Universities Services Centre, October, 1968, with small group leader who was at Peking University between 1958 and 1962.

47. Ibid. This interviewee claimed that at Peking University during the Anti-Rightist campaign, "class chiefs" (*banzhang*), with the written permission of a party secretary, could approach the personnel department with a request for information concerning, say, the problem of "individualism" (*geren zhuyi*). Personnel officers would search the dossiers from an applicant's groups, excerpt relevant sections from them and supply copies for the "class chief" and the small group leaders under his or her jurisdiction. Personnel department cadres were all said to be party members and access to them was strictly regulated. See also Barnett, op. cit., pp. 213-14.

48. The use of generalized quantitative or qualitative quotas at the onset of a campaign has been a feature of nearly every major campaign since the Rectification Campaign of 1942-44, and it is based on principles that were enunciated at that time: "Wherever there are masses, there are in all probability three groups: those who are comparatively active, those who are average and those who are backward. In comparing the three groups, the two extremes are in all probability small, while the middle group is large. As a result, leaders must be skillful at consolidating the minority activists to act as a leading nucleus and must rely on this nucleus to elevate the middle group and capture the backward elements." Boyd Compton, op. cit., p. 178.

49. Whyte, op. cit., p. 14.

50. These hearings are to be distinguished from annual reviews for party cadres and nonparty government cadres described by Barnett, op. cit., pp. 50-52. They are also more formal proceedings than the summaries and evaluations noted in Whyte, op. cit., pp. 49-51. The hearings described by my informants most closely approximate those Barnett describes for County "X" in the course of the Sufan Campaign, except that they apply to nonparty personnel. Barnett, op. cit., pp. 170-72.

51. The description Barnett gives of the dossiers (Barnett, op. cit., pp. 49-50) applies to nonparty personnel as well. Until the Cultural Revolution, at least, dossiers were begun upon a person's entry into institutions of higher education or first unit of full-time employment.

52. Reviews of the dossiers for "reversal of verdicts" occurred sporadically in the period after 1949. Gordon Bennett, "Political Labels and Popular Tension," *Current Scene* 2 (1969): 3.

53. The term "status degradation ceremony" and the place of "accounting" in such a ceremony is drawn from Harold Garfinkel, "Conditions of Successful Degradation Ceremonies," *American Journal of Sociology* 51 (1956): 420.

54. As Peter Berger notes, "Language builds up semantic fields or zones of meaning that are linguistically circumscribed. . . . Within the semantic fields thus built up it is possible for both biographical and historical experience to be objectified, retained and accumulated. The accumulation, of course, is selective, with semantic fields determining what will be retained and what "forgotten" of the total experience of both the individual and the society. By virtue of this accumulation a social stock of knowledge is constituted which is transmitted from generation to generation and which is available to the individual in everyday life." Peter L. Berger and Thomas Luckmann, *The Social Construction of Reality: A Treatise in the Sociology of Knowledge* (Garden City: Doubleday, 1967), p. 41. Language in

use in the small group recruitment process is, in this sense, built up and objectified out of a zone of meaning into a dossier entry—a selective biographical account of the total experience of the individual and the group. As a dossier entry, this account forms a "stock of knowledge" available for transmission in the next round of recruitment.

55. The "snowball effect" describes recruitment by affiliation. Snowballing occurs when all those affiliated with a recruit or potential recruit become targets of recruitment themselves, and they, in turn, make their affiliates available as recruits. For its use in the Great Purge, see Connor, op. cit., p. 405.

56. G. William Skinner and Edwin A. Winkler have developed a more complex schema for distinguishing phases in the campaign cycle, starting with "normalcy" and continuing to "mobilization," "high tide," "retrenchment," "demobilization," and return to "normalcy." Crucial decisions undertaken during a campaign are likewise dimensionalized and related to each of the phases in the cycle. Skinner and Winkler, op. cit., pp. 423-25.

57. On "shaming" see Lifton, op. cit., pp. 424-25.

58. The thesis of educability or malleability is treated at length in Donald J. Munro, "The Malleability of Man in Chinese Marxism," *China Quarterly* 48 (1971): 609-40.

59. Robert Loh, *Escape from Red China* (New York: Coward-McCann, 1962), pp. 86-87.

60. Ibid., p. 98. See also Ezra Vogel, *Canton Under Communism: Programs and Politics in a Provincial Capital, 1949-1968* (New York: Harper and Row, 1969), p. 80.

61. James R. Townsend, *Politics in China* (Boston: Little, Brown, 1974), p. 213.

62. Harrison, op. cit., p. 474.

63. Interviews indicate that some students remained in local villages under the supervision of a brigade's public security cadres. Barnett, op. cit., pp. 389-94 and 399-403, describes brigade public security organization and sanctioning but does not make mention of the role of outsiders as recruits to deviant statuses in the villages.

64. Martin King Whyte, "Corrective Labor Camps in China," *Asian Survey* 13 (1973): 253-69.

65. Harrison, op. cit., p. 608n.

66. Barnett, op. cit., p. 2.

67. Nationalist sources claim as many as 40 million students were sent down to the countryside between 1949 and 1965 (Harrison, op. cit., p. 474). On the assumption that this figure is inflated by at least 10 million and that no more than two-thirds of the resultant number were sent down as a result of political campaigns, one arrives at a figure of 20 million. On the further assumption that the number of youth sent down to the countryside comprised no more than half those who participated in campaigns, this figure changes to an estimated 40 million campaign participants. With the addition of party and state cadres and nonstudent civilians not holding cadre statuses, the number of campaign participants comes close to 60 million. The absence of confirmed statistics forces one to engage in guesswork of this kind, but it should make clear that campaigns do not embrace the totality of a population.

68. The logic of "pricking," "swimming," and "watching" as sources of evidence for the charge of witchcraft is spelled out in Currie, op. cit., pp. 19-20. On the relationship between arrest and guilt during the Great Purge, see Connor, op. cit., p. 407.

69. The classical treatment of "accounts" and the accounting process can be found in Stanford M. Lyman and Marvin B. Scott, *A Sociology of the Absurd* (New York: Meredith Corporation, 1970), pp. 111-43.

70. Harrison, op. cit., pp. 494-504.

71. Mao's "disappearance" for fifty days is discussed in William F. Dorrill, "Power, Policy and Ideology in the Making of the Cultural Revolution," in *The Cultural Revolution in China*, ed. Thomas W. Robinson (Berkeley: University of California Press, 1971), pp. 81-82.

72. The Chinese text and English translation of the sixteen-point decision are reprinted in "Decision of the Central Committee of the Chinese Communist Party Concerning the Great Proletarian Cultural Revolution," *CCP Documents of the Great Proletarian Cultural Revolution, 1966-1967* (Hong Kong: Union Research Institute, 1968), pp. 33-54.

73. The early roots of factionalism are traced in Gordon A. Bennett and Ronald W. Montaperto, *Red Guard: The Political Biography of Dai Hsiao-Ai* (Garden City: Doubleday, 1971), pp. 66-78.

74. Ronald N. Montaperto, "From Revolutionary Successors to Revolutionaries: Chinese Students in the Early Stages of the Cultural Revolution," *Elites in the People's Republic of China,* ed. Robert A. Scalapino (Seattle: University of Washington Press, 1972), p. 591.

75. A brief biographical sketch of Jiang Qing is contained in Hao-jan Chu, "Mao's Wife—Chiang Ch'ing," *China Quarterly* 31 (1967): 148-50.

76. The application of techniques of civil war recruitment will be discussed further along in the chapter. Suffice it to note here that my argument rests on an assumption that political terror serves differing functions at different times and under varying conditions. That thesis is presented in more systematic form in Dallin and Breslauer, op. cit., pp. 5-9.

77. The text of Jiang Qing's speech can be found in "The Quarterly Chronicle and Documentation," *China Quarterly* 32 (1967): 212-16.

78. The link between the dismissal of Yang Chengwu and the escalation of violent conflict in 1968 is discussed in Stanley Karnow, *Mao and China: From Revolution to Revolution* (New York: Viking, 1972), pp. 424-25.

79. Alan P. Liu, *Political Culture and Group Conflict in Communist China* (Santa Barbara, Cal.: Clio Press, 1976), p. 21.

80. According to Stanley Karnow, Xie Fuzhi, minister of public security, in a report of October 2, 1966, claimed that Red Guards had arrested 21,770 landlords, rich peasants, counterrevolutionaries, and other evil elements and estimated that some 900,000 reactionaries had been subjected to Red Guard harassment. Karnow, op. cit., p. 209.

81. Ibid., pp. 179-92. Accusations that work teams had engaged in "white terror" mounted after December 1966, though evidence that physical coercion was actually used is sparse. See Dorrill, op. cit., pp. 94-102.

82. Bennett and Montaperto, op. cit., pp. 81-82 and Baum, op. cit., pp. 378-79.

83. Karnow, op. cit., p. 209. Dai Hsiao-Ai reports that confiscated goods were turned over to neighborhood street committees rather than to public security. Barnett and Montaperto, op. cit., p. 82.

84. "Ten Regulations of the CCP Central Committee Concerning Grasping Revolution and Promoting Production" Draft, December 9, 1966, *CCP Documents of the Great Proletarian Cultural Revolution,* op. cit., p. 134.

85. This characterization of Lin Biao, Jiang Qing, and Chen Boda as "radicals" echoes that of Thomas Robinson. Thomas W. Robinson, "Chou En-lai and the Cultural Revolution in China," in *The Cultural Revolution in China,* ed. Thomas W. Robinson, op. cit., p. 188.

86. "Directive of the CCP Central Committee Concerning the Great Proletarian Cultural Revolution in the Countryside" Draft, December 15, 1966, *CCP Documents of the Great Proletarian Cultural Revolution, 1966-1967,* op. cit., pp. 137-42.

87. "Some Regulations of the CCP Central Committee and the State Council Concerning the Strengthening of Public Security Work in the Great Proletarian Cultural Revolution," January 13, 1967, *CCP Documents of the Great Proletarian Cultural Revolution, 1966-1967,* op. cit., pp. 173-77.

88. The role of students in campaigns is partly reflected in Whyte, *Small Groups,* pp. 100-01. Students were principally witnesses to the recruitment of faculty and staff until

the onset of the Anti-Rightist Campaign in 1957, in which they joined faculty and staff as targets.

89. Bennett, op. cit., pp. 7-8.

90. Ibid., pp. 8-9.

91. Ibid., p. 8.

92. Ibid., pp. 12-13.

93. An official directive of January 1967 prohibited further "reversals," but evidence exists that the movements to "reverse verdicts" continued at the local level despite the official cancellation. Richard Baum, "Elite Behavior Under Conditions of Stress: The Lessons of the 'Tang-ch'uan P'ai' in the Cultural Revolution," in *Elites in the People's Republic of China*, ed. Robert A. Scalapino, op. cit., p. 554n. See also Liu, op. cit., p. 178.

94. Bennett, op. cit., p. 7n.

95. Richard H. Solomon, *Mao's Revolution and the Chinese Political Culture* (Berke—ley: University of California Press, 1971), pp. 268-329.

96. Neal Hunter, *Shanghai Journal: An Eyewitness Account of the Cultural Revolution* (Boston: Beacon, 1969), pp. 111-31.

97. For a good example of the use of dossiers in the making and unmaking of a heroine, see "The Case of Hsiang Hsiu-li," *Chinese Sociology and Anthropology* 2 (1971): 155-81.

98. This point is implicit in Thomas Robinson's description of Zhou Enlai's defense of Chen Yi and Tan Chenlin against Red Guard attacks. Robinson, op. cit., p. 263. See also Lowell Dittmer, *Liu Shao-ch'i and the Chinese Cultural Revolution: The Politics of Mass Criticism* (Berkeley: University of California Press, 1974), p. 350.

99. Victor H. Li, "The Evolution and Development of the Chinese Legal System," in *China: Management of a Revolutionary Society*, ed. John M. H. Lindbeck (Seattle: University of Washington Press, 1971), pp. 249-50.

100. Ibid., p. 249.

101. Calls to desist from seizures of secret documents, interference with productive labor and transport, and clashes with the PLA and between factions were notable for the lag in compliance with which they were attended during this period. The relevant documents are contained in *CCP Documents on the Great Proletarian Cultural Revolution*, op. cit.

102. Liu, op. cit., pp. 82-92.

103. Parris H. Chang, "Provincial Party Leaders' Strategies," in *Elites in the People's Republic of China*, ed. Robert A. Scalapino, op. cit., pp. 514-16.

104. On the confusion among contending groups and the "polycentrism" to which it gave rise, see John Giddings, "The Prospects of the Cultural Revolution," *China After the Cultural Revolution: A Selection from "The Bulletin of the Atomic Scientists"* (New York: Random House, 1969), pp. 68-69.

105. See Liu, op. cit., pp. 82-91; Karnow, op. cit., pp. 367-89; and Baum, "Cultural Revolution in the Countryside," op. cit., pp. 448-50.

106. Karnow, op. cit., pp. 344-51.

107. Ibid., pp. 429-43.

108. "Here is the Shih-ching Detention House," *Chinese Sociology and Anthropology* 2 (1970): 211-14. Karnow, op. cit., gives additional examples. The use of direct, physical coercion in recruitment was, however, also evident in the Four Cleanups Campaign after the promulgation of the "Revised Draft of the Later Ten Points" in September 1964. The use of some of the Cultural Revolution's more pejorative labels dates from this same period. Richard Baum and Frederick C. Teiwes, *Ssu-ch'ing: The Socialist Education Movement of 1962-1966* (Berkeley: Center for Chinese Studies, 1968), pp. 28-32.

109. Bennett and Montaperto, op. cit., p. 87.

110. William Hinton, *Hundred Day War: The Cultural Revolution at Tsinghua University* (New York: Monthly Review Press, 1972), pp. 162-70.

111. Another term was "monster exhibit" (*niu lan*). Bennett and Montaperto, op. cit., p. 128.

112. Hinton, op. cit., p. 220.

113. Townsend, op. cit., p. 135.

114. "Report by Mao Tse-tung at a Meeting of the Central Committee of the Communist Party of China, Peking, June 6, 1950," *Current Background*, June 13, 1950, p. 3. "Party members must penetratingly realize that new methods must be employed in the current rectification movement, namely, that the campaign should be a movement of ideological education carried out seriously, yet as gently as a breeze or mild rain. . . ."

115. Bennett, op. cit., p. 8.

116. Philip Bidgham, "Mao's Cultural Revolution: Origin and Development, Part I," in *China in Ferment: Perspectives on the Cultural Revolution*, ed. Richard Baum (Englewood Cliffs, N.J.: Prentice-Hall, 1971), pp. 19-29.

117. Bennett, op. cit., p. 14.

118. Robinson, op. cit., pp. 234-36.

119. Baum, "Cultural Revolution in the Countryside," pp. 471-72.

120. Robinson, op. cit., p. 221.

121. Karnow, op. cit., p. 240. The shift in Mao's strategies in dealing with his subordinates is documented in Michel C. Oksenberg, "Policy Making under Mao Tse-tung, 1949-1968," *Comparative Politics* 3 (1971): 342-43 and 353-55.

CHINA'S MASS CAMPAIGNS AND
SOCIAL CONTROL
Gordon Bennett

Social control" and "deviance" do not exist as abstracts. It is only meaningful to speak of someone controlling someone else, and to speak of deviance through someone's eyes. This is why sociologists have found elusive a consensus on what behavior should be judged deviant enough to merit society's control. Engels once suggested that "in the course of their migrations the Germans had morally much deteriorated, particularly during their southeasterly wanderings among the nomads of the Black Sea steppes, from whom they acquired, not only equestrian skill, but also gross, unnatural vices."[1] How many Germans shared Engels's moral concern is unknown. And even if it were known we would be no closer to a case for justifying social control of these migrants' "unnatural vices." Justifiably or not, however, communities do define standards of acceptable thought and behavior, and do act on many levels to enforce them and teach them to their young. The easiest working concept of "deviance," then, is whatever behavior a particular community determines to depart from established standards, however arrived at. The easiest working concept of "social control" is whatever steps that same community takes to guarantee conformity to its standards, and also to guarantee preservation of them. One especially important feature of these definitions is their inclusiveness. "Deviant" behavior by elites that merits "control" by ordinary people is just as much part of the process as is the reverse. Unfortunately, the terms "deviance" and "control"

Research funds were provided by the University Research Institute of the University of Texas at Austin, by the Social Science Research Council, and by the National Endowment for the Humanities.

stimulate a one-way vision of authorities controlling the powerless. That happens, of course; but many situations occur, in China and in other societies, where boundaries of socially acceptable behavior are drawn around politicians, and communal enforcement of those boundaries is reasonably effective.

China's campaigns (*yundong*) are highly organized mobilizations of mass commitment to push over barriers to proletarian dictatorship and socialism. Almost everyone in China regularly is involved in one campaign or another, a small one if not a big one. Campaigns are so common to the Chinese people that they appear routine, however counterintuitive it may seem that a short-lived, intense mobilization of activism ever could be routine. Familiar campaign rituals include study of leading articles in the official press, small group discussion of how those articles' messages apply to local reality, specification of deviance, criticism and self-criticism of deviant persons, and public struggle to oppose them and reform them. *Yundong* in China are as common as elections in America; they comprise an institution that is first experienced by school-children, is known to everybody, and is accepted by elites as a political arena.

Oddly, the literature in this area is not far advanced. China's mass movements are ubiquitous, and we have many fine case studies. What we lack is a general analysis of the phenomenon as an institution. My own monograph, *Yundong: Mass Campaigns in Chinese Communist Leadership* (Berkeley: University of California, Center for Chinese Studies, 1976) stops well short of exhausting the subject.In particular it fails to touch upon how connections between mass movements and political participation affect social control. Here my purpose is to extend the analysis of the monograph to include propositions about possible *yundong*-social control relationships, and to evaluate these propositions with interview data gathered from emigres in Hong Kong in 1975.

The respondents are not known to me to be representative of any characterizable population in China, though the sample is obviously skewed toward people who were highly dissatisfied and strongly motivated to leave China. Thus the empirical findings reported here do not necessarily reflect modal tendencies in China recently. Data from such a sample give a worm's eye view of political life in China, and from disgruntled worms at that. Nonetheless, data acquired from systematic interviews do take us a step beyond the evidence on these points we have at present. The total sample size is thirty-seven. Everyone was asked the same thirty-five open-ended questions, phrased identically. Each interview lasted about six hours, over two or three sessions. Most respondents are male native-born peasants from Guangdong province. Others include skilled workers, technicians, teachers, a doctor, and a psychologist; their work locales immediately before coming to Hong Kong were Kwangtung, Kwangsi, Fukien, Hunan, Chinghai, Inner Mongolia, and Peking. Seven are Overseas Chinese. Fifteen of the others have bad class backgrounds, and fifteen good (three workers, nine poor or lower-middle peasants, and three middle peasants). Four are women. Two are PLA veterans. The interviews were conducted in whatever dialect was native to the respondent by a research assistant who I am confident grasped the nuances of each question. I have filed each interview by a two-letter code that I use to name informants in this report.

A general relationship between *yundong* and social control of deviance, if one exists, is certainly not simple to identify. Campaigns bring more control in some situations, less control in others. At least five factors modify this relationship: 1) *Groups involved on each end of the control relationship*. The question here is, who is trying to control whom? Any given campaign at any given time may involve, for example, a declared goal calling for local poor and lower-middle peasants to control local production brigade cadres, and a real situation of one coalition of factions trying to control another coalition. We would expect that a campaign's effectiveness in promoting control would vary considerably among diverse arenas such as these. 2) *Expected duration of the control effect*. 3) *Whether the control object is attitudes or behavior*. 4) *Strength of anticipation effects*, or the degree to which people adjust their speech and behavior in anticipation of campaigns yet to come. Not only past experience, but future expectations, must be considered. 5) *Degree of democratic political participation*. If *yundong* participation in China is merely ritualistic (a view common in Western scholarship), then we must regard campaigns as an instrument of state control, a tool with which leaders manipulate people. If participation is genuinely democratic (the official view), then we must regard campaigns as an institution that joins popular interests with central political power to restrain the pyramiding of political resources by party organizations, administrative agencies, and military commands whose self-interests are narrower than those of the bulk of the population. Or, as a third possibility, if mass movement participation is democratic for some people sometimes (the correct view, I believe), then we must ask for whom, and when? In the section following I will analyze these intervening variables individually.

GROUPS INVOLVED ON EACH SIDE
OF THE CONTROL RELATIONSHIP

Cadres, specifically local cadres, most attract informants' attention. Generally their view is that local cadres were vulnerable during mass campaigns. AO's (worker) contrary statement is the exception that proves the rule: "Cadres don't get in trouble during campaigns, because their relationship with higher authorities is special." Typical was the view that cadres rather easily could become criticism or struggle targets. AA (self-employed) points out that everyone became more guarded during a movement, "especially older cadres with complicated histories." AS (landlord) recalls that a team in his brigade lost a cadre in the 1968-69 Campaign to Clean Up the Class Ranks; that cadre's successor "acted strictly according to official procedures" (*cheng gong ban shi*) and dared not "seek personal gain illicitly while holding a public post" (*ying si wu bi*). AZ (lower-middle peasant), the object of repeated recruitment efforts to be a cadre, including requests to be a Four Cleanups work team member and to be a production team leader, nevertheless decided to "put down his staff and retire to the life of an ordinary peasant" because he felt cadres were more vulnerable than others to mass campaigns. AF (peddler) presents an interesting contradiction. Speaking as a former cadre (he was deputy team leader in 1969), he claims he was sensitive to campaigns: "I did not strongly criticize members of the team who stole collectively-owned goods, or who pilfered fruit from the team, or who were lazy on the job. I worried that when a movement next came along, they would exploit my shortcomings to get back at me." That is, as a cadre he believed he was vulnerable. Later, however, speaking as an ordinary team member, he claimed the opposite: "Ordinary team members are unwilling to speak out against cadres because they fear later retribution, so I can say that movements have little effect in educating cadres." As a non-cadre he also believed he was vulnerable. The apparent contradiction suggests a hypothesis. Local cadres whom everyone expects to enjoy long tenure in office can discourage potentially damaging public criticism. However, those who generally are thought likely to serve only a short while feel more exposed to criticism. Anyone who witnessed criticism of a local cadre for corruption during Four Cleanups, again during Clean Up the Class Ranks, and yet again during One Strike and Three Oppositions would be most unlikely to doubt that cadre's staying power were corruption to be opposed a fourth time.

Besides insecure cadres, certain well-defined categories of deviants also are especially threatened by *yundong*. AE (lower-middle peasant) feared punishment for his illicit private peddling (*zou zi fa*). And AC's (poor peasant) fear of campaigns rose after he was arrested for speculative private trading and the Public Security Bureau declared him to be an "element currently under supervision" (*xian guan fenzi*).* "Sometimes with no cause I would be made a struggle object. Even if one's 'cap' were removed, it could easily be put in place again." BG (merchant and landlord) and BK (poor peasant) both feared having their plans to to to Hong Kong discovered during a movement. Finally, AN (rich peasant) recalls that in the course of each movement a few people doing illegal activities were sent away for "labor reform" (*da yi pi zhua yi pi lao gai*).

Reports by these informants suggest that both local cadres whose positions are insecure, and also well-defined, publicly known categories of deviants are most easily controlled by campaign criticism.

---

*This was to last three years. AG was not allowed to communicate by mail with people in or out of the country; he was deprived of his civil rights (*bei chiduo gongmin quan*) and as a criminal element he was no longer considered a regular team member. "It was like being in prison but without the prison."

EXPECTED DURATION OF THE CONTROL EFFECT

Most respondents emphasize that few movement results last. AI (middle peasant changed to counterrevolutionary) is an exception in believing results endure: he cites persons whose class labels were found to be fraudulent during 1968-69, very few of whom have returned to their old status (*zai ye buneng fuyong le*). But the typical view in the sample is that old ways pop up again soon after a campaign ends. AR (rich peasant) says:

> *Yundong* are effective, I would say completely effective. The CCP emphasizes that all is possible once class struggle is grasped. Take production, for example. Without mass movements it drags along at a snail's pace (*tuotuo lala man tuntun*), but as soon as a movement comes along, everyone is active. Without movements, there is corruption and stealing and all manner of things (*shemma dou chuxian*). As soon as a movements starts, no one dares engage in such activities. From this we can see that there are results but also that they suffer reversal over time. The CCP uses *yundong* to push forward revolution, production, and social progress. Every sector depends upon movements to advance its work.

Many add the corollary that because the results suffer reverses, *yundong* must be repeated over and over to achieve the importance they have in Chinese leadership. BA (Overseas Chinese small businessman) says, "*yundong* are effective but not for very long, so it is necessary to have one follow upon the heels of another (*yin ci yundong jiu yao yige jie yige gaoxiaqu*). *Yundong* are never finished; people must not be allowed to relax, or to lose their vigilance." AZ (lower-middle peasant) feels "because results get reversed, there must be many of them." AV (landlord) believes, "since former attitudes sprout again, new movements must come." AT (middle peasant) says, "if the results were long-lasting, then more movements would not be needed."

WHETHER THE CONTROL OBJECT
IS ATTITUDES OR BEHAVIOR

Only five respondents explicitly express the opinion that *yundong* influence attitudes. Two speak vaguely: AZ (lower-middle peasant) says movements "lead to changes of thought among people in each class," and BC (Overseas Chinese) says "people's consciousness is raised." Two others repeat the widely held idea that the effected attitude is caution in the public presentation of self: AP (Overseas Chinese merchant) says campaigns "leave their mark on people's thought" and "lead people to be on their guard," and AV (landlord) says most *yundong* cause people to feel "threatened." But it is AW (poor peasant) who best expresses the observable pattern in the whole sample when he says *yundong* fulfill a "deterrent function" (*zu he zuoyong*): "Each time a movement comes, people slack off less at work, young people are more content to remain in the countryside, and the number of persons going over to Hong Kong is fewer. But as soon as the movement passes, old tendencies are rekindled again (*si hui fu ran*)."

STRENGTH OF ANTICIPATION EFFECTS

Twenty-sevel respondents say they feared future movements, and thought twice about behaving in any way that might be socially or officially unacceptable. Of the other ten, five agreed with AC (Overseas Chinese), a technician: "I had nothing to be concerned about because I had committed no mistake, I could concentrate on my work and not concern myself with politics. But I hated mass movements. They were never-ending." Four feared someone might use a future movement to seek personal revenge. And only one, GH (middle peasant, married woman), said she was completely free of worry about mass campaigns.

The twenty-seven respondents who say they contemplated future movements when deciding on present actions support a clear, strong conclusion. People expect movements to continue, and they expect anyone who missteps to be caught up in them. AS (landlord) recalls, "All that one could predict was that many movements would come in the future, so in thought and action one was perpetually on guard." AX (lower-middle peasant) replies, "Because I knew many campaigns would come in the future, I was always on edge. I tried to keep on everybody's good side, so that even if I made a mistake it would still be easy to pass (*guo guan*)." BK (poor peasant) feels, "Even if one got by this movement, inevitably another would come along that could not be dodged (*biguo zheige yundong que bibuliao yong wo ti zhi di ling yige yundong*)."

The anticipation effect remains as strong as ever.

DEGREE OF DEMOCRATIC POLITICAL PARTICIPATION

People enjoying high degrees of democratic political participation are better able than others to exercise social control. And they are less vulnerable as targets of control, whether during mass movements or not. For present purposes, let the term "democratic" describe voluntary joining in political activities to achieve ends of interest to an individual, ends that may or may not correspond to the higher official design for those activities. Since the most familiar arena for mass participation is *yundong*, I will take vulnerability to campaign criticism and struggle as a leading measure of a low degree of democratic political participation. In turn, the greater the opportunity for democratic political participation, the more likely one is to control in some sense instead of being controlled. At least eight variables influence campaign vulnerability: occupation, age, activism, cynicism, social class label, exit option, friendship havens, and history of deviance.

Occupation

Professionals and technicians are more vulnerable to *yundong* action than other occupational groups. *Yundong* often bring demands for educated people in jobs requiring special training to spend more time involving themselves in current political priorities. During movements it is less legitimate for them to talk about technical constraints. AC (Overseas Chinese), a boiler designer and Grade 13 technician, recalls an instructive episode from the winter of 1971:

> To meet the popular demand for daily-use products . . . the authorities concerned requested that we produce a large number of high-quality, durable, safe, low-cost boilers, and hoped that we would resort to any means necessary to fulfill this duty. To work on technical problems involved, a production meeting was convened attended by the factory party committee secretary, the chairman of the revolutionary committee, important cadres from the personnel and safety section, the production planning section, the financial and accounting section, the labor and wages section, each shop, and our technical section.

> Party Secretary Mao introduced the proposal sent from above . . . and requested that we produce ten 500-kilo and five to ten 2000-kilo boilers in the first quarter of 1972. Our section objected that such a task was impossible given our present technical resources. The administrative and managerial personnel at the meeting felt that we were not putting politics in command. They said our thought was middle-of-the-road and lagged behind the present situation, and that our politics lagged behind the demands of actual developments. We disputed this criticism. I also spoke out against these ideas, saying that I questioned their good intentions in arguing that suggestions for correct implementation put forth by our technical section were middle-of-the-road, and expressed the belief that we must strive for early completion of tasks based on our capacity instead of resorting to impractical methods to solve problems.

This drama is played out endlessly in China; always some politically motivated person is ready to elevate any technical objection whatever to the level of backward political thinking. In this instance, because the debate occurred outside the context of a movement, Secretary Mao and the chairman of the revolutionary committee chose to emphasize that AC and his colleagues in the Technical Section should "rely on the masses and attack difficult technical barriers, but keep their feet on the ground in the process." That is, the two cadre members essentially agreed with AC, except they would not relax the demand that fifteen new boilers be produced in the coming quarter. In a *yundong* context, such moderate responses often are not possible. AC notes, "We technicians usually were left with the feeling that all credit had gone to the leadership and workers while all the fatigue and hard work had fallen on the technicians." If the boilers were finished on time, it was a victory for Mao Zedong Thought and those who propound it. If the boilers were finished behind schedule, then it was the fault of backward technicians who were bound by conventions and bookish expertise.

Professionals' vulnerability has two aspects. The first one is the nature of the work itself. The task falls on their shoulders to explain on technical grounds why the excessively optimistic schemes of nontechnical politicians are likely to encounter problems. BC (Overseas Chinese), a professor of economic geography at a leading university, recalls, "It was hard to avoid mistakes because they always pressed us to strengthen our political study and raise our thought level." This effect occurred most severely in the most radical stages of the Cultural Revolution. AC continues:

> Even though I expressed some dissatisfaction with those colleagues who ignored financial and material constraints and barged ahead with no thought of the consequences (*bu ji cai li wu li di man gan xingwei*), my critics still said my point of view was mistaken. In the Cultural Revolution, while we were cleaning up the class ranks and attacking the small handful of capitalist roaders, I thought that each persons's mistakes should be divided up into political, work, life, and historical problems. But they ignored this point of view and proceeded like left deviationists—they never gave a person a way out; their method was cudgeling people to death with one blow (*yi gunzi da si*).

The second aspect is intellectuals' collective consciousness that their very role in China these days is only half legitimate. This realization leads many to become discouraged, to lose their initial idealism about being important to the building of a new China, and to withdraw into political passivity. Then inactive political participation itself becomes an object of criticism, unless they can appear "active" by voluntarily assuming heavier burdens at work. AC, who had returned to China from Indonesia at age seventeen, goes on to complain:

> In general there were few things that would make me happy. Reality was cruel, fearful, and hard to fathom. Earning a salary and improving one's life would lead some to say one was living like a capitalist. Dressing a little better would lead some to say one was

seeking after or hanging onto a capitalist lifestyle. All of this was diametrically opposed to what I expected and wanted when I returned to China; my desire had been to study hard and contribute my strength to the fatherland.

AC always reacted to the same way to a movement, an approach he called "no questions, no action, no responsibility, and no concern" (*bu wen bu li by guan bu guanxin*). He adopted the method of "burying my head in my work, not concerning myself with other people's business, and having as little contact as possible with other people." During the Movement to Criticize Lin Biao and Confucious, recalls AD (employee, *guyuan*), a water conservancy technician, people were given time off from work to listen to reports on new study documents: "I myself gave all my attention to production and construction, and never took off from work to study the Confucianist-Legalist documents. This movement did not affect me too much primarily because I was busy at the construction site day and night." AI (middle peasant, changed to counter-revolutionary), a primary school teacher, feared movements and tried to avoid criticism by increasing his work efficiency.

For professionals and technicians, vulnerability to *yundong* is high unless they can withdraw into nonpolitical work.

Age

Young people, until they become full-strength workers, are involved least of all with mass campaigns. They remain relatively free from worry about campaign criticism or struggle, and some even feel inspired to become insistent, vocal participants in campaign activities directed at others. Second least involved are the elderly. Seventy-year-old AO (worker) hid in the background during movements, and was merely a spectator. Cadres did not understand him and generally ignored him. One time he was ordered to the front to participate in the struggle. "I had no choice. I had to obey. Everyone was quiet. I had never spoken before. When they raised their fists I raised mine, but I had never raised a finger to struggle against others." AO feels the way to avoid trouble during *yundong* was to have some special relationship (*yuanfen*) with higher authorities. Others could be denounced for any mistake. Fifty-year-old BI (worker) also was apathetic. The most severe campaign he remembers was the Campaign to Clean Up the Class Ranks of 1968-69. Somehow he became associated during the Cultural Revolution with the local "Di Zong" faction, and was sent to a nearby state farm to guard captured members of the opposition "Hong Qi" faction. Afterward, he says, though he never understood why, he was criticized and even struggled for small matters. Finally he applied to emigrate to Hong Kong. With one exception (AJ, poor peasant), the other eight older respondents (those aged forty-five to fifty-five) in the sample express rather mild views of movements.

AZ (lower-middle peasant), for example, gives the opinion that "Each movement is relatively important for Communist Chinese control. *Yundong* bring about changes of thought by each class, they control interpersonal relations among brigade members, they plug up holes and consolidate social order. Without *yundong* the communists would have to worry about China changing color."

For adolescents and people just beginning careers, the likelihood of becoming a movement target is small. Moreover, as late career and retirement approach, provided one has avoided political stigma, the pressure seems to ease once again.

Activism

"Activist" is not a formal bureaucratic position with prescribed duties. Rather, two types of activist are regularly elected: work activists at the end of each year, and *yundong* activists after the end of each movement. In the past the term activist was used broadly to include local cadres. In 1958, for example, in the twelve *xian* of Honan's Kaifeng special district, recognition as "red and expert" activist was awarded to 252,000 persons. Three-fourths of them (186,000) were sent to one of 1,600 local training classes or schools for further political study, and one-third of the trainees (66,000) were declared eligible for party membership; one-fifth (38,000) actually were admitted as probationary members. An overwhelming majority (85 percent) of the new members were "leaders of production teams or in other leadership positions." That is, many were cadres.[2] Nowadays the term activist most commonly is used to designate non-cadres. AM says his team of 160 members had seven cadres and four activists (two women and two men). AV says his team had five or six activists, all of whom were "five kinds of red." And BA reports that his county hospital had five or six activists among eighty employees. Even though new activists are selected frequently, many of the same people are chosen repeatedly.

Each respondent was asked, "Do you think one generally benefits by being an activist?" (*shi bushi bi putong ren de yi*). Almost all replied "Yes," but at the same time noticeably failed to recall a single example of an activist who was rewarded with upward mobility. *De yi* to them means leading a more privileged existence in one's present unit rather than gaining upward promotion. Perquisites include closer relationships with cadres at higher administrative levels, time off from work to attend higher level meetings, early information about coming campaigns, greater opportunity for transfer to interesting temporary duties, less vulnerability to criticism during mass campaigns, and a greater chance to obtain party or Youth League membership. One respondent who himself was an activist confirms these points. After three years at the commune middle school, AW (poor peasant) rejoined his team in 1969 at age eighteen. He was co-opted onto the team committee, assigned to record workpoints, and made responsible for operating and maintaining the team's tractor.

> Activists feel their prestige is high among the masses. They can mobilize and direct other team members. They go often to the commune or *xian* capital to participate in meetings, for which they are excused from work and receive a subsidy. When higher authorities detach some members of the team temporarily to work elsewhere, activists have the greatest chance of being selected. All this leads them to have a very high opinion of themselves (*zi ming bu fan*).

Activist or not, AW could get in trouble during campaigns were he to display a bad attitude or commit a mistake. But he spoke mildly of receiving "suggestions" from the masses, not "criticism" or "struggle." AT (middle peasant) confirms the point that activists are "part of the team leadership," often as members of the team committee.

The minority of respondents speaking favorably usually mention that activists are reliable persons on whom the leadership can depend, and that they serve to set an example for others. These respondents, six or seven at most, feel it is difficult to be an activist. According to AP (Overseas Chinese), a doctor at a public health hospital, their only functions are responding to new calls from the leadership (*xiangying haozhao*) and setting the pace for others (*qi daitou zuoyong*). They dare not speak too "candidly" or "throw their weight around and give commands." AY (Overseas Chinese, female) regards being an activist a burden: "One constantly has to attend meetings, take more responsibility, and be an example in everything. Often one is wronged (*chikui zui duo*)." AU (landlord) believes commune and brigade cadres depend on activists because their "level" is higher than ordinary team members (*shuiping bi sheyuan gao*). Some of these respondents restrict their praise. BD (Overseas Chinese, female) compares "true activists" who concern themselves with "proletarian revolution" with others who are simply opportunists. AX (lower-middle peasant) remembers rural activists as "real activists" who were "relatively pure," but school activists as opportunistic and ambitious to obtain political standing and good work assignments after graduation (usually they failed). Factories, in AX's view, have two kinds of activists: young workers and master craftsmen (*lao shifu*) on the one hand, and technicians on the other. Technician activists fish for political capital. Masters and apprentices are more truly activist. Young workers aspire to raise their wages and job classification (*jibie*). Master craftsmen seek esteem in the eyes of their apprentices. Most respondents, however, do not speak favorably of activists, depicting them instead as opportunists seeking party or league membership whose privileged status makes them imperious and personally intolerable. To AA (self-employed), a machine tool design technician, "Activists in our factory could command, obtain more fruits of the factory's sideline production, and spend less time working on the farm our factory operated. This showed the leadership's care for them, and made them feel very self-satisfied." In BC's eyes, activists have a spiritual commitment (*jingshen jituo*) to overcome their political shortcomings to obtain party membership: "Those ambitious to join the party sought to appear active in every way. Some of them went overboard and talked with great exaggeration (*biaoxian de kuakua qi tan*)." A few respondents speak more bluntly. BG (merchant and landlord), an institute graduate, despised activists. "They regularly reported classmates' activities to higher authorities. Especially lamentable was that as students they wasted precious time on political activities." BI (worker) was even bitter:

> Activists pretentiously consider themselves officials. As we say in Guangdong, "What use has a lion for a big nose?" (*shi gan da ge bi*). They were fond of moving their mouths but not lifting a finger. They were incapable of setting an example for others. They were divorced from the masses. It got so that production ceased to advance and we became backward. These conceited activists used every criticism and struggle session to scare people. Their only concern was their own prestige. I despised these activists who applied Marxian-Leninism to others and liberalism to themselves.

AN (landlord) agrees, "Activists attack other people to elevate themselves." My own research failed to reveal such instances, but recent interviews in Hong Kong by Ivan and Miriam London of Brooklyn College contain reports of retributive beatings administered to unpopular activists after a movement.[3]

Activists' vulnerability to mass movements themselves, however, is very small.

Cynicism

Informants were asked if they thought of themselves as being "cynical" in the sense of suspecting others' motives (*nin bu xin shiren zuo shi xi youyu chengyi huo bu cun sixin de ma*). All but two say they acquired such an attitude after leaving school and beginning work. Afterwards, in the phrase employed by several of them, they consciously adopted the worldview "If one does not look out for himself he will be cursed by heaven and earth" (*ren bu wei ji tian zhu di mie*). Seven informants say they acquired this attitude at age twenty or older, and fifty-year-old BI (worker) claims he was twenty-eight before he grew cynical. Usually respondents stated that growing cynicism was followed by growing political passivity. A pattern emerges. Youth are capable of considerable dedication to public life, many abandoning this orientation only in their twenties. But when they do lose it, for whatever reason, their participation in movements becomes guarded. According to AG (poor peasant): "Since all these last few years I have been used and cheated by other people, it has made me see more clearly how to get along in society. And in politics it has led me to adopt an easygoing attitude." Similar feelings are expressed by AB (worker):

> Especially during mass movements these last few years I have come to understand that activists seek to gain political capital. Only after the Cultural Revolution did my understanding take shape. This was the time when I really began to understand things. I learned many lessons as I watched some people voice complaints and suppress others, and watched some people actively scheme to do in others. With these realizations I studied how to give the appearance of activism while being passive in reality, or to follow the main current.

Cynical attitudes may not affect one's vulnerability to movements, but such attitudes do depress democratic participation. Cynics feel it is not worth the risk.

Social Class Label

Class plays a major role by bringing ritual struggle in some places to landlords, rich peasants, former Guomindang officials, and others of bad class background. The sample of respondents included some with this experience. AS (Overseas Chinese merchant) reports that class pariahs in his district were known as "old movement hands" (*lao yundong yuan*) and had been struggled in every *yundong* since land reform. AH (landlord) "lived in constant fear of *yundong*." AQ (landlord) was taken to his brigade town for study or for struggle every time a movement came along. Not every landlord was drawn in mechanically. AS was "perpetually on guard." And AU feared if he brought harm to anyone then they would use the next campaign for revenge. Rich peasant informants report less mechanical treatment. AN describes himself as an "ordinary team member who came from a bad family class background." He disliked *yundong*, and made every effort to avoid them. And even though he "feared" *yundong*, he felt there was no way to prepare and "behaved recklessly" (*li yu xun xin you maoxian qu gan*). AR recalls only that he feared committing mistakes because then a future *yundong* would bring much trouble. "If one movement failed to catch you, the next one would" (*guodeliao zheige yundong guobuliao ling yige yundong*).

For nonpariah classes, however, social class label seems a less discriminating variable. Among the unstigmatized, attitudes, levels of participation, and behavior vary little by class. Each respondent, for example, was asked, "Who were your closest friends? Please list one to five persons." The twenty respondents whose replies are categorizable by class label listed a total of fifty-four close friends, twenty-four of whom were roughly of the same class and thirty of whom were distinctly higher or lower (twelve higher, eighteen lower). Only one respondent, AU (landlord), volunteers a tie between social class and activism when he suggests that people from bad class backgrounds find it harder to convince others their activism is genuine. I must add that ties between the interview data and this second point are not strong.

Pariah classes are extremely vulnerable to *yundong*. Among the remainder of the population, campaign vulnerability may not vary significantly by social class.

Exit Option

Does knowing one can leave China change one's attitudes toward *yundong*? Or, short of that extreme, does knowing one can go somewhere else in China alter one's perspective?

Several respondents describe jobs away from home that often lasted for extended periods. Even pariah class elements could exercise this option. AS (landlord) worked on state farms and mines. AV (landlord) worked outside for eleven years (he called it *gao shang jiao*). And AU (landlord) left his team in 1967 to work (*zuo san gong*) first at a *xian* level brick and tile factory for two months, then at a nearby state farm for three months, then at a state forest for four months; before settling down at a job inspecting tiles at a commune level factory, he worked for a while transporting lumber. One's security in these outside jobs, however, is fragile. AX (lower-middle peasant), a technician, left his job at a radio factory in April 1971 simply because he did not like it, and wandered on his own as an unregistered person (*hei ren hei hu*); later in 1971 his university returned his registration (*huji*) to his original production team. And AT (middle peasant), who had learned the tailoring trade from his father and uncle, set up a "sewing station" in a nearby brigade. But in 1974, during a movement to oppose taking the capitalist road, he was accused of "going it alone" and compelled to return to his team to be a simple farm laborer.

A reasonable hypothesis is that the local exit option may absolve one from participating in small movements, but exercising it can increase one's vulnerability to bigger or more pointed ones. Thoughts of exercising the Hong Kong option only induce apprehensiveness that the plan will be revealed.

Friendship Havens

Personal friendships seem relatively undisturbed by *yundong*, though the reasons for this are not at all clear. I have not discovered whether an informal norm protects close friend intimacies from campaign explotation, or whether friends are chosen in the first place to minimize the threat that intimacies will be revealed during a mass movement. No respondent speaks of holding back from criticizing a friend in a struggle meeting, or of defending a friend against an attack; those rituals seem to have a dynamic of their own. Not one informant describes a situation in which a friend was brought up for public criticism and he, the informant, faced with having to say something, experienced a conflict of interest. Nor did any informants recount instances where they themselves were in the dock and one of their friends felt pressured. But friends do provide important relief from interpersonal suspicions and tensions induced by movements. Most respondents say they spent almost all their free time with friends or lovers; these were the only people with whom they could talk sincerely. Asked about their relationships with their closest friends, most informants report meeting frequently (if they did not work together) and talking without restriction about any topic at all—personal or political, sensitive or safe. Friends frequently helped each other tide over temporary economic difficulties, and often friends would go together to seek outside work or to engage in illicit peddling. All this respondents contrast sharply with the minimum contact and reserve characterizing their relations with people who were not their friends. Small groups of close friends, therefore, are safety valves, or escapes, from the relentless pressures of life in larger and more politicized groups.

AF (small peddler) is a farmer who spent his spare time in the evenings with friends watching movies, playing musical instruments, chess, and poker, and watching traveling dramatic performances. "Just talking or strolling with my friends was fun. Especially fun was talking with my friends about what life would be like in Hong Kong. AB (worker) recalls:

> Usually I wiled away the time playing the guitar and other musical instruments and singing with my friends. We didn't sing revolutionary songs but rather currently popular Hong Kong tunes. And it wasn't only us that did this. Many Kwangchow young people could hum several Cantonese or Mandarin popular songs. Sometimes we would go so far as to organize a sort of concert. For this we would go to the Gaoshang residential area of Dongshan district, an area with only one family to a house. This I can say I regarded as fun. Only in this way could we leave the boredom of the week behind and do something interesting.

AC (Overseas Chinese) gives an interesting description of what not having close friends is like:

> I was closest to workers in our technical section. I knew others in the vicinity of our dormitory, but we never got to the point where we could talk openly on any topic. Everyone in our section was just an ordinary worker except the section chief, who was a party member. He did only political work, and had no understanding of technical matters at all; he was an outsider leading insiders. Those living near my dormitory mostly were coworkers from the shops. We talked about life's problems, about work, and about national affairs

from a favorable standpoint. The reason I didn't talk openly with them is that I feared one of them might denounce me for saying something I shouldn't have (*jianju shuo guai hua*).

Friendships were a haven. A reasonable hypothesis is that they provide individuals with valuable charges of morale and with strength for coping with the demands of public life.

History of Deviance

To the authorities, any past transgression or any past instance of receiving struggle and criticism during a campaign is a stigma, an "almanac glanced at through one's old age" (*yiben tongshu di dao lao*). Persons so stigmatized, according to AB (worker), "were called upon by name to participate in every mass campaign, or their old account would be resettled" (*fan jiu zhang*). To ordinary team members, however, the type of transgression makes a difference. They care little about strictly political crimes, feeling these are the concern of the authorities. They feel very angry whenever an affair results in personal losses for them, but are satisfied with public criticism as long as only public or collective property is taken. Inside they say to themselves, "This person is a smart operator," and "These methods aren't bad," and their reproach subsides. Some respondents mention moral failure, especially illicit sexual acts, as a type of wrongdoing that arouses people's ire. But examples where such mistakes were forgotten, or the miscreant's situation even attracted sympathy, weaken the force of the statement. According to AE (lower-middle peasant):

> In 1960 the secretary of our brigade party branch . . . abused his authority by appropriating for his private use some of the brigade's property, and by flirting with women. As a result he was made an object of struggle during the 1960 San Fan campaign; people were very angry with him, and members of the brigade beat him physically during the struggle. Some members of the brigade even wanted to beat him to death. He was sent away for "labor education," but after he returned to his family he mended his ways and the brigade forgot about this ugly affair of the past.

AG (poor peasant) recounts the incident of a band of street youth (*jiedao qingnian*) in a commune town who operated a pickpocket ring on public buses and rural markets; two women in the group "freely engaged in lovemaking." When they slipped up and got caught, people beat them angrily. Nevertheless "some team members and residents sympathized with them saying they took this path only because living was difficult; even the two women's prostitution was said to have extenuating circumstances" (*qing you ke yuan*).

A special situation was brigade members' tolerance of corruption by a cadre member whose leadership had brought prosperity to the brigade. According to AF (peddler), even Party Secretary Chen Hua of Shengshi brigade (Shaqi commune, Zhongsham *xian*, Kwangtung) whose extraordinary corruption and life of ease was exposed during the Socialist Education Campaign, and who committed suicide after his arrest, was a case in point. Chen's house had electric lights, an electric fan, and a telephone; he repeatedly flogged brigade members.

> But except for the flogging the members of the brigade did not have bad feelings about Chen. No small number of them said that in spite of Chen's embezzling such a large sum of money, while he was secretary the value of a workpoint in our brigade had been very high (ten points earned between 1.1 and 1.2 *yuan*), and brigade members made a pretty good living.

A reasonable hypothesis is that while the stain is permanent on one's official record, deviance can be rubbed out in the eyes of one's peers. Still, a past record of deviance depresses opportunities for democratic political participation.

SUMMARY AND CONCLUSION

Main points of the arguments are summarized in Figure 1. Participation variables are related to the object of "social control." Other variables are related to the effectiveness of "social control."

All else being equal, cadre members who are expected to hold office only temporarily are more likely to be touched by criticism from ordinary folk than members whom everyone expects will be around for a while. And anyone who is knowingly operating beyond the pale of the law (for example, selling on the black market, or planning to go to Hong Kong without permission) fears his or her activities will be revealed and punished in the next *yundong*. Short-run effects are more clearly observable than long-run effects. *Yundong* more strongly affect behavior than attitudes. Anticipation effects remain as strong as ever. And interview data from this sample of respondents suggest the following determinants of degree of democratic political participation by nonelites in mass campaigns.

Professionals participate less actively than others, and by the nature of their work are more vulnerable to criticism and struggle. Youth up to the age when they are counted as full-strength workers are involved least with campaigns, old people involved next least, and young workers just beginning their careers next least. The gradual process of achieving recognition as an "activist" raises participation. But activists' influence over their peers stems less from their ability to genuinely set an example than from their widely perceived role as political opportunists acting as conduits to higher authority. After adopting

SUMMARY OF THE ARGUMENT

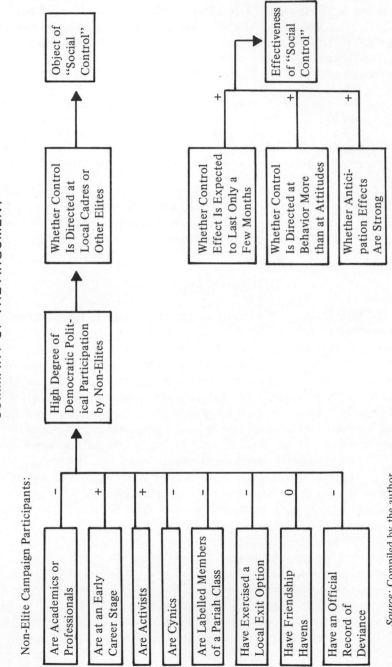

Non-Elite Campaign Participants:

- Are Academics or Professionals — (−)
- Are at an Early Career Stage — (+)
- Are Activists — (+)
- Are Cynics — (−)
- Are Labelled Members of a Pariah Class — (−)
- Have Exercised a Local Exit Option — (−)
- Have Friendship Havens — (0)
- Have an Official Record of Deviance — (−)

High Degree of Democratic Political Participation by Non-Elites

Whether Control Is Directed at Local Cadres or Other Elites

Object of "Social Control"

Effectiveness of "Social Control"

- Whether Control Effect Is Expected to Last Only a Few Months (+)
- Whether Control Is Directed at Behavior More than at Attitudes (+)
- Whether Anticipation Effects Are Strong (+)

Source: Compiled by the author.

138

a cynical view of people's private motives for public behavior, one recoils from *yundong* and begins to feel that active, altruistic participation is not worth the personal risk. Except for members of pariah classes, who are struggled against routinely, official social class category makes little difference for individual participation in mass campaigns. The "local exit option" can absolve one from participating in small movements, but exercising the option for any length of time can increase one's vulnerability to larger and more intense movements. Close personal friends affect participation very slightly if at all. However, time spent with friends does provide an important psychological haven from inexorable public demands. And, with few exceptions, a record of past deviance increases vulnerability to *yundong* action by authorities, but not to retributive action by peers.

In the decades ahead, were mass democratic *yundong* participation to lessen in Chinese politics and the anticipation effect to diminish, we could then expect to see less control of illicit private economic behavior, less control of unwanted population movement, less persecution of pariah classes, and more power for local cadre members as their authority came to derive from their organizational position alone. These specific forms of social control very probably would not outlive the disappearance of *yundong*.

NOTES

1. Frederick Engels, *Origin of the Family, Private Property and the State* (New York: International Publishers, 1942), pp. 61-62.

2. John Wilson Lewis, *Leadership in Communist China* (Ithaca: Cornell University Press, 1963), p. 118.

3. Letter from the Londons to the author, December 15, 1975. Two Kwangtung peasants interviewed in 1973 mentioned ambushing and beating a village cadre member who had initiated struggle meetings and overacted harshly during the proceedings. A sack was thrown over his head to blind him to the identity of his attackers, and he was beaten "within an inch of his life." He was laid up for over a month. When he reappeared his behavior was "relatively restrained." A young Canton resident interviewed in 1975 explained that residents' committees in his district did not apply themselves to cleaning up "speculators' organizations" in the area because if they showed too much enthusiasm, their children would be waylaid and beaten.

8

LAW AND PENOLOGY: SYSTEMS OF REFORM AND CORRECTION
Victor H. Li

It is not difficult to describe the Chinese attitudes and approaches toward reform and correction, but it is very difficult to find a satisfactory way to relate the Chinese experience to the West's. This difficulty is due in part to the understandable emotion attached to terms such as "thought reform" and "thought control." American society has fixed ideas about the institutions and techniques which should be employed to control and correct deviant behavior. Many of these ideas range from idealistic to naive to plain incorrect. For example, the very use of the terms "criminal law" and "penology" evokes images of prisons, probation officers, parole boards, and the like, focusing one's attention on the courts and the formal criminal process. This attention is misdirected for the study of American society and makes no sense at all for the study of China. It is often implied that the American penal system is actually engaged in the reform of deviants. Whatever this system might do in the way of deterring potential offenders, punishing deviants, or isolating dangerous persons from the rest of society, there is almost nothing done to help a person reform.

The entire field of comparative legal studies needs to be reformulated into broader and less Western-oriented terms. Instead of the traditional approach of "comparing" particular legal institutions and principles, one might ask: What are the desired norms of behavior for various segments of society? What persons or institutions determine these norms? By what process are these determinations

Originally published in Michel Oksenberg, ed., *China's Developmental Experience* (New York: Praeger, 1973). Copyright The Academy of Political Science, Columbia University. Reprinted by permission of the Academy of Political Science.

made, and on what rationales are they based? After the determination is made, how are the norms characterized and articulated? How much discretionary power is granted to lower levels to supplement, amend, interpret, or adapt these norms to local conditions? Finally, how are the norms communicated to the various segments of society? What means are used to influence the public to adhere to these norms? What is done when a person fails to adhere? These questions are framed without reference to a particular society, theory of law, or preexisting set of legal institutions and practices.

While all of these questions form a unified whole, this paper will deal primarily with the last three. First, these questions will be applied to the American system—in part to start with something familiar and in part to lay the foundation for comparisons with the Chinese approach. The Chinese attempt to handle the same three questions will be described, and then the possibility of transferring useful ideas from one system to the other will be considered.

THE WESTERN MODEL OF CRIMINAL LAW AND PENOLOGY

There is no question that the United States is a society based on law. Its larger law libraries boast of housing hundreds of thousands of books, each describing in excruciating detail what one can and cannot do in particular circumstances.

To have so many laws is not unlike having too few laws or even no laws at all. In either case, the layman has great difficulty learning the rules which purport to govern his conduct. That is, because of the sheer volume of material, he probably cannot find the precise law applicable to his case. Even if he does find an apparently appropriate law, he cannot be sure that there are not still other laws which are equally applicable or which alter the meaning of the law he has in hand. Obviously, even if he finds all the applicable laws, he cannot be sure that he properly understands their meaning. Finally, even if he understands their meaning, there is no assurance that he will have the opportunity or the legal standing to put his knowledge to use. It is clear that if a layman could deal adequately with the legal system, this country would not need its 400,000 lawyers (with another 100,000 in law school). And if the market is any indication of one's usefulness, the high income of the legal specialists accurately reflects the vital role they play in American society.

One possible, though impractical, solution to the problem of the layman's ignorance of the law is to undertake an active program of public education about law. This is not being done, except perhaps for areas such as traffic regulation or drug abuse. Two leading legal educators have written:

> Law schools . . . are focused almost entirely upon the training of
> professionals in the law. But, as this report seeks to stress throughout,

the law is everybody's business. Not the least of the factors contributing to the contemporary crisis in respect for and enforcement of
the law is the almost complete lack of understanding about the legal
process among the public at large, and its younger members in
particular. Nowhere in the United States is there an effective
program for legal education of the citizenry—a most dangerous condition for a democratic society that looks to its people to make its
own laws, and in large part relies upon voluntary compliance with
those laws.[1]

Instead of instituting an educational program, the United States has
adopted a much simpler and cleaner solution: it has defined the problem out of
existence by creating the legal fiction that "everyone knows the law" and that
"ignorance of the law is no excuse." If these statements were taken literally it
would prove most troublesome and unworkable. Fortunately, they are not.

To begin with, many of the substantive provisions of the criminal law are
in fact known by most people. It is not necessary to cite chapter and verse of the
criminal code to know that one should not hit another person, or throw a rock
through a window, or take money from a cash register, even if one feels like
doing so. All this is part of a person's general knowledge, whether it is derived
from childhood socialization or from watching detective programs on television.

At the same time, there are clearly many areas where general knowledge
and beliefs are not congruent with the provisions of the criminal law. These
include matters involving private and public morality (e.g., obscenity, sexual
practices, use of some drugs, and some "political" offenses), as well as matters
on which the law itself is complex or unclear (e.g., disorderly conduct, insanity,
and conspiracy). In addition, moving away from conventional criminal law and
into areas where the government's use of police power is backed by criminal
sanctions (e.g., health and sanitation regulations and the regulation of labor and
business practices), the layman's knowledge of the law becomes more and more
tenuous. This is especially true when no criminal sanction is involved but a
citizen is trying to force the state to take or desist from taking a particular
action (e.g., a change in zoning ordinances, greater or lesser welfare benefits). As
the legal fiction that everyone knows and therefore can presumably use the law
becomes more fictitious, the legal system becomes less viable and less able to
govern conduct.

A second technique is also used to soften the provisions of the criminal
law in cases where a literal application would lead to an "unjust" result. These
cases include situations in which a person is truly and understandably ignorant
of the law, the law itself is unclear, or the legislators had contemplated a different set of circumstances at the time they enacted the law, even though there
is now a technical violation of the legal prohibitions. In such cases, various
officials are granted a wide range of discretionary power concerning how to
apply the law, and even whether or not to apply it. For example, if two persons

get into a heated argument on the street, a policeman may ignore them entirely, he may tell them to break it up and go home, or he may charge them with a range of offenses, including disorderly conduct, assault and battery, disturbing the peace, and interference with an officer in the performance of his duty. At the police station, the two persons might be sent home, booked for some or all of these offenses and sent home, or booked and locked up. The public prosecutor then might choose to drop all or some of the charges, or might bargain with the offenders to plead guilty to some of them in return for dropping others and recommending a light sentence. The judge may accept or reject these recommendations, and if the offender is found guilty, may impose a relatively heavy sentence or may suspend the sentence entirely. Depending on the nature of the case, probation officers and parole boards have similar latitude. How each of these officials chooses to act depends on the character of the official and the offender, but also on a judgment by the official concerning what would be a "correct" disposition of the case, given the overall circumstances.

This liberal use of discretionary power adds a human element to an otherwise mechanical process and also provides the flexibility necessary to adapt rigid, formal rules to diverse, concrete situations. At the same time, it causes some serious problems. In many areas, including the criminal process, little is known about the extent and manner in which discretionary power is exercised, and consequently there is little control over its application. For example, how often does a policeman decide not to take formal action against an apparent offender? On what basis is this decision made? How does the prosecutor decide what cases to prosecute and what charges to bring? How does the plea-bargaining process, which disposes of some 80 percent of the cases reaching the courts, function? Is the system of discretionary justice, however desirable it may be, so pervasive and uncontrolled that the legal system in practice bears only slight relation to the formal legal system on the books?

Given this situation, however oversimplified here, how does this society, particularly through its legal system, attempt to govern conduct? Much of this work is handled through the childhood socialization processes during which a child learns what is "right" and "wrong." Beyond that, however, American society basically leaves people alone. That is, there exists an informal and continuous process of socialization wherein a person interacts with the people around him, and tries to make his behavior conform to their expectations, or, at least, tries to minimize conflict and unpleasantness with them. Aside from this generalized application of peer pressure, there is not a deliberate and structured attempt to inculcate values or to shape the conduct of adults. (For obvious reasons, religion and commercial advertising are not considered here.)

The overall effect of this system is that, however society operates in practice, in theory the state tends not to enter into or interfere with the ordinary activities of individuals. Clearly, this is an oversimplification since the state may enter into some areas but not others. It is not possible to draw clear lines between complete "interference" and total "noninterference." Nevertheless, the range of permissible behavior is, on the whole, quite wide. Minor deviations from the accepted norms are ignored, tolerated, or controlled and corrected through some informal means when the state is not a direct participant. Moreover, all of this is highly prized in the United States and is often described as a major aspect of democracy and freedom.

This freedom, however, has a price, although very likely a worthwhile price. When an adult begins to deviate from "proper" conduct, no systematic and effective effort is made to correct him. As the transgressions become more serious, still little is done—whether out of an affirmative philosophical conviction that noninterference is desirable, an institutional inability to cope with a problem of this magnitude, or a basic indifference to the well-being of others so long as their actions do not directly affect oneself.

In any case, at some point the transgressions become so serious that the state intervenes. Then the roof falls in, as the entire majesty of the law is visited upon the malfeasant. Put another way, up to a certain point a person is free to do as he wishes; he gets little encouragement or help to correct his conduct, even though his actions are undesirable and grow progressively worse. Finally, this person commits a "crime." While the exercise of discretionary power by an official provides some leeway for the case, basically the offender has fallen off the edge of a cliff where the state and society had left him too much alone and he loses much of his control over his own fate.

Note that the story basically ends here. If charges against the offender are dropped, he is returned to the top of the cliff. But having been returned to his original situation and given virtually no guidance or assistance, it usually is only a matter of time before he falls off again.

If charges are not dropped, the offender is moved through a legal process with which he is almost entirely unfamiliar and which he usually cannot afford financially. Should he be exonerated, he is returned to the top of the cliff as before, though this time possibly with a social stigma that makes him less able to reform. Should he be convicted and sent to prison, the situation becomes practically hopeless. The statistics on recidivism show that virtually no one is reformed as a result of this treatment. Indeed, some have suggested that jails and prisons are a kind of graduate school for criminals where their original values are reinforced and their professional skills are sharpened. Upon release, the offender carries a social stigma, generally has learned no socially useful skills, and usually returns to the milieu where he first developed his deviant tendencies. In a sense, this person is now beyond the pale, and never really gets returned to society.

THE CHINESE MODEL OF CRIMINAL LAW AND PENOLOGY

Like the West, China relies heavily on law, although very likely most Western as well as Chinese observers would not describe the situation in these terms. There are only a few items in the Chinese system that were proposed and passed by some legislature, that are formally designated "laws," or that resemble laws as they exist in the West. Nevertheless, using the questions posed at the beginning of this paper, there are many items which, in the sense of the term used here, could be called "laws." They are found not merely in law books, but, more importantly, in mass-communications organs such as the *People's Daily*. They are not usually labelled "law" and are not phrased in legal terminology. Yet they define in greater or lesser detail what is permissible conduct, provide means for ensuring that the desired norms of behavior will be followed, and describe the consequences of noncompliance. This is law. These laws have played a major role in bringing about the great changes, both in institutions and in attitudes, that have taken place in China since 1949.

The Western and Chinese legal systems differ, however, in that the West uses the legal fiction that everyone knows the law, while China tries to make this fiction a reality.[2] This is accomplished in part by making the normative rules of conduct readily accessible to the public, and in part by keeping the rules simple and free of technicalities so the layman can understand and apply them. Most important, the Chinese have undertaken a vigorous and thorough program of public legal education. With the exception of young children, everyone is a member of one or more "small groups" which are composed of about twenty persons who are closely affiliated through their employment, place of residence, or other ties. In addition to other activities, these groups engage in a number of hours of "study" each week; a substantial portion of the study sessions deal with matters falling under the rubric of law. Several hours a week times fifty-two weeks a year times twenty-three years, plus the hours spent in continuous, intensive study during campaigns and similar times, yield a great deal of specific knowledge about the law. Moreover, an effort is made to apply the general principles examined to the actual living and working conditions of the members of the group. This application of theory to practice not only enables the discussants to understand better the general principles, but also helps to explain ambiguities, fill in gaps, and provide an opportunity for the introduction of local initiatives and variations.

As second major difference between the Western and Chinese legal systems is that the small groups not only educate the public about law, but also play an important role in legal enforcement. They are extremely effective in bringing to light any member's deviations or incipient deviations from the accepted norms of thinking or behavior. Groups are formed of persons with close ties who must spend considerable time together. Thus, as a person's thinking begins to deviate, this is quickly observed by other members of the group during the course of study sessions or other activities. Similarly, one who steals would be unable to enjoy his newly found riches since the people around him would know or suspect how he had acquired them.

The discovery of deviations and crime is only one step in the enforcement and correction process. If a person truly loves his neighbor or truly is his brother's keeper, then he has a moral and social duty to correct his brother's shortcomings. If truly no man is an island and the actions of each person directly affect the lives of all others, then the "group," however defined, has a real and direct stake in controlling the actions of its members. This is entirely contrary to the Western approach of legally, though possibly not morally, discouraging the intrusion by one person into the lives of others, except when something very serious is involved. In place of the "officious intermeddler" rule in most Western tort law and the consequent unwillingness of bystanders to go to the aid of a person in trouble, the Chinese (and, indeed, all the socialist countries and a few others as well) impose on the citizenry a legal duty to go to the rescue of a person in distress. Similarly, comments and criticisms made about another's life-style or work-style are regarded, in the ideal case, as proper exercises of a social duty to one's fellow man, not as invasions of privacy or as meddling in the affairs of another. No legal limitations are imposed on "standing" to raise a complaint or to sue, and there are no "victimless crimes" since these acts directly harm all of society.

The process of enforcement and correction begins with the first efforts at studying new laws. During the course of study, a person learns both the specific provisions of the law and also their rationales. Presumably, doubts or questions one may have are raised and are argued out within the group. This process not only clears up most of the ambiguities, but also produces a common understanding among all members of the group as to the meaning of the rules. There will still be areas where, by design or by inability to do better, the group will be unable to figure out what conduct is desired of its members. These areas, however, are relatively small. They tend to concern changes in policy, and hence by definition tend to involve a degree of uncertainty until all the changes are completed. In these areas, the group must tread carefully, and probably ought to seek further clarification and instruction. In any case, all members of the group are in the same predicament, and hence within the group there is little problem of lack of notice or of the imposition of an unknown standard.

At this point, a person understands the meaning of the rules and accepts the underlying rationale. He then slowly internalizes the norms of behavior prescribed by these rules. If doubt or misunderstanding arises, additional study is carried out which may clear up these questions or which may produce a new common understanding.

There is no enforcement problem for those who have internalized the norms. Others who have not done so might still adhere to these norms in order to avoid the unpleasant consequences which result from their violation. Such persons would not present much of an enforcement problem, although the group must be watchful for violations and must be sure that the enforcement and deterrent system is functioning properly.

Finally, there are persons who, for a variety of reasons, violate the desired norms. The handling of these persons shows another major difference between the Western and Chinese approaches to correction and reform.

Most people do not commit serious crimes without warning. Such actions are a part and perhaps the culmination of an entire pattern of dissatisfaction, unhappiness, or confusion. This pattern is manifested in many ways and grows gradually, with minor problems becoming increasingly serious. The Chinese, through the small groups, treat these symptoms of unhappiness and possible deviation as soon as they appear. The effort is to solve problems before they get entirely out of control, somewhat like treating a physical disease.

As a person begins to express improper thoughts or deviant tendencies, others will try to "help" him. This takes the form of criticizing the incorrect actions and explaining what would be correct. It also involves discovering and curing the root causes of the problem. For example, a person might be sloppy in his work and consequently damage production. He is criticized for his carelessness, but also he is given additional technical training to improve his skills. Moreover, other aspects of his life are examined to find the root causes of his difficulties. Perhaps an unhappy marriage is adversely affecting his work; if so, the factory group must find means of "helping" his family life.

If the offender does not respond, the group increases pressure. Criticisms grow harsher and longer. More and more persons join in as the scope of the criticisms increases. At some point, the employer and the neighborhood apparatus formally take part. Finally, the threat of criminal sanction is made; the public security or some other state enforcement agency becomes involved; and then the criminal process is invoked.[3]

This gradual process differs considerably from falling off the edge of the cliff. The principal effort is to stop the decline as early and as quickly as possible. Since problems attacked early are much more easily resolved, this effort is successful in many cases. At the same time, an attempt is made to return the offender to the good graces of society. This is possible, partly because problems are attacked before the offender has strayed too far or caused too much damage. In addition, a rationale for the cause of the deviance is given which allows everyone to accept the idea of nearly complete reintegration. Wrong thinking and misinterpretation of facts are due to a combination of subjective factors within the person (e.g., capitalist tendencies) and external factors that exist in society (e.g., poverty and unequal distribution). One ramification of this approach is that no offender should be blamed for all his actions, since some portion of the offense might be traceable to external factors. If care is taken in one's phrasing, it is possible to condemn an act without condemning the inner man. Consequently, in dealing with offenders, even serious ones, there is no need to begin with a bias against their basic characters or to regard the offenders as basically incapable of being reformed. This is an oversimplification, of course, since there are biases against the basic character of persons having bad class backgrounds.

Nevertheless, it still means that the Chinese accept much more readily the possibility of reform and of perfectibility.

A second ramification is that some external factors must be corrected. Society in general and the offender's peer group in particular must take active steps to rehabilitate him. Merely returning the offender to his original circumstances after meting out criticism or punishment would be quite improper. The group must alter the undesirable external conditions, and must continually "help" and supervise the offender so that he does not begin to deviate again.

Most important of all, the Chinese appear to accept as a given that, when confronted with a clear distinction between good and evil, most people will choose the good. Hence, there is no great surprise at and no great resistance to the idea that most people are completely reformable. An offender can analyze why and where he went astray, state that he now recognizes his past errors, and promise to sin no more. While he will continue to be supervised, the group can accept with relative ease what he says and allow him to rejoin it as a full-fledged member.

This discussion of the Chinese system of correction and reform does not include a description of the handling of serious criminal offenders. That subject has been dealt with in considerable detail elsewhere.[4] Suffice it to be said that the handling of serious criminals differs in degree but not in kind from the handling of minor offenders. Serious criminal offenders constitute only the barest tip of the correction and reform iceberg. The great bulk of the work in this area concerns minor offenders of the type described above. It may well be true, if one does not take things *too* literally, that there is basically no crime in China. Attacking problems at an early stage and across a wide range works. Moreover, it would require quite an unusual person who could resist the social pressures which are systematically applied to him as his deviations increase. This is especially true since discovery of deviations is nearly certain and escape from "help" and supervision is nearly impossible.

THOUGHT REFORM AND THE AMERICAN PENAL SYSTEM

"Thought reform" has a bad connotation and usually reminds people of brainwashing and 1984. It should be noted, however, that American society is thoroughly familiar with thought reform both in concept and in method. The childhood socialization process is an obvious example. First-year law school (and perhaps many other educational situations) and advertisements are two other equally striking though less obvious analogies.

The Chinese use the term "thought reform" to describe an approach to dealing with behavior. It is not limited to deviant behavior. Instead, the basic question is how do you get people to behave in a particular way when either they disagree with you or they have been ignorant of your wishes. All the problems of communication, internalization, and supervision which were previously discussed apply here.

Given the shambles of the American penal system and the relatively healthy state of the Chinese system (at least in its ideal form), the question arises whether there are concepts and methods developed in China that can be applied in the United States. On the whole, the answer is no. Thought reform will work only in China.

The problems that arise are both practical and philosophical. On the practical side, there does not appear to be a willingness to devote sufficient human and material resources to improving the United States penal system. That being the case, the Chinese approach, which requires a massive input of resources, cannot be used. Is there the will to spend thousands of hours in study sessions so that "small groups" can help formulate local norms and communicate these norms to all members? Is there the will to spend more thousands of hours to implement the system, to criticize deviant conduct, and to supervise offenders? And is there the will to invest the tremendous amount of money that is needed to "correct the external conditions" which were part of the causes for deviations in the first place and which thereafter contribute to recidivism? Of course, the practical and the philosophical considerations are not separable. Resources are not expended in this way in part because philosophical and political priorities are different in the United States.

There also seems to be doubt whether criminals are reformable, and hence there is an unwillingness to spend large resources in this area. Perhaps this attitude is due to the fact that Americans think of "correction and reform" not as it applies to early and minor offenders, but only in relation to serious offenders who might well be unsalvageable. Even the Chinese do not claim that everyone can be reformed. This attitude may also be traceable to certain strands of the Judeo-Christian tradition which contain the notion of "original sin" and have little faith in the intrinsic goodness and ability of man. In any case, it is considered dangerous when there are no external standards or law to restrain and channel man's "natural" urges. Thus, when a person is placed under the control of his small group, it may be an invitation to arbitrariness and localized tyranny. The Chinese view the same situation as a fine application of the concept of the mass line. The difference lies in whether one believes that an "unbridled" small group will tend to act properly or improperly most of the time.

Finally, on both practical and philosophical grounds, it is probably felt that the Chinese system entails the loss of too much privacy and freedom. The line between loving one's neighbor and busybodying is quite thin at times. And even if the collective life is preferred over individualism, it would still require considerable time to learn the techniques of properly loving one's neighbors.

Throughout this paper, the Chinese system has been discussed in its ideal state with little mention of how it works in practice. There are not enough data for a thorough exploration of this question, although the author's prejudices are that the ideal and the practical do not differ greatly in this area. Some questions can be raised, however, which suggest that thought reform may not be working well even in China, so why import it here.

The opportunity for reintegration into society is a vital aspect of the system of reform. Without this, all incentives to reform are negative in character. In the years immediately following 1949, the Chinese could tell deviants that they were products of the old society and that this accounted for much of their evil behavior. They were then told that this was a new society and, if they reformed, they could have a full share in building the new China.

Twenty-three years later, it becomes increasingly difficult to say that errors are due to external conditions rather than to subjective factors. Hence the bulk of the blame is due to some flaw in the character of the offender. At the same time, as the revolution stabilizes, it becomes harder to correct the external conditions. Consequently, an offender is quite likely to be returned after criticism or punishment to much the same conditions that contributed to producing his earlier deviant tendencies. Moreover, as revolutionary ardor cools and the situation becomes more settled, less effort may be devoted to the thought-reform process. The result could be that the systems of correction and reform will become more perfunctory and therefore more coercive and less effective.

NOTES

1. Thomas Ehrlich and Bayless Manning, *Programs in Law at the University of Hawaii: A Report to the President of the University* (Honolulu, December 1970), pp. 12-13.

2. For a more thorough discussion of the development and functioning of the Chinese legal system, see Victor H. Li, "The Role of Law in Communist China," *China Quarterly*, no. 44 (October-December 1970): 66-111; see also Stanley B. Lubman, "Form and Function in the Chinese Criminal Process," *Columbia Law Review* 69 (April 1969): 535-75.

3. On the formal criminal process, see Jerome A. Cohen, *The Criminal Process in the People's Republic of China, 1949-1963: An Introduction* (Cambridge: Harvard University Press, 1968). For a discussion of group study, see A. Doak Barnett, *Communist China: The Early Years, 1949-55* (New York: Praeger, 1964), pp. 89-103.

4. Allyn and Adele Rickett, *Prisoners of Liberation* (New York: Cameron Associates, 1957); Andre Bonnichorne, *Law in Communist China* (The Hague: International Commission of Jurists, 1956); and Harriet Mills, "Thought Reform: Ideological Remoulding in China," *Atlantic Monthly*, December 1959.

9

DEVIANCE, MODERNIZATION, RATIONS, AND HOUSEHOLD REGISTERS IN URBAN CHINA
Lynn T. White, III

Let us confess it. There is an intellectual attraction to deviance. Nonconformist motives are as fascinating as normal ones. Deviant citizens can show us just as much about the bases of social integration as can their more upright colleagues. Indeed, some students begin with great expectations that the common ethics of action in any society can be thrown into clearest relief by studies of groups that rebel, by behavior at the margin. These students think to find what social rules are by seeing what they are not, by seeing how they are violated. From research on norms so basic they provoke a reaction when crossed, a fuller understanding of social integration might be gained. In fact, we can draw part of the design of this rug by looking only at the fringe on its edges.

DEVIANCE AS MAINLY OFFICIAL:
SOCIAL CONTROL AS MAINLY MOBILIZATION

The subject of deviance has concerned some major social thinkers. Emile Durkheim's classic study, *Suicide*, treats only a single kind of deviant behavior. Its determinants were found in the moral constitution of a society as a whole, which he characterized as egoistic, altruistic, or anomic. A few more recent writers, such as Robert Merton in *Social Theory and Social Structure*, explain many other kinds of deviant behavior by characterizing the ways that social groups and society as a whole relate norms to goals. Talcott Parsons, in *The Social System*, is even more general. He explains deviance by categories so comprehensive they could be used to talk about any type of action at all. His famous "pattern variables" can be attributed to individuals' habits of deviant or other behavior, as much as to the norms of groups or whole societies. Parsons (who often deviates far indeed from common ideas in his search for analytic science) finds it helpful to think of deviant behavior in terms of a matrix with at least four separate dimensions and twenty-four cells, and to typify it by its activity or passivity, its alienation from or conformity with norms, its social or normative object, and its societal, group, or individual level. In addition to these "directions" which deviance can take, and in addition to the patterned conventions with which deviance is counteracted, Parsons also insists we should look for the "strains" in the social system that give rise to such behavior in the first place— and finally for the established structures that provide fields of opportunity for deviant action.[1] Surely this is not a simplistic view of the matter, whatever else may be said of it. It is valuable here mainly because it suggests that similar concepts can be used to study deviance and other behavior. The fullest categories with which to think about deviance and normal action in a community have become nearly indistinguishable.[2]

Maybe something was lost as attention spread to more types of deviance and more levels that define it. Durkheim's original interest was to find in specifically deviant behavior a test to determine the kind of general bond that unites members of a society. When discussions of subsocial groups do not show the relation between those groups and society as a whole, this interest is sidetracked. Quite recently, some scholars have in effect returned to Durkheim's linkage. They show how the norms and structures of deviant groups are created by society itself in a "labelling" process.

Not only have sociologists generally neglected to apply any sort of deviance theory to the Chinese case; they have not even inquired whether data from that country—which is too important to be ignored in any serious comparative effort—might suggest refinements or even changes in these theories, which were developed to describe the West.

A quick consideration of the second omission gives rise to some suggestions. First, China is changing quickly. Modernization is not just a matter of oil derricks, steel mills, higher literacy, and tractors. Ideas modernize too. China's social norms have gone through obvious short-term fluctuations in recent years. Since these norms are the criteria from which any kind of deviance must be measured, the analyst's job in China is not the same as it was in lands that have had more time to change. Are we sure that in an urgently pressed, revolutionary country, whose spokesmen often call for new types of action, we will find many norms stable enough to provide a standard from which deviance can be measured? A founder of the Chinese Communist Party, Chen Duxiu, expressed the problem bluntly:

> We really don't know which, if any, of our traditional institutions can be adapted for survival in the modern world. I would rather see the destruction of our "national essence" than the final extinction of our race because it is unable to adapt. The Babylonians are no more; what good does their civilization do them today?[3]

To the extent norms change in a discontinuous and quick way, there are implications for concepts of deviance and social control that were developed to describe societies that could move more slowly.[4]

All this will affect the ways we do research. The nature of most of our data from China forces us to return willy-nilly to Durkheim's notion that any kind of deviance, properly understood, is a trait of society as a whole, and so sheds light on normal behavior too. Durkheim's link is made very actively by the government in China, even if we analysts may have good reasons to resist it in that form. The trouble is that we can seldom find how a "typical" individual or small group in present-day China would define deviance without reference to the political system there. If we want to know what definitions the government uses, we can find them in any Chinese newspaper. In China, the state is the "moral entrepreneur."[5] The government's approach to the relation between deviance and integration is not impartial science, but is very active in policy.

By means of a single, unified set of institutions—including the household and ration systems on which this paper concentrates—the Chinese government is simultaneously trying to control deviance and strengthen society by mobilizing individuals' positive energies. In China the enforcers of social guidance become nearly identical with the offices and customs that encourage people to take any public action. Research on these institutions, therefore, can tell us how normal people tick, not just how deviants do.

Modernization has strengthened this pattern in China, but it is not without a history there too. Donald Munro, in Chapter 2 of this book, points out that the Chinese traditionally define "thought" (*sixiang*) as public. The main form of social control and guidance in that country, and in many others, has long been before-the-fact socialization, not after-the-fact arrest.[6] In Communist China, the role of prior education for social control is emphasized more explicitly and consciously than in the West. More kinds of activities, both legitimate and otherwise, are considered to be matters of government concern. Distinctions between political and other sorts of deviance are often irrelevant to contemporary Chinese perceptions. "Politics takes command" of both deviance and mobilization—and although I, by my own frankly liberal lights, see that as a social problem, there is no need to import Western normative distinctions into the analysis. The notions of the government are the most obvious standards in Chinese society now. They are also the main relevant Chinese data we possess. Most of the chapters in this book have naturally used them. Since we are going to do this anyway, we should say so.

It must be clearly appreciated that there are drawbacks to employing definitions of the sort proposed above. They are practical as tools of research; indeed, the old nets catch few fish in China. But their use, even if it is necessary, should be only tactical and heuristic. Deviant and normal action are zero-sum phenomena. But deviance and official control are not. We must remain conscious of the extent to which the available data from China imply that they are. We can use such data; but we should point out the implications of the way they were selected for us. When this is done heuristically, much can be learned. In the long run we must relate the Chinese situation to other places comparatively. A means to do this can already be suggested. The usual functionalist concepts of deviance presume some general stability, of which relatively fixed norms are an important aspect. When a system changes, norms at different levels of society may become less coherent in practice. If norms become very diverse, the "political system" often campaigns to strengthen nerves of communication for norms, to re-create a community and language in which people give reasons for their very new types of public behavior. This function of encouraging individuals, groups, and the nation to act in some common cause is different from the more standard, bureaucratic goal of specifying the goals of action exactly. The former function has not been much studied in the West, because it has really been less salient there in recent times than in China. It is more important in countries undergoing forced modernization. To hold a quickly changing system together while allowing it to change, the collective agency of the state does two separate things. First, it urges each level of society to work with full local energy, so that vaguely prescribed norms have some active implementation (they result in action only when they are communicated). Second, the state tries to prescribe those norms as definitely as it can (they result in concerted action only when they are specified).[7] Higher levels want to create more social resources at lower levels, but they also want to determine how those resources will be used. The communication and specification of norms are different tasks, and they often conflict with each other in practice.

In countries like the United States, the bureaucratic, norm-specifying job is the more salient one. But in developing China, the two aims have been phased over time. Very famous political campaigns are the result. Movements like the early Great Leap or the early Cultural Revolution encourage citizens to change their vague communal self-identifications and to commit themselves to common but nonspecific norms. Such campaigns could begin to accomplish their communitarian goals because rules were not spelled out precisely. These were periods of great normative disorganization; and although they may have been useful for some social purposes, they were dangerous for others and certainly could not be permanent. After the campaign phase of such cycles, bureaucratic coordination again becomes the main concern. These phases make the job of studying deviance and control difficult in China, since the meanings of the concepts are constantly changing. Exploration of these topics in China may, however, serve in the long run to expand their usefulness by showing how they apply under conditions of quick normative change.

THE USES OF HOUSEHOLD REGISTERS

Enough of theory. We will now outline the structure of means by which ordinary Chinese city dwellers obtain social goods like schooling, employment, shelter, and food. The framework of opportunities for Chinese city folk is connected in many ways with the urban rationing and household registration systems. They are, in fact, the main sources of urban mobilization and deviance control there. It will be useful to begin with a description of the current registers and of their functions. Then the historical evolution and varieties of household counting will be discussed. Finally, the specific conditions under which the system is effective or ineffective for changing citizens' communal self-identifications can be induced from these empirical data.

Household registration books (*huji bu*) are legally required for all residents in Chinese cities. The exact format of a household book may vary from one city to another, because registration is administered at the municipal rather than the national level. Such a book will ordinarily contain one page for each member of a house. This page is a form, including entries for the person's name, any alias, the birth date, occupation, place of work, family background (*jiating chushen*), individual status (*geren chengfen*), level of education (*wenhua chengdu*), marital status, religion if any, and ancestral place of origin (*jiguan*). The head of the house is reponsible for keeping this whole book up to date, and for reporting births, deaths, or other changes to the local public security station, so that the police's copy of the book can be amended too.[8]

Anyone who sojourns in an urban area where he is not registered, even for a single night, is supposed to be reported to the security officers of the local street or residents' committee by the head of the household in which he stays. But in fact, this rule is ordinarily honored in the breach, except when campaigns are being conducted to enforce it.[9]

This registration system is far more than a continuous census. Its functions extend far beyond ordinary public security and the control of clearly criminal deviance—although it is of use for these regular police tasks. Its more important functions apply to all citizens of a city, not just criminals and political discontents. Valid household registration is necessary for any urban resident who wishes to obtain a regular job, school admission at any level, housing, or rationed food and clothing. For example, employment in a Chinese city can be of many different types. Especially in the late 1950s and early 1960s, urban newspapers referred to firms called "spontaneous houses" (*zifa hu*) or "underground factories" (*dixia gongchang*). These are either illegal or are legitimized only by low-level residents' groups, and they hire workers without requiring evidence of household registration.[10] But if a person hopes to obtain any really respectable urban job, with good pay and union membership, he must show current residence registration before he can be hired. If a youth hopes to attend any regular school from a kindergarten to a university, the same document must be shown before he can matriculate.

If a person wishes to rent urban housing, the local real estate management bureau, which in most cities owns or jointly owns almost all residential space not connected with jobs in state enterprises, must be shown residence approval papers stamped by the police before rental arrangements can be concluded.

Staple food and basic clothing rations are also tied to the census system. Ration tickets for grain and cloth are issued only against presentation of household registers. And if jobs, education, shelter, clothes, and food are not sufficient incentives for the people living in cities to register, a host of minor services also depend on registration. For example, if a couple wishes to become married, the valid household book of each partner must be presented before a marriage license can be issued. The household system is the basic identification of each urban Chinese person from the time he obtains his birth certificate until the day of his death.

Of course urban residence can be legally changed in China. The procedures for this are not simple. If a family wishes to move from one place to another, it can report its desire to the local police station. Cadres will investigate any debts the household may have contracted, and they will ask all of the family's employers whether the move should be allowed or not. If these approvals are forthcoming, the local police station requests a "moving certificate" (*qianyi zheng*) from its superior, district-level police headquarters. The household must possess this document before any physical facilities for moving are made available—and also before residence registration in the new place can be confirmed.

Sometimes a single member of a household will go to a new place to join the army, attend school, transfer to a state farm for national construction, go to a May 7 cadre school, or the like. In this case, the individual may obtain a "temporary household" (*linshi hukou*) in the new location. Ordinarily, the public security unit of his new employing agency will contact his old police district to have his name removed or temporarily removed from the book of his family. This office will also arrange registration in the new police district. Military units, and boarding institutions such as universities and many companies, maintain "collective household registration" (*jiti huji*) to which new names can be added easily.

HISTORY AND VARIETIES OF RESIDENCE REGISTRATION

Household registration is not new in China. Before describing in more detail the main function of this system—food rationing—it is necessary to give some historical background to the topic, approximately from the Zhou to the Cultural Revolution. Such a description will have to be a bit sketchy for the first two millennia or so. But the reader is urged to appreciate clearly that residence registration long predates the communists in China.

Beginning from ancient times, the functions of most Chinese cities were so thoroughly intertwined with rural life that separate urban population registers would have been pointless. Cities were commonly divided into specialized districts for religious, economic, and administrative purposes.[11] After some groups of shrines, shops, and offices were surrounded by walls during the Zhou and Han periods, and as these agglomerations developed over time, large cities like Changan and Loyang developed, no doubt equalling Rome in size. The revival of the empire after the assimilation of many kinds of Tatar invaders created even more resplendent and cosmopolitan cities, containing more tax bases and security risks; and the first full efforts at bureaucratic registration developed in early medieval days. The Tang-Song period saw the development of collective responsibility systems for public security, which became the "*bao jia*" system of later times.[12]

Song household documents were registers of wealth for assessing taxes and corvee equivalents.[13] The government listed households rather than individuals as its subjects. Each house was given a grade according to its land and other riches. Rural officials were particularly eager that city dwellers should be easy to locate, so that imposts could be levied on them effectively and country people would not have to bear all the tax burdens. But urbanites moved about more frequently than peasants, and registraion was difficult to enforce.

The first Ming emperor ordered a compilation of "yellow registers" (*huangce*) throughout China to make the labor service and tax systems more equitable. This was the most thorough effort of the sort for many years.[14] The late Ming and Qing governments maintained these records only sporadically, in most parts of the country. Qing magistrates were supposed each year to give a door placard to each household, indicating the name, age, and occupation of the family head, plus the names of other residents in that house.[15] Copies of this information were to be kept by the heads of the hundred-household organizations called *jia*, and also in the local magistrate's office; but again, such regulations were commonly neglected.

The city of Shanghai, which will be our main example here, has a mixed registration history because its most prosperous districts were built under the influence of foreigners. For a century after 1845, foreign and Chinese city governments coexisted in Shanghai. The mix of several legal jurisdictions in this somewhat atypical, but largest, Chinese city made residence control ineffective. The first systematic registration covering all parts of the city was carried out under Japanese occupation. The collaborating Chinese city government issued "citizens' cards" (*liangmin zheng*) to provide a means for its soldiers to check on people's movements. After the war, the Nationalist authorities in Shanghai issued "identity cards" (*shenfen zheng*), but the communists before 1949 excoriated this police system so vehemently that they could hardly retain it in the same form after Liberation.[16]

For security, employment, and rationing reasons, the communists nevertheless issued "residents' cards" (*jumin zheng*). These were not given to each person, as the Nationalist cards had been, but were assigned to each head of household (variously called *huzhang, huju,* or *jiazhang*). In Shanghai during the communist period, there has not been any personal identity card. No document has been required systematically of all individuals. But in Canton, an "urban resident's certificate" (*chengshih jumin zheng*) has sometimes been required. In areas along the coast, a "frontier defense district resident's certificate" (*bian fung qu jumin zheng*) is needed. Travel between some border districts is legal solely for holders of "border defense district passes.. (*bianfang qu tongxing zheng*), which are valid only for specified areas. Boat households are issued proof of their status; and when they are registered with the militia coast guard for passage to and from Hong Kong or Macao, they are given special cards to that effect.[17]

It is impossible to separate the early communist household cards from preparations for the ration system, but the certificates issued before 1954 had two other uses that were ostensibly their main purposes: they helped identify spies and wanted persons, and they served as proof of legal residence for unemployment registration. In the period immediately after 1949, restrictions of this sort were often carefully enforced. In order for anyone to buy a railroad ticket in Shanghai, the purchaser had to show identification. If he could not prove his residence in the city on the basis of old or new documents, he could be sold only a one-way ticket to elsewhere.[18]

By early May 1951, a more thorough migration control system had already been evolved for Shanghai. New arrivals to the city were divided into three groups: those who had legally "moved in" (*qianru*), those "from elsewhere" (*waiqiao*), and those "traveling" (*luxing*). Such regulations were apparently intended to prevent landlords and rich peasants from avoiding the land reform struggle movement by coming into cities and losing themselves so that the authorities could not find them. The legally "moved in" people and the temporary "travelers" were not the problem in this regard. The regulations were directed toward people whose intentions in the city, if legal, would categorize them as "from elsewhere." New arrivals were required to report within three days if their legal residence was in China, and within five days if they came from abroad.[19] At first, household books differed considerably in format from one place to another in China. But by July 1951, because of land reform, the national Ministry of Public Security issued regulations for some standardization of procedures in all cities—although the uniform system was not fully applied in Shanghai until June 1955, well after rationing had begun.[20]

FOOD RATIONING: VARIATIONS OVER TIME IN THE EFFECTIVENESS OF CONTROL

We will now concentrate on the relation between household registration and food rationing, for the sake of focus in tracing the further history of this whole system—and more important, for the purpose of discovering when an important type of social control works and when it does not. Analogies to other functions of the household system will be evident as we progress.

Each urban police station since the early 1950s had a "household registration section" or "household registration group" (*huji ke* or *huji zu*). This agency had theoretical charge of all residence and ration matters in its ward. In many places it issued monthly tickets (or for some commodities, less frequent tickets) in the names of the commercial companies that sold supplies. But in practice, the wards were quite large and inefficiencies developed. People complained that they had to wait too long at police stations when they came for nonurgent matters.[21] Ration tickets were therefore increasingly issued by commodity companies directly, on the basis of the public security documents shown to them.

The amount of paperwork involved in these systems was staggering. Tickets for some foods in periods of shortage had to be handed out two or three times each month, to each household, as supplies came to the city and their amounts were known. When the commodity companies took over ticket distribution, they also took over the management of very long lines. To rationalize this system and save congestion at coupon offices, work units such as factories began acting as agents of the heads of households whom they employed. For these people, as well as for workers living in company dormitories, the guard sections (*baowei ke*) of the production units were actually in charge of handing out tickets, either directly to the ultimate consumers, or to buyers of food in canteens where they ate.

Commodity companies still distributed the real goods. These state enterprises were supposed to follow plans, by allocating the full ticketed amounts of their products to the ration system and by allowing no leaks even at the lowest retail levels. But in cities full of clever bourgeois accountants, such rules could not always be enforced. The whole complex of laws and regulations surrounding household registration and rations was not watertight. It was nevertheless quite effective as a residence control in times of partial shortage, when the supply of available commodities was restricted.

Food management stations (*liangshi guanli suo*) are often the procuring agents for retail grain stores, but they are also the only wholesale sources of supply for many other local stores selling nongrain foods. The stations ordinarily issue all food ration tickets for a specific area. In a fully developed system, many kinds of food coupons would be included in a single "food book" (*liangshi bu*) supplied by the station.

The possible kinds of ration tickets are legion; but in prosperous times, supplies or prices are high enough to make many of them unnecessary. The most important coupons are generically called "grain tickets" (*liangpiao*). These monthly chits usually indicate that they are valid for a certain amount of a specific grain, usually rice or wheat. Conversion into other starches is possible according to fixed rates at the official stores. Other monthly rations are available in exchange for meat tickets (*roupiao*), which are also specialized for pork, fish, beef, lamb, and sometimes other meats; these are also usually convertible in the same way, at rates determined by supply. Tickets have sometimes been necessary to buy sugar (*tangpiao*) and edible cooking oil (*shiyou piao*). Cakes and many kinds of specialties have been rationed by "nonstaples tickets" (*fushipin piao*). The coupons issued by local food stations change from time to time, and they represent one of the most common interactions that people in Chinese cities have with their government.

Local companies under the Ministry of Textiles usually make only annual distributions of cloth tickets (*bupiao*). Fuels are rationed by coupons such as kerosene tickets (*shuiyou piao*). Tobacco and other luxuries have sometimes been sold only against chits like cigarette-purchasing tickets (*xiangyan goumai piao*). A wide range of items like bicycles, radios, and other light manufactures were distributed, in times of shortage only, by means of industrial goods tickets (*gongyepin piao*).

From the end of 1957 to July 1966, some people could obtain Overseas Chinese purchasing tickets (*Huaqiao goumai piao*). These coupons were available whenever relatives abroad remitted money into China. In some cities such as Shanghai, Amoy, Swatow, and Canton, where Overseas Chinese dependents are concentrated, this fact reduced residence control somewhat, because it increased the general level of local consumption. Hard currency transfers to leftist banks outside China could be remitted to a domestic branch of the People's Bank. A recipient would collect Chinese money at the bank according to fixed exchange rates, and at the same time obtain certificates containing ration tickets in proportion to the amount of money changed. These certificates could be used only at special Overseas Chinese stores (*Huaqiao shangtian*) in the area where they were issued. The range of goods available in such stores, which only Overseas Chinese could enter as customers, was better and wider than the selection in ordinary shops. Because Overseas Chinese sometimes could not use all the commodities they could buy in this way, their excess goods appeared on black markets.* The exact impact of this on Shanghai's ration control system is difficult to measure.

Not until long after Liberation was the ration system so full-blown as the account above may suggest. Household registrations, the heart of this system,

---

*I held four interviews in Hong Kong emphasizing the ration system in November and December 1969, January 1970, and February 1972. The text above tries to suggest the considerable variation in the systems used at different times and places, while emphasizing the general effect on residence control during periods of economic shortage. The interviewees together had residential experience in Shanghai, Canton, Swatow, Amoy, and Peking. Two of the respondents had Overseas status, and two did not.

have not been easy to collect for any of the governments that have made the attempt. The communists' special forte has been to mobilize people, rather than to count them. It was not until 1953 that the new government first tried to take a thorough census. In the spring of that year, Shanghai census cadres began to study previous registration records to prepare for their survey.[22] Over a period of several months, more than 3,900 registration stations were set up in the city under district-level supervision; on November 23, 1953, the actual enumeration began. Registration forms were distributed in both functional and residential groups. Spot checks were made to encourage the completeness of this census. But because the enrollment was associated with policies from which individuals derived no immediate benefit, such as upcoming elections and police controls, and because its implications for rationing were not yet obvious enough to encourage compliance, some residents not connected with any major work place may well have been missed.[23] Shanghai residents away at the time of the census for less than six months were registered as permanent in Shanghai. Those absent for more than six months were supposed to register elsewhere, although notations could be made of their absence in the Shanghai household they would join if they returned.[24] Although the 1953 urban census was no doubt incomplete in details, it was by far the most impressive effort of its sort that had been made there up to that time. It laid the basis for a much more thorough check on urban population than most countries have.

Household registration, census work, election work, and rationing were largely the same process. Not only were rations the most important economic element in this set of policies; they also affected ordinary citizens' daily lives most directly. Before rationing began, agricultural taxes and free market supply restrictions had been the main methods by which the government could restrain urban use of staples. "Unified purchase and distribution" (*tonggou tongxiao*) of grains was first introduced in some areas during September 1953. Its stated purposes were to cut consumption, stabilize prices, prevent black markets, and support industrialization. As Chen Yun, the vice-chairman of the Central Committee and vice-premier, later explained to a National People's Congress, this rationed and centralized system of wholesale supply was "only a temporary measure," and it would be cancelled as soon as production in each region could meet demand. But Chen made a momentous understatement in reporting that this cancellation would "not come very soon."[25]

By March 1, 1954, the grain market at least in Shanghai was completely under state control, and capitalism was officially restricted to nonstaples.[26] The new State Food Company authorized 1,498 rice shops in Shanghai to act as its sales agents. On the twenty-fifth day of every month, each of these shops submitted a distribution plan. After bureaucratic approval, grain was issued to fill it. The company promised to pay a handling fee "approximately equal" to the profits that these should could have made if they had set their own retail prices. For the first few months, while the system was being prepared and used experimentally, the total state grain allotments to Shanghai increased markedly.[27] Uniform prices for various grains were instituted all over the city, and the government advertised that the new prices would be slightly less than they had averaged in fully private rice stores before the change. Rations for grain, cooking oil, meats, and cloth were instituted in this manner almost simultaneously.

The mechanism of rationing was thus allowed to consolidate itself for more than a year before major austerity drives began on the basis of the system. By March 1955, however, the national grain shortage and a quickening of the socialization campaign caused the ration system to be oriented for the first time toward savings.[28] The immediate reason for the necessity of this 1955 campaign was simple: there had been severe flooding the previous year in the East China region, especially in northern Kiangsu, and rice supply was short.[29] The Shanghai party committee called a meeting of key cadres from many fields on March 24, to hear comrades in the municipal food bureau (*liangshi qu*) give reports on the need for austerity training in factories, schools, hospitals, and offices.[30] Every organization had to call its workers into conference, where they were told to eat less. More than 10,000 collective units in Shanghai drew up "consumption plans" and submitted them to the Food Company.[31]

In this time of shortage, when rationing first meant saving, there were still many ways in a large city to evade the regulations. In late June, the Shanghai Public Security Bureau arrested a gang of fifty-three illegal entrepreneurs who had organized a supposedly "Taoist" secret society to transport grain from counties in Kiangsu. The leader of the group lived at various residences in Dongai, Dafeng, and Xinghua counties in Kiangsu north of the Yangtze. The grain salesmen of this combine included a good many boat people, who were apparently also engaged at the same time in legal transport. Other retail agents operated under cover, in enterprises like embroidery stores or tailor shops; still others were ordinary hawkers "peddling carrots."[32] A Shanghai functionary of this organization was caught with many grain order forms, and no less than fifty-six different kinds of counterfeit chops. These were both public and private seals, with which he could force documents from fourteen separate government bureaus. (The number of chops per office therefore averaged four.) By using such seals, this entrepreneur had manufactured more than one hundred fake household certificates to obtain extra rations. He was also equipped to turn out orders and bills for large interprovincial grain shipments.

The rice shortage was so severe that the government instituted "family grain consumption plans" (*jiating yongliang jihua*).[33] Actual reductions in family grain use seem to have been distributed almost on a quota system among many groups in Shanghai. Newspapers did not say directly that each group received a quota, but they did announce that, "Now when good discussions are held in basic level organizations, a "certain" (*yiding di*) result has been achieved."[34] Shanghai's boat people have such mobility that many kinds of official policy are difficult to enforce among them. But because of their special function of transporting food, the government clearly wished to emphasize this particular movement among them. People living in boats were especially propagandized to make "refined calculations" of the food they would need.[35] In June, the city's grain use was down another 24 million catties.[36]

By August 1955, after the first harvest was being delivered from double- and triple-crop fields in East China, the worst of the crisis was over. The campaign abated somewhat, but the institutional structure for encouraging low rations was not abandoned. As the structure of the system became regularized under a regimen of adequate but fairly frugal consumption, the government set forth a "provisional method to supply the food quotas in cities and towns" (*shizhen liangshi dingliang gongying zhanxing banfa*).[37] Under this nationwide plan for cities' consumption, individuals' grain quotas were calculated according to differences in physical energy required to perform various jobs. Job information was available for all persons covered in the household books, so these data could easily be taken into account when ration cards were issued.[38] Intensive surveys during the autumn of 1955 were made to determine how work categories should be used to compute fair rations—but the surveyors almost always found that the earlier quotas had been irrationally high.

The fall of 1955 saw the introduction of Shanghai's first "purchase cards" (*goumai zheng*) for nonstaples. Beginning September 1, cards were necessary to obtain some dishes at restaurants and cooked-food stands.[39] Even New Year's cakes and long noodles were now to be covered by ration regulations.

In the first few months of 1957, the grain shortage was alleviated by careful distribution and better production. There nevertheless came to be a general lack of "supplementary foods" (*fushipin*) and "daily use products" (*riyongpin*). The reasons for this are not entirely clear. For some nonperishable commodities, the shortages may have been caused by general inventory depletions in the period 1954-56, when many industries were under financial and supply pressure to make the transition to socialism. The official explanation no doubt also has some merit: that 1956 wage reforms had increased total purchasing power. For either or both of these reasons, 1957 saw the only kind of inflation that can occur with fixed prices on goods that are not rationed. The supply of them was exhausted.[40]

Early 1957 also saw another intensification of the food austerity cam-campaign. The local trade unions' paper proudly announced that Shanghai by February had some 7,200 lunch groups of twenty-five people or more. No less than 60 percent of these groups delivered unused foods to the state on a regular monthly basis—and within the groups, possibly on a planned basis. Standard-form accounting had also begun in 80 percent of the lunch groups by that February.[41]

Legal free markets hamper the enforcement of ration procedures and reduce their residence-control effect by making money rather than legal household status an important source of livelihood within the city. Shanghai's legal free market in pork lasted until September 10, 1957. When it was closed by a decree of the state council, Shanghai buyers were forbidden to visit rural villages to purchase either pork or living hogs. Transportation companies were forbidden to carry pork on behalf of peasants or individual merchants. A major reason given for this change was that all meat should be checked by the city's public health bureau before it was sold. But the actual cause apparently lay in the need to keep tabs on rural slaughtering and urban deliveries, so that the whole urban management system could be more effective.[42] Local food stations were also instructed to recheck the sizes of households in their neighborhoods— and not to leave that continuing inspection job entirely to the public security system.[43]

By 1958, however, the bureaucratic simplification and send-down movements had hampered enforcement of rationing and population control in the urban area. Changing investment patterns created many low-paying, temporary, contract jobs in Shanghai, and rural people could move quite freely into the city. Police stations did not have enough personnel or resources to investigate the economic merits of local factory managements' decisions to hire more employees. In practice, they honored factories' requests that household registrations be transferred from rural areas to cities. Many new economic units were formed, and the ration system had to be extended to them, but it was impossible to keep the household records accurate in a time of high labor recruitment and migration. Sometimes workers were criticized for moving, but they received permission to do so anyway. Residence control was so weakened by the breakdown of the household system—and by the abundant harvests of 1958—that immigration to cities was nearly unrestricted during the Great Leap period.

The main dikes against this flood of migration were still institutional. In fact, the latter part of the Great Leap laid foundations for the more political and more thorough kinds of population control that flourished in the mid-1960s. The lives of city people increasingly centered around their work places. In no case was this change more pervasive or visible than in the mundane matter of obtaining daily "bread." During the Great Leap, for example, Shanghai Bicycle Plant built dormitories for 1,100 of its workers (800 men and 300 women). They together constituted a single collective household. The dining hall could serve all of them at once. Food was rationed by price, rather than by ticket, within the unit. For example, workers could choose four-tael, six-tael, or eight-tael boxes of steamed rice at any meal as they pleased, and they could choose other courses at ten, fifteen, or twenty fen, just as if they were in a restaurant. They paid at the end of the meal. A single official, leading a force of twenty watchmen and clerks, took care of both security and personal affairs, and he also arranged ration rights for the whole collective. The dormitory contained about 73 percent of the factory's work force.[44]

When food shortages became evident in mid-1959, an attempt was made to revitalize the rationing system out of necessity. Structural changes within the system at that time formed the basis for a more complete household control later, but residence records in 1959 were inadequate to allow cadres to construct an efficient and fair rationing system of the sort that the quickly developing shortages really required. A few pre-Leap holes in the regulations were nonetheless now closed. Previously, some important kinds of food, especially for children, had been obtainable without ration cards. When the pinch came at the end of the decade, there was simply no surplus to allow these exceptions.

By 1960, a lack of agricultural inputs for industry had also caused unemployment in the city. Laid-off workers no longer could eat in their factory canteens. Restaurants therefore became crowded with people who could no longer live under institutional auspices. Long lines formed for tables at all public eating houses. The Shanghai government estimated that over 1 million people in the city were looking regularly for food in restaurants in late 1960.[45] It became necessary to enforce the distinction between permanent residents and unregistered people so that food-preparation service could be rationed, as well as food itself. The government issued special coupons to registered householders, allowing them to obtain restaurant tables without so much waiting in line.

The shortage of fuel for home cooking also gave the restaurants an unusual appeal in 1960. By the following year, the food supplies had become so low that the government did not even have enough resources to award the permanent residents very effectively. It was difficult, under these circumstances, to expect much compliance with the household registration rules. According to one report, it was announced on May 1, 1961, that until further notice there would be no more meat for sale in Shanghai.[46]

Some reports, whose credibility might be considered low except that many of them appeared together at this hard time, suggest, a minor revival of several old kinds of deviance in Shanghai: prostitution and illegal dealing in gold and foreign currencies. The scope of these activities in 1961-62 was very limited by pre-1949 standards. Their occurrence nevertheless showed the extent of the food problem. Prostitutes reportedly accepted commodities and ration tickets as well as money in exchange for their services, and they plied their trade near amusement halls, parks, and special stores. The clientele consisted mainly of seamen, who could obtain goods in foreign ports, and privileged persons whose jobs or Overseas Chinese status gave them extra rations. Unemployment also spurred the rate of gambling in these undertain times. Card games were popular, because in contrast to Mah-Jongg they were not noisy and so did not attract the attention of cadres who had the delicate job of policing this situation.[47]

Food supplies became quite sharply better in early 1963. Already by spring, the government was able to remove some commodities from the ration list, and there were price reductions for many items.[48] People who were not engaged directly in production still got fairly low allotments; for instance, student rations at the Shanghai Teacher's College in 1963 ranged from twenty-five to thirty-five catties of rice per month.[49] But supplies steadily improved into the next year. By 1964, it was clear that shortages had helped in the long run to solidify discipline at least among legal food outlets. Now the price decreases helped to drive illegal entrepreneurs out of business.

By the spring of 1965, the real effects of ration controls even for non-staples were gradually beginning to vanish. Cigarettes came off the rationed commodities list, the price of soap went down and its availability went up, and hard goods like radios and kitchen utensils also had price reductions.[50] The New China News Agency proudly reported that in Shanghai the prices of 139 kinds of manufactured goods dropped 7 percent to 24 percent from mid-1963 to mid-1965, and the prices of pork, eggs, and sugar products went down as much as 30 percent.[51] Even the cloth situation improved toward the end of that year. Although all cotton and most wool items still required coupons, the increased production of synthetics helped to satisfy the demand for cloth.

By the end of the year the grain allotment for ordinary housewives was over thirty catties.[52] It was proclaimed that "the supply and distribution arrangements had made speculative actions almost impossible." Plentitude proved to be the best nostrum against black markets. It was now "possible for residents to purchase all their requirements without fear of being late."[53] By the spring of 1966, nominal grain rations had not actually gone up much, but the continuing and reliable supply of nonrationed subsidiary foods, including some starches, made it quite easy for anyone to live in Shanghai without legal residence status, if only he had some money. Grain and cooking oil were now the only rationed food products.[54]

Under these conditions of prosperity, residence controls declined from their 1963-64 levels. State-defined norms were clear as always in official statements. But deviance increased, and even became a kind of "cultural revolution," because the practical rules of conduct of many different groups became inconsistent. Rustication (*xiaxiang*) has a close connection with the residence registration functions that are described above. Change in the police books was, after all, the legal essence of rustication. The *xiaxiang* program was an early casualty in the confusion of norms that new prosperity introduced to the household system. Youths stayed in the cities to hold meetings that supported rustication. Or if they were already in the countryside, they returned to the city to criticize the street and school cadres who had sent them out, on bases that would have required their return to the boondocks.[55] Small communities and families were temporarily served on the basis of the norms of a large communalism.

By this point, it should be unnecessary to continue our narrative further, because the structure of this main social control and guidance system in Chinese cities should be already evident. Enough data have been presented above to give us some hope of answering the question: Under what conditions does this kind of system work effectively? And when does it collapse? The history above has emphasized the control of careers and residence by rations particularly; but despite that focus, it may be able to suggest some of the specific conditions under which deviance or communal consensus flourish in urban China.

DEVIANCE CONTROL AND MEDIUM PROSPERITY

When the national economic fluctuation that affects Chinese cities is in a doldrum stage, as it was during the early 1960s, the government can offer few incentives for urban people to take the occupations and residences that planners feel would be best for national development. Many sorts of deviance abound when prosperity is low. The ration system during the early 1960s was in the law books, but the black market supplied many important goods. Firms were cutting back their staffs due to a lack of raw materials, and the unavailability of jobs created no incentive for registration to obtain them. Education was no doubt an alternative to employment; but in fact this was the zenith period for "mass schools" (*qunzhong xuexiao*) run by local committees, and they usually did not require residence documents. Unemployed people sometimes became students when they had nothing else to do. Immigration to cities was controlled less efficiently during this period than in any other. Deviance, from government goals at least, was rampant in clubs of "social youth" (*shehui qingnian*) whose members were largely unemployed adolescents not wanting to rusticate. As we have seen above, some treaty port vices were resurrected in their old haunts during this period, and law enforcement in the economic field was largely suspended. Above all, the household books were not kept up to date, and no one could get much more food by registering with the police.

The considerable prosperity of the mid-1960s, when supplies for urban consumption were at a high level in 1965-66, also caused a lack of residence control. This was only somewhat less severe than in the earlier hard times, and it dominated many practical aspects of the ensuing Cultural Revolution for most urban people. Some jobs were available, but the placement systems run by unions had become so institutionalized that there were almost as many political problems from this recruitment structure as there had been from shortages in hard times. Much the same difficulty prevailed in the education admissions system, which shortly collapsed in its entirety. These recruitment problems contributed to the struggles among factory and school groups that soon followed.[56] Many important goods had been taken off the ration lists, and the amounts of rations had been raised considerably because of good harvests. An immigrant from the country thus had little incentive to register; his legally resident family or friends could share their own large rations to provide him sustenance without difficulty.

Urban China's social control system, based on residence registration, has worked best when there was a medium level of prosperity, because only then did the government have means to restrict personal mobility between residences and jobs, and the people did not have so many resources that they found it in their interests to evade the restrictions. In 1956-58, and then again during the recovery of 1963-64, the officials had some rations to give, but citizens still really needed the tickets because there was no great surplus. Some housing was built, which could thus be distributed to people on the registration books. Some new jobs were made available as raw materials from the countryside were supplied. A middle level of prosperity, rather than a high or low one, maximized the government's leverage to control the types of deviance it dislikes in city dwellers. The level of social guidance has varied over time.

CONCLUSION

Material constraints can have nonmaterial effects. We are talking here not only about rations and controls, but also about the sense of community that makes people structure their actions for the goals of groups larger than themselves.[57] That sense of community is a major control on deviance and a guide for individuals' actions. During some periods in the recent histories of Chinese cities (for example, during the Korean War), many citizens may really have identified with the nation as a whole more readily than before. At other times (for example, during the job and commodity shortages of the early 1960s), their objects of political identification clearly ebbed to smaller groups. To some extent, such changes in the value structure behind social control and guidance were induced by official propaganda. But as the data on household controls suggest above, the effects of other government policies—especially in the economic sphere—are at least as important. The levels of community whose goals guide action are created by "goods" of both the ideal and the physical kinds.

The speed with which such communities change is not fast. A history of residence policy, or any other policy, almost unavoidably emphasizes campaigns and change. But ordinary citizens alter their basic foci of communal identification only very slowly, despite the temporary moves by which they may respond to immediate pressures. The system for deviance control and social community in China's cities has had its ups and downs. These fluctuations are real, but they do not affect people so strongly as a narrative description of policy changes in this system alone might imply. Quick changes in the way the residence system interacts with other government programs are not so important, in the long term, as the fact that the residence books exist at all.

It must be evident that there are some practical implications for long-range development policy in the particular residence-based method the Communist Chinese have used for social control in their cities. The method has implications that go beyond purely intellectual interests.[58] It entails the restriction of freedom of some levels of community for the expected greater or later benefit of other levels. Many kinds of questions are in order about the efficiency of this present sacrifice for long-term social goals. But no attempt need be made to answer them here.

Residence restrictions have certainly been imposed in other countries than China. But strangely, this whole genre of policy has hardly been studied at all. The most obvious comparison is the USSR's "passport" system, but Russianists have apparently paid little systematic attention to that.[59] The partial, problematic kind of pressure on careers which governments can attempt to apply through residence systems provides economic and social planners with a powerful tool to direct individual energies toward community purposes. But if, as is possible during the next few decades, several of the world's large, developing semidemocracies move toward tighter systems (of whatever political complexion), and if they attempt to lower deviance and raise social production in their cities by residence and job controls, the effects of such policies on individuals' values may prove to be mixed. Local incentives to act for common goals will be most steadily sustained by a supply of goods that neither dips so low it includes no surplus to inspire common action, nor rises so quickly that individuals might do as well acting alone. The campaign method by itself does not accomplish this. A balance must be struck between the benefits of phasing mobilization and control goals over time and the benefits of providing a steady stream of resources to encourage individuals and small groups to work increasingly for the public good.

NOTES

1. See Emile Durkheim, *Suicide*, trans. J. A. Spaulding and G. Simpson (Glencoe: The Free Press, 1951); Robert K. Merton, *Social Theory and Social Structure* (Glencoe: The Free Press, 1957); and Talcott Parsons, *The Social System* (Glencoe: The Free Press, 1951). A fuller argument for the joining of discussions of legitimate and deviant opportunity structures for action can be found in Richard A. Cloward, "Illegitimate Means, Anomie, and Deviant Behavior," *American Sociological Review* 24 (April 1959): 164-76.

2. Distinctions between the terms "community" and "society" do not seem necessary in this essay; they would obscure the fact that the Chinese state is now trying to change both by a single, unified set of policies. If such distinctions are to be made, a four-part model is preferable. See Werner S. Landecker, "Types of Integration and Their Measurement," *American Journal of Sociology* 56 (January 1951): 332-40.

3. Quoted in Lucien Bianco, *Origins of the Chinese Revolution, 1915-1949*, trans. Muriel Bell (Stanford: Stanford University Press, 1971), p. 42.

4. The modernization of ideas is discussed for another purpose in Ishwer C. Ojha, *Chinese Foreign Policy in an Age of Transition: The Diplomacy of Cultural Despair* (Boston: Beacon, 1969). The main interpretation is Joseph R. Levenson, *Confucian China and its Modern Fate*, 3 vols., (Berkeley: University of California Press, 1965).

5. Howard S. Becker, *Outsiders: Studies in the Sociology of Deviance*, rev. ed. (New York: The Free Press, 1973).

6. Compare the distinction between *chientu* and *chiench'a* (before-the-fact and after-the-fact) types of accounting in Franz H. Schurmann, *Ideology and Organization in Communist China*, rev. ed. (Berkeley: University of California Press, 1968).

7. See my "Shanghai's Polity in Cultural Revolution," in John W. Lewis, ed., *The City in Communist China* (Stanford: Stanford University Press, 1971), p. 367.

8. Robert Tung, "People's Policemen," *Far Eastern Economic Review* 53 (August 18, 1966): 319-31; and interview, Hong Kong, December 1969.

9. Ibid. (interview).

10. On "spontaneous houses," see New China News Agency (hereafter NCNA), Shanghai, November 13, 1956.

11. See Chou-yun Hsu, *Ancient China in Transition: An Analysis of Social Mobility, 722-222 B.C.* (Stanford: Stanford University Press, 1965), p. 137.

12. See John K. Fairbank, Edwin O. Reischauer, and Albert M. Craig, *East Asia: Tradition and Transformation* (Boston: Houghton Mifflin, 1973), pp. 77, 100, and 107.

13. Brian E. McKnight, *Village and Bureaucracy in Southern Sung China* (Chicago: University of Chicago Press, 1971), Chapter 6.

14. Ping-ti Ho, *Studies on the Population of China* (Cambridge: Harvard University Press, 1959), pp. 3-4.

15. T'ung-tsu Ch'u, *Local Government in China Under the Ch'ing* (Cambridge: Harvard University Press, 1962), Chapter 9.

16. Interview, Hong Kong, December 1969. The government on Taiwan still issues *shenfen zheng*.

17. Interview, Hong Kong, October 1969.

18. Otto van der Sprenkel, ed., with Robert Gullain and Michael Lindsay, *New China: Three Views* (New York: John Day, 1951), p. 105. This restriction on ticket buying was apparently lessened after the mainland was unified militarily. After rations were introduced, however, travel was convenient only for people who had applied for special ration cards that could be used at restaurants and hotels throughout the country.

19. *Shanghai gongshang ziliao (Materials on Shanghai Industry and Commerce)* 2:36 (May 5, 1951): 1303.

20. *Xinwen ribao* (hereafter XWRB), June 5, 1955, cited in John F. Aird, "Population Growth," in Alexander Echstein, Walter Galenson, and Ta-chung Liu, eds., *Economic Trends in Communist China* (Chicago: Aldine, 1968), pp. 220-21.

21. Ibid. and *Laodong bao* (hereafter LDB), October 5, 1956.

22. *Renmin Ribao* (hereafter RMRB), June 10, 1953.

23. See NCNA, Shanghai, November 28, 1953, where the census procedures are outlined in some detail and the possibility of systematic flaws can be readily seen. The speed of the campaign was one of its most spectacular features. About 280 stations in populous Puto District estimated that they had registered more than half the district's population in only three days. Puto has factories, slums, and workers' housing. In such a situation, the possibilities of intentional and unintentional double counting and noncounting are large.

24. NCNA, Peking, July 8, 1953.

25. Ibid., September 23, 1954.

26. NCNA, Shanghai, March 1, 1954.

27. Ibid. says that the amount of grain shipped to Shanghai from November 1953 to January 1954 was 62 percent more than in the corresponding period in the previous year.

28. For excellent background on this, see Thomas P. Bernstein, "Cadre and Peasant Behavior under Conditions of Insecurity and Deprivation: The Grain Supply Crisis of the Spring of 1955," in A. Doak Barnett, ed., *Chinese Communist Politics in Action* (Seattle: University of Washington Press, 1969), pp. 365-99.

29. XWRB, July 10, 1955.

30. NCNA, Shanghai, March 26, 1955.

31. NCNA, Shanghai, May 17, 1955.

32. RMRB, June 28, 1955.

33. XWRB, July 5, 1955.

34. Ibid., another article.

35. XWRB, July 8, 1955.

36. XWRB, July 6, 1955.

37. XWRB, August 31, 1955.

38. RMRB, September 5, 1955.

39. XWRB, September 1, 1955.

40. *Qingnian bao* (hereafter QNB), Shanghai, January 11, 1957.

41. LDB, February 4, 1957.

42. XWRB, August 28, 1957.

43. XWRB, October 8, 1957.

44. Interview with an Indonesian Overseas Chinese who failed to enter university in Shanghai and became an odd jobber in the Shanghai Bicycle Plant. Other sources indicate that at some plants chits for the mess hall were all bought together at the beginning of each month.

45. "Interview with a Translator from Shanghai," *Current Scene* 1, no. 6 (July 10, 1961): 3.

46. Letter written in the fall of 1961 by a German businessman resident in Shanghai, sent to Santa Cruz, California, printed in the San Francisco *Chronicle* and reprinted in the *China Mail*, Hong Kong, March 28, 1962. See also Edgar Snow, *The Other Side of the River: Red China Today* (London: Victor Gollancz, 1963), p. 538. These reliable reports are of malnutrition, not starvation.

47. Edgar Snow, op. cit., pp. 535-36, quotes a secretary of the Shanghai People's Congress to the effect that gangsters had been eliminated in Shanghai, although the official conceded that a few prostitutes might be operating "as rare cases."

48. "Shanghai Newsletter" column (hereafter SHNL) of *South China Morning Post*, Hong Kong, May 18, 1963.

49. Interview with a Shanghai person who studied at the Specialized Teachers' University, Huangp'u District.

50. SHNL, May 28, 1965.

51. NCNA, Shanghai, April 24, 1965. But an ex-resident disagreed, saying that food prices rose slightly since the 1950s, although the tags on manufactured goods went down.

52. Interview with a Thai Overseas Chinese from Shanghai.

53. SHNL, February 2, 1965.

54. SHNL, June 8, 1966.

55. A speculative essay is my "Shanghai's Polity in Cultural Revolution," cited in note 7 above, p. 366. On increased localism see ""Local Autonomy in China during the Cultural Revolution: The Theoretical Uses of an Atypical Case," *American Political Science Review* (forthcoming).

56. See "Workers' Politics in Shanghai," *Journal of Asian Studies* (forthcoming).

57. See Landecker, op. cit.

58. See Norman Uphoff and Warren F. Ilchman, *The Political Economy of Development* (Berkeley: U.C. Campus Paperback, 1971), Part I, for a superb definition of development policy science.

59. The classic on Soviet urban politics, Merle Fainsod's *Smolensk Under Soviet Rule* (Cambridge: Harvard University Press, 1958) and the more recent contribution by William Taubman, *Governing Soviet Cities: Bureaucratic Politics and Urban Development in the USSR* (New York: Praeger, 1973) both discuss local elite politics, not local mass politics. I am unaware of any full treatment of the Soviet residence or rationing systems. Comparisons in other countries, ranging from East Germany to Japan, might also be interesting; but very little has been done on the relation between low-level job and residence economics and levels of community control.

10

WORK INCENTIVES AND
SOCIAL CONTROL
Charles Hoffmann

INTRODUCTION

In our efforts to understand the changing policies and practices of China's leaders as they attempt to move toward defined revolutionary goals, it may be helpful to look at how work incentives have taken their place in the CCP's strategy to shape a modernized revolutionary society. In the larger context of this volume, which is aimed at exploring social control and deviance in the PRC, this paper has several objectives: 1) to help understand changing Chinese work incentive systems in both economic and ideological terms, 2) to see how social controls have been devised and modified in the context of revolutionary goals to reinforce the new and weaken the old incentive mechanisms as a revolutionary incentive system is shaped, and 3) to identify varieties of deviance from the new social norms and to see how they have been contended with.

Social control over individual and group behavior for or by society must focus on the perennial tension between collective and individual interests. Social stability hinges on a reasonable resolution of these often conflicting interests, and in China that social stability further has to be fashioned in a setting of heavy ideological commitment to collective styles and modes and the inferior but not consistently negative position given to individual interest. This is signally important in incentive mechanisms since the individual as producer has usually had his or her individual recompense linked to his or her work performance. In pressing to develop collectivist incentive mechanisms and, ultimately, a fully assimilated collectivist work ethic, the Chinese ideologues and party leaders, as apt social controllers, must utilize the propensity to conform to accepted social norms—at a time when old values and behaviors are being exorcized—as well as exploit the need for individual self-esteem to internalize a new set of social values.[1]

As we look at Chinese incentive systems and their development and transformation we should be aware of the broad process of social control in any
society. Societal means for controlling behavior vary considerably and are frequently not readily discernible, especially to the outsider. The formal mechanisms of control are more easily identified, though the problem of intended vs.
actual operation is always a vexatious one. Sometimes of greater importance,
especially in providing the cement that is essential for a robust, stable social
structure, are the informal social controls that reinforce in aversive or positive
ways the desired behavior. In this network of dynamic environments, social
control is exercised constantly through a variety of institutions, values, and both
formal and informal media, including public opinion, law, belief, religion,
personal ideals, art, ceremony, illusion, personality, social values, markets, producing units, and advertising.[2]

Whatever the systems of social control, there are limits to the exercise of
that control—limits, of course, that are not absolute but that are relative,
temporally and culturally. Social controls that persistently threaten the interests
of individuals and groups to the breaking point or that conjure up intense negative expectations that jeopardize people's fundamental needs are likely to upset
social stability and generate wholesale deviance and disloyalty. Within any
system of social control the individual and the basic level group must have some
sense of fulfillment and self-realization if a modicum of social harmony is to
obtain. In one context, deviance may be seen, therefore, as a consequence of
conflict between individual perceived needs and social controls that frustrate
those needs. Extensive group deviance often leads to rebellion and revolt, and
random individual deviance is characteristic of all societies in varying degrees.
In China the problem of deviance is made somewhat more difficult to assess by
the rapidly changing norms imposed by revolutionary goals, by the seemingly
contradictory policies that have been put forth, and by the considerable number
of surviving values from the old society that often are in sharp conflict with new
revolutionary values.[3]

As we analyze incentives in China, we should keep this social control
framework in mind together with the following basic analytic framework on
motivation. People are motivated by a variety of factors, all of which in some
way propel the individual actor to perform, alone or in groups, at different
levels of quality according to a perceived or sensed gain, material or otherwise,
to be derived either from the overall performance process itself or as a reward
for the quality and quantity of measurable units of performance. Motivation
thus has intrinsic and extrinsic elements, though a particular culture or sub-
culture may emphasize one or the other.

The intrinsic elements include gain or satisfaction that arises generally in
the work process and broad outcome. For the individual this includes personal
satisfaction from a job well done, overcoming physical or conceptual obstacles,
improving skills, etc., or satisfaction from the successful attainment of group or

societal objectives, from working closely and effectively in a group, from contributing to the group's development process, etc. Guilt or fear in a group or personal context may also be part of the psychodynamics of intrinsic motivation.

Extrinsic motivation, on the other hand, is more task-oriented: the reward is not *in* the process of production but *for* the specific outcome or output (performance result) of the individual worker or work group. This is seen in its extreme form, piece rates, where the actual unit of output is directly linked to the unit of payment (wages), and other aspects of the worker's contribution to the work process are ignored or assumed to be mechanically linked to the output unit (i.e., one has to work well in the production process to have a high output rate).

Clearly, in any work situation both intrinsic and extrinsic elements (negative and positive) at some time operate together and there are overlaps, reinforcements, and contradictions. But in modern industrial societies the emphasis, in varying degrees, is on extrinsic motivation schemes. This is patently a function of the profit indicator and the market pressures for cost minimization. The analysis of incentives, therefore, usually proceeds on the assumption that extrinsic motivation must be a major determinant of work behavior and that any system ignoring this precept is in conflict with human nature and thus "irrational," though some concessions are often made to the possible positive effects of improved working conditions. We plan to analyze incentives in this dualistic framework with the expectation that such an approach will help throw considerable light on what Chinese social controllers have in mind in their incentive policy prescriptions.

The use to which this suggested framework can be put becomes more apparent if we consider the ideological and economic constraints within which the CCP has propounded its changing policies aimed at guiding the social process in the right direction and at a tempo appropriate to the estimated social limits. Incentive policies and practices must be shaped within the context of fundamental ideological goals and values as well as economic and cultural realities. The ultimate goals of the revolution are clear, and significant material inducement to generate worker and peasant enthusiasm is not consonant with those goals of shaping communism. Given the rejection of development with ramifying material incentive systems,[4] the CCP must either use coercive mechanisms or design new incentive systems. The intrinsic-extrinsic analytic framework should help us explore their efforts more effectively.

The ideological goal of advancing through socialist stages to communism via a revolutionary modernization process is not blueprinted in a detailed way, yet important elements of the objectives and process have been made explicit. The Chinese talk about closing the "three gaps," and this objective reveals the heavy commitment to a future egalitarian society. The gaps—now quite wide—between mental and manual labor, town and country, and worker and peasant must be eliminated before communism is possible, and the task of achieving this condition foreshadows a social control agenda cutting a wide societal swath. The elimination of the first gap means taking on such perennial issues as bureaucracy, status, role, division of labor, and individual vs. collective interest. The second gap addresses itself to the global search for new kinds of population concentrations and organizations of a modernized society other than what we know as urbanization. The third transformation issue poses problems touching on specialization, self images, and overcoming powerful traditional rural social forces. Cutting across all three is the question of the kind of work ethic and motivation that can feasibly be shaped given the powerful continuities of the past and the Maoist vision of a communist society of the future.[5]

Other ideological elements surround and support the egalitarian thrust of Maoism. Eliminating the three gaps is a process that occurs concomitantly with the transformation of the mode of production and the superstructure of society. The transfer of the ownership of the means of production to society is only one of several imparatives. The distribution process must also be converted from commodity production to production for use: the market mechanism and the law of value (profit indicator) have to be superseded gradually, as ownership of all the people (state enterprise) spreads and economic planning extends to cover larger areas of production. At the same time, social relations in factories and on farms must be reoriented to the requirements of the collectivist work style. As for material incentives, the socialist remuneration principle (payment according to one's output) is to be replaced by the communist principle (payment according to need). The transition calls for the creation of new incentive mechanisms, the raising of the people's proletarian consciousness, and the development of new political, educational, and other superstructural institutions as society industrializes and modernizes in a revolutionary way. The fact that bourgeois elements from the past as well as new class interests persist in reinforcing "bourgeois right," which is a function of the continued existence of commodity production, mandates continuing vigorous class struggle and the conscious exercise of dictatorship of the proletariat against these lingering reactionary forces and attitudes.

The economic context that CCP leaders have to deal with if they are going to succeed in changing behavior certainly complicates their task. China's factor endowment mix of scarce capital and land and relatively abundant labor means that labor must be more effectively utilized if capital and land and their fruits are to be generated in rising amounts. This also means that labor must be powerfully motivated to work responsibly and imaginatively, to upgrade skills, and to move where needed as the economy develops. In other words, an enormous labor force, largely untrained in modern skills and techniques and coming mainly from peasant origins, has to be trained in occupational and technical processes essential to modernization and deployed to the various parts of the economy using motivational mechanisms that minimize material reward and emphasize instead collective and social aims, processes, and values.

Thus, in guiding China from and through socialism to communism and its newly designed work ethic and style, the CCP leaders are faced with the formidable challenge of drastically changing behavior—which means overcoming worker and peasant dependence on age-old extrinsic material recompense for work input and outcome with new social incentives and collectivist relations on the job. As extrinsic material incentives are soft-pedaled, heavier reliance on intrinsic social incentives is imperative and there is a compelling need to internalize the new revolutionary values and provide major nonmaterial payoffs in gratification in the work process and in the new social relations that are shaped. Such psychic income is of course not meant to take the place of satisfying basic material needs, which are planned to rise slowly over time. But if extrinsic material incentive is to be eliminated, some other set of functional incentives must take its place.

We review below how CCP leaders have dealt with and continue to deal with this exercise in mass social control aimed at maximizing collectivist conformity and minimizing deviance from the highly valued new norms. First we review the patterns of incentive mechanisms for the period to the Cultural Revolution; then we cover the period since that momentous series of events. Next, we look at the changing roles that cadres, technicians, workers, and peasants have been called upon to play in the new evolving incentive environment. Finally, we analyze the problems of deviance that have arisen from the new motivational institutions and roles in factories and communes.

THE CHANGING PATTERNS OF INCENTIVE MECHANISMS

1949 to 1965

Before the Cultural Revolution, incentive policy and practice changed considerably both in response to the transformation of China into a socialist society and to the major changes in development strategy that adverse experience with the Soviet model dictated. During the entire period efforts were made to find incentive mechanisms that were consistent with the socialist principle of remuneration—payment according to the quantity and quality of work. These efforts were carried on while the development strategy was radically modified from one emphasizing the rapid growth of heavy industry following Soviet experience to one giving agriculture the highest priority and stressing proportionate development. This latter strategy was fashioned completely only after the Great Leap Forward (GLF). After the experience of the First Five-Year Plan (FFYP) seemed to mandate a drastic strategy change as bottlenecks, unemployment, slow agricultural growth, and other economic problems cast a shadow on China's development, the GLF was a first attempt to design a Chinese development model less dependent on the market mechanism and more in keeping with China's particular factor endowment mix and the Maoist vision of the road to Communism. In the adversities that followed the near debacle of the GLF, there was both retrenchment and return to some of the devices of the FFYP and settlement on the new strategy to "take agriculture as the foundation and industry as the leading factor."[6]

In this period of zigzagging policy in which land reform, socialization of industry, collectivization of agriculture, introduction of the commune during the GLF, consolidation, adjustment, and economic recession after the GLF followed one another, varied incentive systems were experimented with first, to help rehabilitate industry and agriculture, next to establish and build a socialist remuneration system, and finally to lay the foundation for a communist work ethic. Incentive mechanisms were expected to contribute both to worker and peasant behavior fostering attainment of short-run economic and political goals, and the cultivation of proletarian consciousness through the introduction of new incentive modes and their extension or discard as experimentation proved successful or not.

Not only did the CCP leaders shape and reshape development strategy and implement socialist work incentive schemes, but they also had to get in motion an effective economic planning mechanism as the foundation of a socialist and future communist society. The market existed as an allocative mechanism following the "law of value" (profit indicator) and thus had to be contended with, while commodity production and exchange necessarily continued. Market elements had to be retracted and the law of value qualified as conditions permitted, and economic planning had to be extended. In the field of labor allocation and incentive, CCP leaders substituted nonmarket (direct) means for dealing with deployment and motivation of labor.[7]

While CCP leaders were formulating and implementing such policies, they also had to respond to a series of pressing and unexpected problems. Unemployment, inherited from prerevolutionary China, persisted despite expectations that the CCP's programs would provide work for all. Peasant migrants to the cities, unhappy with conditions in the countryside and attracted by rising wages and the urban allure, perversely swelled the city labor pool, which was rising anyway as city population grew. Industrial expansion was not rapid enough to absorb the natural growth, let alone the flow from the country. Another problem was lagging agricultural production during the FFYP and the sharp drop in grain output after the first surge of the GLF petered out. There was also spreading official concern over the perpetuation and spread of "bourgeois attitudes." Clearly the motivational and allocative mechanisms in operation were not effecting the kind of social controls desired and in many instances were actually stimulating deviation from ideological and economic norms.

Looking at the evolving incentive mechanisms during this period, some light may be thrown on how establishing socialist work incentives and laying the foundation for a communist or proletarian work ethic affects workers' and peasants' social behavior. Attempting to implement incentive mechanisms consistent with the socialist remuneration principle involved modifying existing and devising new mechanisms. Emphasis was placed on extrinsic or external kinds of mechanisms, though certain new types had some important intrinsic elements that were more heavily stressed during the GLF.[8]

Material incentives developed and extended in agriculture and industry reflected a continuing reliance on external or extrinsic motivation linking work performance directly with income. Nonmaterial incentives, for the most part, were cultivated in the same way. This pattern was modified, however, during the GLF when greater efforts were made to lay the foundation for the communist work ethic and to experiment with broader incentives in which the intrinsic or internal motive force was more prominent. After the GLF there was widespread reversion to the patterns of the 1950s, though radical party groups continued GLF patterns and mechanisms where they could.[9]

In both agriculture and industry material incentives were rationalized, strengthened, and extended following Soviet practice and the socialist payment principle. Wages were standardized with an eight-grade system (first grade, least skilled: eighth grade, highest skilled) predominating throughout industry and aimed at stimulating greater work input and attention to improving skills with a view to promotion to a higher grade. Piece rates and bonuses were superimposed on this system to heighten the drive to work harder and upgrade skills. By 1957 about 42 percent of industrial workers were on some kind of piece-rate setup. This type of payment scheme was further developed ideologically from individual to group modes, the premium pay being linked to the whole group's performance and the individual distribution of premiums often left for the group to decide.[10]

Technicians and cadres also had their pay scales rationalized, though they reached to much higher levels than workers' scales. (E.g., the highest pay for a skilled worker was about ¥125 a month, while the highest scale for cadres and technicians was somewhat under ¥800 a month.) Higher level technicians and cadres also received perquisites such as better housing, services in kind (use of cars), better medical care, special vacation facilities, etc. Another type of payment—monetary awards for inventions, innovation, and improvements—was directly linked to the value of the proposal in saving money or generating greater output. The cash amounts ranged up to ¥10,000.[11]

In agriculture the pattern was the same. Since the cooperatives and later the communes were collective rather than state enterprises, income was not wages but shared distribution of output. The workpoints system evolved: as in industry and following extrinsic motivation modes, peasants were graded by skill, and to each grade attached a specific number of workpoints (least skilled, five workpoints; highest skilled, ten workpoints). Piece rates were integrated into the system with standard workpoints for a skill level being augmented if work norms were exceeded by specified amount or proportions. During the GLF, communes modified the workpoints mechanism with a supply-wages system in which workpoint distribution was used for only a portion of the total income (or grain) distributed (anywhere from 30 to 70 percent), the remainder being distributed on a per capita basis following a schedule of absolute amount of grain related to age, difficulty of work, etc. The supply part of the system introduced into the socialist remuneration mechanism a communist element with an intrinsic quality.[12]

The nonmaterial incentives of the period were mainly extrinsic and individual. But they also contained intrinsic elements, and over time these latter were stressed as an aspect of a broader effort to change the work environment so that it became an important part of an intrinsic motivational mode. During the 1950s certain nonmaterial incentives of the extrinsic and individual type were extended following the Soviet experience: model and advanced worker and peasant awards, token competitive awards (dragons, red flags, etc.) for individuals and groups, emulation contests for individuals and groups, conferences for outstanding workers and peasants, etc. These mechanisms were mainly competitive and distributive, their effectiveness depending on keen individual and group rivalry and on the restriction of the awards if their value was not to be debased.[13]

Some of the nonmaterial incentives developed during the period, however, did not fall into the mold just sketched; they concerned themselves more with changing the work setting and style of work and creating positive work attitudes through involvement in day-to-day processes and decisions—in this regard they were important in their intrinsic or internal motivating thrust. These incentives, which were mainly cooperative and by their nature involved groups rather than individuals, were usually introduced through elaborate political education campaigns. If they had any claim to heightening peasant and worker enthusiasm, that claim rested on raising the level of group solidarity and identification so that contributions to group objectives (say, meeting certain production quotas or designing a new machine) in themselves fulfilled salient individual needs. These mechanisms were really forms of implementing the mass line: mass production review meetings, mass meetings to deal with a variety of specific objectives (productivity, cost reduction, output problems, design, innovation, etc.), criticism/self-criticism meetings, technical intraplant and interplant exchange meetings, advanced-backward group meetings, mass projects, worker participation in management, mass merit evaluations, mass decision-making, and so forth. An important part of the factory setting was having new communist elements injected into it as the commune had with the supply-wages system.[14]

Factory and agricultural cooperative (and later commune) environments were modified in other ways to encourage new proletarian work styles and social relations between workers or peasants, on the one side, and cadres and technicians on the other side. The large and small group involvements of workers and peasants discussed above were one set of mechanisms that required social behavior different from the conventional. Other mechanisms included cadre participation in physical labor on a regular basis, formal criticism sessions dealing with cadre and technician performance, and the development during the GLF of three-in-one combinations in which workers (or peasants), cadres, and technicians would work together handling specific work problems rather than relying on one hierarchic authority to resolve a particular issue in his or her specialized jurisdiction.[15]

So far as labor allocation within and between work units was concerned, early in the period wages and wage and income differentials did play a role in deploying labor within and between economic sectors. There was still a labor market in the early 1950s; even later, when moving about looking for a job became illegal, income differentials attracted workers and peasants to the better (higher paying) jobs. Labor assignment was instituted as the approved means of deploying labor and labor bureaus carried out this function, if somewhat imperfectly, as the old method of social control, the market, still exercised its influence through wage income differentials. Income gaps continued through the period, reinforcing the value of certain kinds of careers in contradiction to the ideological rhetoric extolling the role of worker or peasant. The spread between workers' and peasants' incomes widened until the GLF, when it may have stabilized for a while. After the GLF the situation was somewhat erratic due to severe economic contraction, and with recovery, inequalities spread again. The differentials between workers and cadres and technicians increased during the 1950s, probably stabilized during the GLF, and then continued to grow. Before the Cultural Revolution maximum skilled worker pay was often less than half cadre and technician maxima; average worker pay was about one-fifth the cadre-technician maxima.[16]

1966 to Date

Incentive mechanisms have been cultivated since the Cultural Revolution with much attention to a proletarian work environment and style. The goals and spirit of communism have been trumpeted in various campaigns to reinforce intrinsic motivational modes and to forestall backsliding into heavy dependence on traditional material incentives, which have been held in check selectively. The social controls exercised formally and informally in the basic work units have been reinforced through struggle techniques focusing positively on accepted proletarian incentive modes and negatively on conventional incentives such as wages. One cadre admitted that he "often wittingly or unwittingly considered 'material incentives' as 'tangible means of control'" when the issue of control rests ultimately not with material recompense but with the social relationships in the plant, an inherently internal or intrinsic mode of control.[17]

In industry, wages have been modified in several ways. Piece rates have generally been eliminated, though they probably still exist in some factories. Bonuses have, similarly, been retracted; in one plant when they were eliminated ¥5 was added to the standard wage scale, thus avoiding negative effects and equalizing the income impact with a greater proportionate increase going to the lower wage grades. Wage increases made available in 1971 applied only to the workers in the lowest three wage grades, leaving the basic scales untouched and raising the average slightly from the bottom rather than all along the line.[18] Invention awards, which had been cut back somewhat in the early 1960s, seem to have been abolished altogether. Certainly the policy to hold wages in tight rein (the "rational low wage policy"), even as China's economic growth proceeds apace, is being adhered to at the same time as ideological campaigns attacking "bourgeois right" and backsliding are pressed.[19]

The post-Cultural Revolution pressures to telescope incomes and attack material incentives in industry have also been felt in the communes. The clarion call to "learn from Dazhai," the model commune brigade, has been accompanied by strident campaigns against "workpoints in command" and the "bourgeois" preoccupation with private plots to the neglect of commune activity. Results in the countryside have apparently been somewhat different than in urban factories: the denunciation of material incentives has not resulted in piece rates being as widely withdrawn as in factories. Large numbers of communes use material incentive mechanisms, which are still a long way from the ideal Dazhai pattern in which peasant incomes are not as mechanically linked to individual output as in the standard workpoints scale. Cadres still are under pressure to shape peasant behavior to the ideological norms in which revolutionary commitment drives the peasant to carry out commune tasks with energy and devotion. In those communes where piece rates and workpoints are still clearly necessary to stimulate proper work performance, the cadres deplore but accept the reality of low levels of political consciousness, which may reflect poor commune productivity as well as the powerful cultural continuity of the past.*

The more persistent and intense social pressure to de-emphasize material and extrinsic rewards for work after the Cultural Revolution has been especially strong on cadres and technicians. While their salary scales do not appear to have been formally revised downward, the practice has been to push the maxima down to almost half of their former levels. In factories, the maxima now range between ¥150 and ¥225 a month, one and a half to two times the workers' maxima and only about half or a little more of the highest salaries paid in the PRC (¥400 a month). In July 1975 Vice-Premier Deng Xiaoping disclosed to a

---

*Two communes in Kwangtung province I visited in July 1973 used piece rates to a considerable degree. One used them especially during peak periods and soft-pedaled them at other times.

group of Japanese journalists that his salary, at the crest of the salary scales, was ¥400 a month, a top level of income paid, he asserted, to about one hundred persons in China. He also indicated that the next lower income level, ¥300, was received by only several thousand persons. He considered the gap between the ¥60 which is the average for workers and the top salaries in the PRC still to be too great.[20]

In factories the patterns of higher wage scales for cadres and technicians than for workers are violated in interesting ways: the highest paid person may not be the top manager (chairman of the revolutionary committee) but rather a senior worker, a physician, or an engineer. For example, in the Shanghai Irregular Shape Steel Tube Plant in 1973, the highest pay was ¥125 a month to a senior worker. The chairman of the revolutionary committee who managed the plant received ¥108 a month, probably the wage he was receiving when he took over his leadership position.[21]

Cadres have in the past also benefitted from perquisites giving them favored treatment on housing, transportation, superior schooling for their children, etc. The mandate since the Cultural Revolution has been to eliminate or reduce these as ideologically anathema. Though it is quite likely that special privileges are still enjoyed by many bureaucrats, expectations are that cadres' public morality is high, and given the means and penchant for criticism and the campaigns against "bourgeois" behavior, it is quite probable that more cadres behave "properly" now than when the issue was on the back ideological burner. When I was in China, persistent inquiries on the incidence of private use of a factory's passenger cars by leading cadre members occasioned exasperated protestations that such a practice did not happen and if it every did it would become a matter of wide public discussion and criticism.[22]

As for competitive nonmaterial incentives such as designating model individuals and groups, token awards, intergroup emulation drives, and the like: some of them continue, though they are overshadowed by greater emphasis on cooperative incentives and the development of intrinsic modes embodied in the ongoing work process. Model workers receive awards, sometimes posthumously, that are widely publicized in a noncompetitive fashion; outstanding factories are similarly feted. Often the accolades are collectivized when the recipients are cited en masse. Emulation meetings for exchanging experiences, especially the ideological ones, have been widely promoted on regional lines.[23]

One important outgrowth of the Cultural Revolution which significantly changes the social environment and attempts to redirect the aspirations of young people is the revolutionization of education. Not only are Chinese youth expected to link their education and training to serving the people, but they are also required to accept being assigned where they are most "needed" by the people. The process of sending middle-school graduates to work in communes, factories, or PLA units before being eligible to apply for admission to universities and their usual return to these work units after completion of education are an important part of labor allocation by assignment rather than through the differential wages (pricing) of a labor market. Career selection is not left to individual choice based on expected future earnings; instead "success" is to be measured by the commitment and competence with which one serves wherever he or she is assigned, thus setting up a radically different set of life expectations.[24]

The Dazhai production brigade in Shansi province and the Daqing oil fields in Heilungkiang province have been widely publicized as models of the kind of revolutionary spirit and behavior all Chinese should emulate. "In agriculture, learn from Dazhai," and "in industry, learn from Daqing." Though in both of these models the standard extrinsic material incentive mechanisms have been in operation (in the Dazhai brigade efforts were made during the 1960s to infuse collectivist behavior norms into the process of workpoint determination), the principal motivational strategy is the development of revolutionary enthusiasm and its internalization through the cultivation of new work modes that yield intrinsic rewards at the same time as improvement in material living conditions is effected.[25] The success stories of Dazhai and Daqing encapsulate the principal elements of ideology and organization that have to be combined effectively if social control of the work environment is to bear the proper fruit.[26] These elements include struggle (against natural and social barriers), proper organization and leadership, perseverance, self-reliance, the "correct line," serving the people, the mass line—all geared to "grasp revolution and promote production."[27]

The prominent attention given to the Dazhai and Daqing models and the extension of mass campaigns and political education based on their experience since the Cultural Revolution must be seen against a broader canvas of positive efforts at social control. Two important motifs that must be taken into account are the extension of a more or less guaranteed minimum level of living for peasants and workers, and the cultivation of "new socialist things" which change the work environment. Both of these policies in recent years have been developed, as important movements to contain conventional motivational mechanisms and prevent backsliding into "bourgeois" practice and behavior have been mounted and pressed (e.g., anti-Confucius-Lin Biao, dictatorship of the proletariat, and bourgeois right movements).[28]

The development of a floor of basic necessities for all Chinese workers and peasants is an important incentive element aimed at building a secure socialist environment in which noncompetitive social relations conducive to high levels of work input and initiative can flourish. This floor includes a set of basic goods and services that have been accumulated over the years for workers and more recently have been extended in the countryside to cover the fundamental needs of peasants. For workers the array includes social insurance and subsidized food, clothing, housing, transportation, cultural and recreational activities, and education. Peasants still have a considerable distance to go to reach the extent of worker coverage, but they are secure in cooperative health care, old age benefits, cultural and recreational activity, education, housing, and food. Thus a general, broad system of social security has been developed which gives each person or family the right to the basic necessities of life, and this right is being internalized and expanded as material levels are raised. Work, therefore, is performed as a social obligation rather than an individual necessity.[29]

Thus, since the Cultural Revolution the work environments of peasants and workers have been changed considerably in terms of sets of motivating mechanisms. The old material incentives have been modified and the extreme extrinsic reward elements (piece rates and bonuses) have been eliminated or drastically reduced. The new incentive elements, dwelling more on intrinsic recompense through cooperation and closer social relations, have been set in motion more widely. Now the roles of the actors in the work setting are being reshaped out of these opposite processes.

CHANGING ROLES OF CADRES, TECHNICIANS, WORKERS, PEASANTS: THE WORK SETTING

To appreciate more fully the major transformation in work attitudes and motivational dynamics being essayed in China, we look now at the roles that cadres and technicians play vis-a-vis workers and peasants and the new modes through which workers and peasants carry out their roles. In essence, the Chinese leaders are attempting to set up processes and social relations that are imbedded in daily factory and commune activities essential to serving the needs and wants of the inhabitants of the producing unit as well as those outside who will also enjoy the fruits of production. This means that a system of social control revolving around "serving the people" is being constructed, while the old system geared to maximizing profit and motivating with extrinsic instruments is being phased out.

Roles of Cadres and Technicians

The roles that workers and peasants play in factories and communes are determined to a considerable degree by how cadres and technicians are expected to and do in fact act out their parts. To the extent that the Maoist concept of a non-self-perpetuating bureaucracy free of the elitist ethos is realized, the "hired hand" mentality is expected to disappear and the possibilities of genuine worker and peasant self-management are expected to be increased. Furthermore, if cadres and technicians are effectively integrated into a collectivist human organization of the plant's or commune's division of labor, worker and peasant self-realization and activity to that end are more likely to be attained.[30]

Supervisory and technical personnel in the Chinese factory and commune are now called upon to carry heavy responsibilities without the expectation of considerable extrinsic reward either in material compensation or in assurance of rapid promotion and stellar careers. Their task is to serve the factory or commune well, and they know that serious failures invite dismissal from their leadership positions. Moreover, leaders are expected to be humble, work readily and cooperatively with workers and peasants, and display proletarian virtues. Here is one Chinese image of an exemplary factory leader:

> Like the rank-and-file workers, Chen Shih-jung wears an ordinary gray cotton suit, lives in a simple flat and cycles to work from his home to the mill in the city's outskirts. Before being told, we would never have spotted him as the top leader of the . . . Mill. This slim, middle-aged cadre joined the revolutionary struggle against Japanese aggression . . . when he was a boy of 13. Today, he is secretary of the mill's Party committee.[31]

The requirement that leaders behave in certain ways is buttressed by a set of institutional arrangements calculated to develop leaders of this type. These arrangements touch on the leaders' material recompense (direct and indirect), work styles and commitments, political and human awareness, responsiveness to criticism, and other aspects of their tasks in the social process of the factory or the commune and its numerous extensions.

So far as salaries in factories are concerned, cadres and technicians have graded salary steps analogous in form to the eight-grade wage scales used to compensate workers. Before the Cultural Revolution, these cadre and technician scales rose to maxima three and four times those for industrial workers. Since then, in line with Maoist mandates, pay for cadres and technicians has been telescoped and maxima in factories now range between ¥150 and ¥225 a month, one and a half to two times the industrial workers' maxima, and only about half the highest salaries paid government leaders in the PRC.[32]

On communes cadres' incomes have also been reined in. Depending on their level, they are paid either by the team in workpoints or by the state according to cadre wage scales. In the former situation cadres usually receive the top of the scale (ten workpoints in some instances, up to twelve in others). In the post-Cultural Revolution period, tighter rein has been kept on cadres' workpoints, reducing them in total; those paid according to state payments scales have had reductions as those scales have been cut back.*

---

*These generalizations were obtained by the author in the PRC in July 1973, and have also been reflected in the literature.

The Maoist expectations on leaders' behavior include humility, sensitivity to workers' and peasants' working conditions, awareness of the actual production process, etc. Chairman Mao was quite clear in demanding cadre participation in manual labor as an ongoing collectivist requirement:

> It is necessary to maintain the system of cadre participation in collective productive labour. The cadres of our Party and state are ordinary workers and not overlords sitting on the backs of people. By taking part in collective productive labour, the cadres maintain extensive, constant and close ties with the working people. This is a major measure of fundamental importance for a socialist system; it helps to overcome bureaucracy and to prevent revisionism and dogmatism.[33]

That such participation in labor will become a regular, meaningful involvement in the work process rather than an occasional, token event is clearly the desired result, with selected workers participating regularly for a short time in managerial positions. (In communes this pattern is also widely developed.) Regularization and reasonably full participation take a variety of forms. One factory pattern is to regularize a particular day of the week as one when cadres work alongside workers on various jobs, dealing with different work problems as they arise. (Public display of cadres' days at physical labor is often required.) Another way is to have a large number of cadres from higher administrative units go down en masse to spend a fixed period at various factories, mines, or communes, engaging in the physical labor aspects of production.[34]

The participation-in-physical-labor program is only one such mechanism aimed at keeping cadres in communication with production realities and developing collectivist styles, and it has been a long-standing practice. A more recent development, issuing from the Cultural Revolution as a more concentrated means for attacking bureaucratism, "commandism," and just plain arrogance, has been the setting up of May 7 Cadre Schools in the countryside, where cadres of all sorts are sent for extended periods, usually six months, to be "re-educated by the peasants" on a full-time basis. On May 7, 1966, during the Cultural Revolution, Chairman Mao issued an instruction that laid the basis for setting up schools where cadres "study Marxism and take part in collective labor in production. They also spend . . . time in the surrounding villages learning about life there. All this helps them to remold their world outlook and better take the stand of the laboring people."[35]

Cadres and technicians in factories also find themselves subject to institutionalized internal and external criticism mechanisms: they must respond to different collective constituencies as well as random individual complaints. Special meetings are held by the factory's leaders to solicit criticisms of the operation of the plant and the cadres' work style. A regular six-month criticism meeting—open-door rectification—is held in some factories to uncover problems through criticism. Ad hoc criticism sessions are periodically called at the behest of the party or revolutionary committee to deal with a pressing problem. Regular visits to enterprises consuming the factory's products are arranged to gather evaluations of the products and service. The factory's trade union group may hold sessions on the quality of political work, labor insurance, safety conditions, welfare, etc. Another form of criticism is the wall newspaper or poster, which appears in specified places in the factory and may be used by anyone to give vent to a grievance or complaint. A very powerful form of external criticism comes into play in a plant or commune when a campaign, such as the Lin Biao-Confucius movement of 1974, is launched throughout the country. The metaphorical criticism given nationwide prominence becomes the vehicle for searching criticism of numerous shortcomings, the local details of which can be utilized to document a more general complaint. For example, "restrain oneself and restore the rites" (used in connection with the Confucius criticism) translates into "putting material incentives in command" (overemphasizing material remuneration) or other such examples of negative practice.[36]

Expanding Roles of Workers

At the same time as cadres' and technicians' roles are more sharply defined in nonelitist and less preferential terms, at the same time as institutional mechanisms are devised to ensure that bureaucrats' consciousness is kept "pure" in the service of the people and that their activities are constantly subject to mass review and criticism, the opportunities for workers to exercise some participatory functions, formally and informally, have been increased. (Workers also play a role as representatives on government bodies outside the factories and on worker propaganda teams overseeing the universities in the locality.) The Chinese factory is a vital experimental organization attempting to adapt technical structure and function to human needs rather than the opposite. A set of mechanisms for such purposes, integrated into the production processes—routine and exceptional—has evolved and is utilized in varying degrees in factories throughout the country.

The Chinese worker is represented on the controlling bodies of the factory, the party and revolutionary committees, and is heavily involved in the criticism mechanisms that have been shaped in China over the last quarter of a century. Formally such devices in themselves do not indicate any startling differences between China and other industrial countries. The Chinese worker's vote has a qualified meaning, since party and revolutionary committee nominees usually need to be acceptable to party officials. The workers' votes, however, probably have a veto power. (More probably nominees who do not command popular support are not put forth.) Criticism mechanisms, unless integrated into the daily processes of the organization, are capable of becoming institutionalized rituals, though the Chinese criticism sessions seem to be quite alive and also seem to serve important purposes. But clearly, periodic voting and criticism would represent minimal kinds of worker involvement.

There are group mechanisms that the Chinese have cultivated since the 1950s that functionally involve workers as well as cadres and technicians directly and indirectly in operation decisions. They are all collective in form, though the group size varies according to the general function and its particular application, and they all change, in some ways, the conventional technical organization of the production process and develop intrinsic motivational modes. Whether through them, as the Chinese claim, "the rank and file [workers] take part in all aspects of management" remains to be seen.[37]

One collective form—the three-in-one combination—has been widely expanded since the Cultural Revolution, though its origins go back to the 1950s. It is a work group that brings together three different kinds of staff (usually workers or peasants, cadres, and technicians, but including other sets too, such as old, middle-aged, and young workers; three sets of cadres from different origins; consumer and producer workers and technicians; etc.) to deal with any number of work functions. Its functional existence aims at simulating creative work styles as well as undermining elitism, bureaucratic exclusivism, one-man decison-making, alienation, and other Maoist targets in the old line technical organization of work. Let us look at some examples, remembering that all factories do not have the same types since local initiative obtains.

First, there is the three-in-one economic management group for a factory. It is made up of workers, cadres, and technicians who participate in all phases of management: welfare, workers' living conditions, technology, production, and finance throughout the plant and at all levels—the plant, the shops, and the work groups. At the plant level the deputy chairmen of the revolutionary committee (cadres), heads of finance, heads of supply and marketing (technicians), and workers' representatives together deal with operating and technical problems as they arise. Similar groups function in the shops and among the work groups in regular and special activities—meetings, investigations, inspections—to assist plant leaders problems and to advise and check on these leaders.[38]

Other three-in-one purposes include cooperation, teaching, learning, and problem solving. Some of the specific uses to which these triple combinations are put are designing and developing new products, technical innovations, technical problems (repairing machines, adapting machines for new use, eliminating flaws in production quality, etc.), technical demonstrations (to transmit expertise from one group to another), evaluating new products, investigations of work performance, revising plant rules and regulations, etc. As the three-in-one groupings gather experience, their scope of activity widens and more members of each constituency get involved.[39]

Another collective form in which workers participate in the administration and management of some Chinese factories is the veteran workers' advisory group. The unit, made up of veteran workers with wide-ranging production experience and with high levels of political consciousness, attends all important party committee meetings and is involved in discussions of major questions affecting plant operations. It also executes investigative and technical tasks assigned to it by the party committee. The technical tasks undertaken include a wide set of issues arising from the various production operations of the plant. The limits of these activities are not clear, since some events occurring in the factory are unpredictable, yet the group may be called upon to assist in handling them if they appropriately can.[40]

Another method for worker input in management processes in some factories is provided in the organization of production groups, basic producing units of around fifty workers. The group has its production and trade union leaders (cadres) but also "five responsible members," workers elected by their peers, to assure worker participation in all decisions affecting the group. In one plant, the five workers are responsible explicitly for political propaganda, work operations, quality of work, accounting, safety, workers' welfare, and daily living conditions. The seven meet regularly on specified days of the week to deal with the work situation and problems that arise. On Saturdays, a general meeting is held with all the workers in the group to discuss production and management questions as well as publicly to commend outstanding workers. The cadre-worker unit involves itself in a wide range of events important to the workers' existence, not just to the technical management of production. For example, the five responsible worker-managers concern themselves, as a group and singly, with the illness of a workers' child (one makes a visit), with criticisms about conditions written on the group's wall newspaper, with personal problems of an individual worker, etc.[41]

Mass movements are also widely used in factories to deal with a variety of plant issues that usually are of a general nature and that lend themselves to inputs from the experiences of the mass of workers. As indicated above, Mao placed a high value on the creativity of the masses, and the notion "from the masses to the masses" is expected to be continuously implemented. Mass movements of wide range have been carried out for many years in PRC factories and elsewhere to accomplish numerous objectives: to lower costs, to raise productivity, to stimulate innovation, to develop aspects of decision-making, to improve proletarian work styles, etc. One factory application of the mass line approach dealt with the problem of changing plant rules and regulations. The workers in a shop met to discuss the current rules and regulations, analyzing strengths and shortcomings and discussing which ones were to be modified, left alone, or dropped. Every worker in the group drafted his or her proposed regulations, which were then coordinated and modified. A final draft was presented to the plant's three-in-one combination responsible for finally producing the new rules. That group edited the final draft and the new rules and regulations were then ready for trial performances.[42]

Workers also provide input in the formulation and acceptance of economic plan quotas or targets. The central planners in the government will set major targets, but their final legitimation requires a feedback process from the operating units via intervening responsible governmental and party agencies so that ultimate responsibility for achieving targets is based on opportunities to affect the setting of targets. Even longer range plans receive worker input. In a Kwangsi mine, for example, the tripling of output over a ten-year period was agreed upon by the miners after mass discussion under the leadership of the party committee. This discussion occurred after some workers expressed the view that such planning was for cadres, engineers, and technicians. The opposite view was raised and the miners were then heavily involved in the planning process. A three-in-one planning committee was organized for the entire mine with subgroups set up for the different work sections. Workers accounted for 80 percent of the committee membership and the ultimate agreement on the long-run target resulted after the process of mass and committee discussion.[43]

Activities of the trade union committees in Chinese factories also afford opportunities and provide channels for worker involvement in plant management. Trade union responsibility covers political and ideological indoctrination, spare time technical and cultural education, plant safety, social welfare and insurance administration, and the like. Workers are involved in study groups by their work group's trade union leader. Discussions of criticism campaigns often focus on factory questions such as "production in command," "bourgeois right," and "material incentives in command." They become a forum for the airing of grievances and criticism of plant policy, and are followed by an agenda for action.[44]

A counterpart to the periodic participation of cadres in productive labor is the assumption of managerial posts in plant departments and offices by selected workers. During the Cultural Revolution "workers' investigation groups" were created in factories to participate in management. The advent of the revolutionary committee put the worker groups in the background, but some revival of similar forms has taken place. For example, in the Shanghai Watch and Clock Parts Plant, worker participation in management positions is being cultivated. In the past the party committee selected workers for such posts at the same time as cadres went down to labor. Now the workers are recommended by their peers, approved by the party committee, subject to study classes in preparation, and then assigned to their posts. A new group of "worker-cadres" is being developed as part of the revolutionary process to eliminate one of the "three gaps," in this instance the gap between mental and physical labor.[45]

One of China's new ways of providing advanced training and education for workers is the July 21 College set up in factories during the Cultural Revolution. Curricula cover an array of technical and professional subjects and areas. These institutions, as well as parallel ones, not only provide workers with greater opportunities to be vertically mobile through advanced training (thus helping to bring an "end to monopoly of technology by a few intellectuals"), but also provide many workers with instructional and curriculum development roles. Educational and technical decisions on the scope, direction, and detailed linkages between actual work in the factory and instructional content are made by workers, technicians, and cadres.[46]

Though we have already discussed the use of wall newspapers in the context of cadres and technicians being subject to criticism, their use from the workers' standpoint bears repetition. The writing of a wall newspaper criticism may be an individual act (though it often is put up by a group of workers), but it usually generates collective responses, both from cadres-technicians and from other workers. In one plant, five workers put up a big-character poster criticizing party committee members for not having recently taken part in labor. The committee members responded with a poster accepting the criticism and calling a meeting to deal with the issue. A particular day for participation every week was announced. In another factory, the party committee decided to pay overtime to workers in response to worker pressure. A group of workers put up a wall newspaper objecting to this, saying, "One should work hard and aim at raising output quickly and not for monetary incentives." The party committee then reversed itself after discussion of the question.[47]

Not only do workers exercise criticism functions through factory wall newspapers, newsletters, and formal criticism sessions, but they also have access to the mass media to voice critical opinions and make policy suggestions. This kind of activity has a two-pronged effect so far as worker participation is concerned: it develops their skills as intellectuals (writers) who can effectively articulate policy positions for their coworkers and themselves and stand as models for other workers to emulate, and it reinforces the practice of looking at factory work decisions critically from the workers' point of view.[48]

Workers also seize important factory design and production initiatives that receive prominent acclaim by authorities as reflecting exemplary proletarian practice. Such initiatives include designing and producing new machines, overhauling and repairing defective or old equipment, building expanded work facilities, assisting backward work groups, reorganizing work groups, etc. For example, recently in the Shanghai No. 1 Machine Tool Plant, a technologically and politically advanced factory, a group of workers took such an initiative when they learned that a costly hobbing machine for making 6.3-meter gears was being ordered from abroad. The group aroused worker response by putting up a wall poster indicating their resolve to design and produce an 8-meter gear hobbing machine, thus carrying out "self-reliance." After they received support from the plant's party committee, the design and building of this machine, the first made in China, was completed successfully in about four months and received wide publicity. In the Shanghai No. 2 Welding Plant, workers constructed workshops and built their own machines. They also undertook to help in new construction projects in the community. In the Hangchow Combined Silk

Dyeing and Printing Plant, workers in a high-tension switch room decided to repair a boiler, insuring maximum safety in a refurbished unit.[49]

Peasants' Roles

Like workers, peasants play a variety of participatory roles. These include representation on party and revolutionary committees and three-in-one combinations, working as veterans to advise cadres and technicians, participation in mass movements in decision-making and problem solving, involvement in production plan resolution, teaching and study at May 7 universities, developing wall newspaper and other criticism modes, and working on peasant writer teams. Variations and extensions of the factory examples we have given abound on communes. In my visit to Huadong Commune outside Canton in July 1973, for example, I observed various examples of peasant involvement in technical work such as design and construction of hydroelectric turbines and farm machinery.

In the above discussion and analysis of the work setting with changing roles for cadres, technicians, and workers or peasants as the case varies, we are faced with a major question for which no solid answer is in our grasp: to what extent do the new roles and modes for greater worker or peasant participation actually function in China's factories and communes? Our answer must be speculative and tentative, since it is based on very little evidence and considerable amounts of nuance and inference. It is quite probable that most or all factories and communes have representative groups on which workers and peasants play some role. It is also probable that a minority of factories (perhaps something over a third) and communes (perhaps something less than a third) have a considerable amount of worker or peasant participation and complementary cadre-technician collectivist roles operating on a major scale. And it is likely that in the remaining factories and communes varying degrees of worker-peasant participation beyond representation and cadre-technician parallel roles are to be found—ranging from very little to considerable activity, depending on the CCP's participation policies.

The extent of worker-peasant and cadre-technical involvement in exemplary collectivist fashion is part of the larger question of worker-peasant activism and the effective implementation and extension of the mass line. The number of worker or peasant activists is relatively small, as is the number of "advanced" factories or communes. Similarly there is a small number of "backward" individuals or units, with most individuals and units falling in the middle. The party's goal is to increase the number of activist workers and peasants and advanced factories and communes over time in order to attain specific as well as general goals. In the area of collectivist managerial style the transformation of the work setting and the social relations among workers or peasants and cadres and technicians is a major objective in the movement toward communism and the elimination of the gap between mental and physical labor. The successful development of the new modes of management described above in some plants and communes is expected to be the basis for these advanced units being emulated by growing number of factories and communes. As the social control techniques devised, experimented with, modified, and extended in the advanced units are introduced and expanded in all plants and communes, more and more units are expected to become advanced.

THE PROBLEM OF DEVIANCE

Any system of social control, if it is to be generally effective, needs to provide formally or informally for the containment of deviant behavior—behavior that immediately undermines desired operational outcomes directly and that, over time, spreads infectiously to nondeviants. Ideally, authorities seek maximum conformity to behavior norms but plan social control mechanisms to deal with the widespread phenomena of nonconformity. Given the variety of less than desirable behavior and the many causes for such behavior, the mechanisms for social control of this perennial societal phenomenon must be inclusive enough to deal with a complex set of events.[50]

In the Chinese context, the problem of deviance must also be seen in the framework of compelling ideological mandates. As a revolutionary society overturning old institutions and ways of life as well as cultivating radically new attitudes and shaping new and markedly different structures and mechanisms, the Chinese environment is particularly confusing to conforming citizens, since they are confronted with old norms and new norms and it is not always clear which ones obtain under specific conditions. For example, in the incentive area the socialist principle of remuneration, which is the basis for material extrinsic work rewards, is set forth as proper and at the same time exhortation to work harder and longer and to reject the notion of "material incentives in command" is widely broadcast. This situation of changing and opposed norms compounds the difficulty of setting up proper means for controlling socially the behavior of the individual and the group.[51]

In fact, CCP leaders are not unaware of the difficulties of living with the old and the new alongside one another. They attempt to come to grips with the problem intellectually and operationally, Mao has said:

> In each thing there are contradictions between its new and its old aspects, and this gives rise to a series of struggles with many twists and turns. As a result . . . , the new aspect changes from being minor to being major and rises to predominance, while the old aspect changes from being major to being minor and gradually dies out. The moment the new aspect gains dominance over the old, the old thing changes qualitatively into a new thing.[52]

The problem of the old and the new and proper behavior in dealing with the resolution of the questions is linked to the broader issue of contradictions and their "correct handling." This opens up the operational issue of handling conformity and deviance through social control. In Mao's view, social control of contradictions takes two paths: one for "the enemy"—counterrevolutionaries, bureaucratic bourgeoisie, and the like—and one for "the people." For the first group the full force of the state is to be used if their behavior is deviant and obstructive. Contradictions among "the people," including deviant behavior, are to be handled carefully:

> . . . in no sense do we mean that coercive measures should be taken to settle ideological matters and questions involving the distinction between right and wrong among the people. . . . In settling [such] matters . . . , we can only use democratic methods, methods of discussion, of criticism, of persuasion and education; not coercive, high-handed methods. . . .[53]

In this context then, deviant behavior is to be expected. It will continue indefinitely and have to be contained by continuing class struggle, an ongoing process to be integrated into the day-to-day activities of all workers and peasants.[54]

In the work area there is a variety of issues, other than random negative deviancy, that may give rise to behavior by workers or peasants that flouts the widely publicized revolutionary norms and affects new or modified social mechanisms, including the array of incentives. These incentives, as we have indicated above, are important social conditioners calculated not only to stimulate greater and more skillful labor input, but also to cultivate the nascent proletarian, collectivist work style and ethos. Deviant behavior in work on the part of groups or of individual workers or peasants takes several forms, including:

1) pressing for increased material rewards (higher wages, bonuses, piece rates, more workpoints, greater fringe benefits, etc.);
2) poor work discipline (absenteeism, lax performance, etc.);
3) defying the law and migrating in search of jobs;
4) labor disputes (conflicts with cadres over work, slowdowns, strikes, etc.);
5) refusal to work; and
6) sabotage.

Since the establishment of the PRC, there have been numerous reports (official and other) of the types of deviant behavior listed above,[55] varying in type, importance, duration, and intensity. They continue to occur. The occurrence of such individual and group deviant behavior is testimony to some dysfunction in the social control mechanisms. The interesting questions, however, since deviant behavior is a universal phenomenon, are what social mechanisms the Chinese use to contain and reverse such behavior and how effective they are in achieving their ends.

In their approach to controlling individuals and groups, CCP leaders over time have attempted to achieve control more through inclusion than through alienation. They have, of course, used and still use both external and internal controls (external and internal to the basic operating groups) but, as one astute student of their ideology and organization puts it, they are concerned about "control of the man rather than of his performance."[56] They have since the 1950s shifted emphasis from external to internal controls, from economic to political controls. We turn, therefore, in our effort to throw light on the developing incentive system as a social control mechanism, to both external and internal patterns of dealing with deviance in work performance.

The array of external controls that have been used in China to help shape work performance follows the usual negative, disincentive patterns shaped in the Chinese mold. Included in this set of punitive methods of dealing with deviant behavior in factories and communes are wage and income loss as penalties, demotion, forced rustication (punitive *xiafang*), labor re-education, labor reform, prison, and other forms of coercion. In this type of negative social control mechanism there is an apparent extrinsic disincentive element. Specific undesirable performance is linked to the negative or punitive sanction with the expectation that such aversive conditioning will deter further nonconforming behavior. The individual's performance rather than his or her ideology is the object of control. This approach, in general, appeared to be more heavily emphasized during the 1950s; in more recent years, some of these mechanisms are still in operation, while others seem to have been abandoned.

Wage and workpoint penalties were built into incentive mechanisms during the 1950s. Various mechanisms, particularly piece rate types, followed the punitive or negative principle formally. For example, in the 1950s, one factory piece rate mechanism took both quantity and quality norms into account. If a certain quantity and quality standard was not fully met, only 92 to 94 percent of the standard pay was given to the worker. If the quality and quantity standards were not attained, no payment was received until that minimum was reached. In practice, however, this most negative part of the mechanisms was often not implemented. On communes, workpoint mechanisms following the same negative reward principle were also set up, but they too were often not rigorously followed. Similarly, demotion stood as an extrinsic disincentive mechanism, although such action was often avoided.[57]

The *xiafang* movement of transferring personnel down to the countryside to labor on farms or in factories was a widespread phenomenon that had different aspects to it at different times. Though it mainly affected intellectuals, technicians, and cadres whose political behavior was unacceptable, and after the Cultural Revolution was used in a nonpunitive context, it was often viewed by workers as a punitive mechanism and it was sometimes used in that way in the earlier period for nonconforming work performance. It served for factory workers as a disincentive for a variety of minor work patterns that violated the set of stipulated work norms.[58]

Where nonconformity or deviance on the job goes beyond the minor misdemeanor type of behavior, the authorities have more formal external means of dealing with the transgressors. According to the severity of the deviance and the discretion of the authorities at the work site, those individuals who violate labor discipline norms can be sent to labor re-education or labor reform units. A network of labor correctional camps set up in the 1950s is used for political as well as other violations of behavior norms and legal statutes. Those subject to labor re-education, the less extreme of the two corrective arrangements, can be sent to such camps through administrative action taken by the offender's work unit and the public security authorities. The job-connected offenses that might subject someone to labor re-education include not being engaged in "proper employment," having the capacity but for a long period refusing to labor, and not obeying work assignments, employment arrangements, or work transfers. The mere violation of codes of work conduct is not sufficient for someone to be sent to labor re-education; there must be numerous violations in the face of "repeated education" for the regulations to be invoked. This has left a wide area of administrative discretion to cadres.[59]

To be subject to formal criminal prosecution, workers and peasants must commit illegal acts rather than fail to carry out labor discipline as in the above instances. Acts of sabotage or counterrevolutionary acts on the job (or elsewhere) subject workers or peasants to criminal prosecution. Upon conviction they are sent to corrective labor camps in the countryside where they are compelled "to reform themselves through labor and become new persons."[60] This type of punitive action against workers or peasants occurs in extreme cases where the element of "contradiction" is between "the people and the enemy."

Beyond reform by labor, in the continuum of negative or punitive actions by Chinese social controllers, there are the extreme actions of sentencing individuals to prisons and detention houses as well as using force by the PLA or police. For example, in a set of fifteen labor disputes, including strikes and violent incidents, in only two were extreme sanctions imposed: in one strike in which cadres were beaten up, two leaders were executed and several others sentenced to prison; in the second, a workers' demonstration at a plant director's office, three of the demonstration leaders were imprisoned as counterrevolutionaries. Clearly, in both instances the "enemy" were being punished.[61] These ultimate instruments of the state stand as potential means and probably act as deterrents, though their deterrence impact is a function of how frequently they are used and how widely that is known to potential violators. The use of troops in serious disorders, however, is an ultimate act aimed at stopping continued disorder rather than a set instrument in the array of disincentive mechanisms.

In the 1950s, as the CCP set up the kinds of external controls just reviewed, controls borrowed from the Soviet institutional armory, it was also developing other means of dealing with nonconforming or less than ideal behavior in factories and on communes. During the GLF and the Cultural Revolution, these techniques were further cultivated and extended. They are now prominently employed as a means of galvanizing workers and peasants (all citizens, in fact) to the tasks necessary to advance revolutionary values and aims. These techniques of social control, aimed at shaping the person as some one who is continually internalizing the established and emerging values of the revolution, are internal in process: they are exercised within the group (production team, brigade, commune, work team, shift, plant) by group members—"insiders" —and they function by drawing the individual worker or peasant more deeply into the group.

As one looks at the methods of internal social control exercised by the CCP to deal with deviancy, an interesting point emerges. They are much the same as the intrinsic or internal incentive mechanisms used to encourage and stimulate workers and peasants to perform better. The internal or intrinsic mechanisms, though tuned to deal with particular problems and achieve specific results, rely fundamentally on involving the individual and the group in the larger purposes of the collective whole—the world revolutionary movements, China, the province, the country, the factory or the commune, the work shift or the brigade. The aim is to socialize the individual so thoroughly that his or her sense of identification with the group becomes an overwhelming internal force in which the values and aims of the group have been effectively assimilated and guide individual behavior. If deviancy involves rejection of the group norms, the antidote is not to reject the deviant, but to work harder to draw him or her into the group, to negate the deviant behavior through more complete identification with the group, and to play on the deviant act as separation from the group with its attendant guilt.[62]

Nonconforming work behavior such as pressing for wage increases and bonuses, being absent from work frequently, or carrying out work tasks in other lax ways is far from uncommon in China. It is dealt with in various ways in which collective behavior aims are projected and reinforced. For example, late in 1974 a factory party committee, after much pressure from some workers, agreed to pay overtime. A group of workers then put up a wall newspaper objecting to the policy change. This objection led to a series of meetings at which criticism of the change in policy and its conflict with Maoist norms was mounted. Eventually the party committee reversed itself and the norm of "politics in command" rather than "wages in command" was reaffirmed and reinforced.[63]

In this episode, as in other departures from norms of revolutionary behavior, the struggle against deviance is socialized in mass meetings triggered by an informal criticism. In similar fashion, as we have seen above, a mass meeting might be called to initiate (and stimulate) participation in a campaign to design a new machine rather than purchase it abroad. Thus, in both instances, the desired behavior is collectively asserted, in one instance to counter and reverse the nonconforming action, in the other to move on to a new application of the principle of group initiative. In both situations motivating workers toward "correct" behavior is achieved socially through unifying rather than alienating actions: criticism sessions and group involvement are the main modes.

In other circumstances of less than expected work performance, say poor levels of output, similar solidifying or unifying processes would be used to achieve the goal of conforming to the norm of responsible, diligent work effort. A Sian factory that had performed well, overfulfilling its production quotas over time, began to be slack, and in the first quarter of 1975 production was adversely affected. After investigation cadres decided the causes were poor ideological and political education. The party committee then developed a set of prescriptions. Over 120 study classes were held, over ninety meetings were held to exchange work experiences, and over 200 articles were written on theory and practice. The study classes were used "to help [workers] correct their errors." Cadres were also subject to worker criticism on their ideological failings. The reported results were enhanced "unity" and improved performance.[64] Here too the style and mode of approach is to focus on positive work behaviors.

In similar fashion, within and between plants or commune brigades and teams, "advanced" units are often used to help "backwardness," which is a euphemism for lax or less than responsible action in production. In other units, backwardness may reflect the need for more training or better leadership. In either case, however, the nonconforming or less than desired performance is approached positively, to provide reinforcement through demonstration by and identification with the "advanced" or exemplary group of workers or peasants.[65]

Role models, positive and negative, are also used in a variety of ways to counteract nonconforming performance and redefine and reinforce the "correct" way, as well as to highlight and reinforce exemplary performance. In all situations internalization of revolutionary values and behavior is a primary objective. Where negative models are used, nonconforming behavior of individuals and groups (with its attendant guilt feelings) is identified as an error of the individual or group but the main onus for the "incorrect" behavior falls on the negative model, say Liu Shaoqi or Lin Biao, who pursued the "wrong" line and misled cadres, workers, and peasants. The latter made mistakes, as all people do, but these mistakes can be rectified through continuous class struggle and through uniting with one another to follow the revolutionary line. Cadres are "urged to . . . deeply criticize the counterrevolutionary line of Liu Shaoqi and Lin Biao as well as their crimes in splitting the party and the revolutionary ranks; repudiate bourgeois factionalism; . . . strengthen revolutionary unity; enhance the sense of revolutionary discipline . . ." and thus avoid and counter behavior that fails to carry forward ideological objectives.[66]

Another example, involving a positive role model directly, occurred in Hangchow, where the Hangchow Gearbox Factory workers and cadres actively interacted with counterparts in the Hangchow Ballbearing Works, which had "lagged in production" and "suffered from the influence of Lin Biao's counter-revolutionary revisionist line and interference from bourgeois factionalism." The Gearbox Factory, a model after the example of Daqing, sent personnel to the Ballbearing Works who conveyed to the plant's party committee concern about their situation and reminded them of party policy requiring certain norms of performance. After this, it was reported, party committee members and workers' representatives were sent to the Gearbox Factory for a "study visit" to see how that factory followed party policy mandates and how the Ballbearing Works could correct its performance. Upon return to their factory these representatives met with cadres and workers to report on their visit and on the measures that had to be taken. Then study, criticism, and wide publicity on what the Gearbox Factory's situation was and how it could be emulated were undertaken.[67] Here, again, the approach was to attempt to unify cadres and workers to solve a common problem that was not theirs alone but belonged to the wider community, which could be depended upon to provide support and instruction.

In more serious deviancy, such as general worker or peasant disaffection that leads to grave production decline or to labor disputes including strikes, internal social controls are also employed. (I indicated above in my discussion of external controls that in such labor conflicts troops might be used in the conventional way to put down disorders.) Our information on serious disaffection or disorder of this sort comes from official sources or outside sources several times removed from the origin of the trouble, and thus has to be used tentatively. Another difficulty is that the events are quite recent so that the information is a first generation flow and still incomplete.

Since early 1975—and possibly going back in a continuous line for Hangchow to early 1974—there have been unrest, lax labor discipline, strikes, and other labor disorder in some Chinese factories. Most official publicity on these events has focused on thirteen plants in Hangchow, where PLA units said to exceed 10,000 in number were sent to the factories to help contain and improve the situation. Reports of similar factory and mine unrest in Shanghai, Hsuchow, Wuhan, Canton, and Nanchang, as well as at points in a number of provinces, have also been received. The causes of the unrest seem to stem mainly from failure of workers to have economic (wage) demands met. In Nanchang the reailway workers became disaffected because bonuses were abolished. "Factionalism"—strife among groups in factories—has been much publicized in the official media and seems to have risen from conflict over material incentive issues.[68]

In complicated circumstances such as these, it is difficult to do more than suggest the techniques that are being used to contain and reverse deviant behavior. Certain patterns are clear, nevertheless, and these will be discussed. First, it is evident that both external and internal social control measures are being put into operation. For example, one report is that "many workers in Hangchow were sent to re-education camps after major strikes and factional battles there."[69] The calling in of the PLA in itself involves both internal and external control, since that organization is viewed on the one hand as a model for production and a unifying agent (a function significantly carried out during and after the Cultural Revolution) and thus is held in high esteem by many Chinese, and on the other hand as a military and security force capable of using its power coercively. Thus, even if the PLA in its mission to restore behavior norms in the factory did not use force—and there have been no reports yet of violence and the use of force—its presence must have had some impact of external (coercive) control on recalcitrant workers.

So far as internal controls are concerned, the authorities, quite predictably, have stressed the social controls exercised by the PLA that are unifying rather than alienating and coercive. The PLA, which has a long history of production and social service and is a quite popular organization, has been reported involved in a variety of activities in plants where labor unrest was widespread. In addition to "participating in productive industrial labor," setting examples for workers by diligent and long-lasting work despite intense hot weather, "carrying out mass work, propagating the important instructions of Chairman Mao," holding discussion meetings with workers, helping "workshops to publish special columns on grasping revolution and promoting production"—in a word acting as model workers and propagandists—the PLA units have also acted out the mandate to serve the people.[70] In Hsuchow, Kiangsu province, the PLA unit assigned to a coal mine carried on some service activities such as acting as barbers, cutting grass in the dormitory areas, and providing health care for the miners.[71]

CONCLUSION

From our above description and analysis of work incentives in the context of social control and deviance in China, certain conclusions seem clear:

1. Looking at the historical development of work incentives since 1949 reveals that the CCP leaders have fashioned an incentive system that is de-emphasizing external or extrinsic incentives such as wages, bonuses, and piece rates and emphasizing internal or intrinsic incentives such as cooperative emulation, mass production movements, collective three-in-one task forces, worker participation in management, and cadre participation in physical labor. The ideological objective is patent: to supersede material incentive, a remnant of

bourgeois society, with social incentives that develop toward the communist remuneration principle of distribution according to need.[72]

2. So far as social control to achieve these incentive as well as other aims is concerned, the goal appears to be to maximize social control at the basic working (and living) level and to cultivate internal rather than external social control mechanisms.

3. Deviance in work settings is a significant problem, perhaps exacerbated by the confusion of changing norms as well as the urgent demands of a new, revolutionary work style and ethos. The social controls aimed at containing and reversing deviant behavior in the work environment parallel those employed to stimulate work enthusiasm: there are external and internal control mechanisms. The external mechanisms are familiar and entail varying degrees of negative social sanctions and coercion, though even these have internal elements. The internal mechanisms to control worker deviance are often the same as those aimed at heightening worker input and output: the use of role models, criticism sessions, and mass meetings and involvements. They focus on uniting the deviant with the rest of the social group through positive actions taken by members of the group.

4. Certain general patterns of changing social control, true in varying degrees for the entire society, emerge in the incentive area. Social controls are moving from one ideal type toward another: a) from an economic to a political emphasis (from the market to direct decisions), b) from an external to an internal emphasis, and c) from the party center to the base operating units, with emphasis on self-reliance. In the movement from one ideal type to another, with both in operation at the same time, the confusion that often prevails may itself generate or encourage deviance. Thus the transformation of social controls is doomed to continuous struggle over clinging to or returning to the social controls scheduled for ultimate disappearance.

5. The CCP leadership, not unexpectedly, is faced with major problems of developing social controls consonant with the long-range objectives of communism. In the incentive area, the attempt to de-emphasize material reward has met resistance, and even where a more ideologically acceptable incentive system is in operation, periodic backsliding occurs. Maoist ideology expects such deviance to continue to occur and relies on heightened awareness of such "contradictions" and continuous class struggle to transform the contradictions while the socialist and communist elements of the system are nurtured. The fundamental question of whether continuous class struggle with succeeding campaigns against "bourgeois right" and other negative continuities of the past can effectively change China's masses without a major upheaval is a still open question about the efficacy of the old and new social controls that CCP ideology dictates and its cadres implement and modify.

NOTES

1. For a classical statement on social control, see Edward Alsworth Ross, *Social Control* (Cleveland: Case Western Reserve University Press, 1969). A view of social control and solidarity that informs my views is Emile Durkheim, *The Division of Labor in Society* (New York: Macmillan, 1933). A useful application of the framework to a most important area of the economy is found in John M. Clark, *Social Control of Business* (New York: McGraw-Hill, 1939).

2. Ross, *Social Control*, pp. 89-375 and Elaine Cumming, *Systems of Social Regulation* (New York: Atherton, 1968), pp. 4-6.

3. See Ross, op. cit., pp. 417-27; Durkheim, op. cit., Robert B. Edgerton, *Deviant Behavior and Cultural Theory* (Reading, Mass.: Addison-Wesley, 1973); and Fred E. Katz, *Autonomy and Organization: The Limits of Social Control* (New York: Random House, 1968).

4. See the CCP's early commitment to a "rational low-wage policy," Charles Hoffmann, *Work Incentive Practices and Policies in the People's Republic of China, 1953-1965* (Albany, N.Y.: State University of New York Press, 1967), pp. 14-15.

5. Some of the ideological elements discussed here and below will be found in Yuan Ching, "An Important Question in Production Relations," *Hung Ch'i*, no. 5, (1975) in British Broadcasting Corporation, *Summary of World Broadcasts* (hereafter SWB), FE4905, May 16, 1975, pp. BII6-BII10; Wu Chang, "Study Some Political Economy," *Hung Ch'i*, no. 8 in U.S. Foreign Broadcast Information Service, *Daily Report: People's Republic of China* (hereafter FBIS), no. 166, (August 26, 1975): E1-E3; Chi Yen, "Ideological Weapon for Restricting Bourgeois Right," *Peking Review*, May 30, 1975, pp. 7-11; Fang Hai, "Smash the Bourgeois Intellectual Fetters," *Hsueh-hsi yu p'i-p'an*, no. 5 (May 18, 1975) in U.S. Consulate, Hong Kong, *Selections from the People's Republic of China Magazines* (hereafter SPRCM), no. 825 (June 16, 1975): 5-10; and Yao Wen-yuan, "On the Social Basis of the Lin Piao Anti-Party Clique," *Peking Review*, March 7, 1975, pp. 5-10.

6. For an official view of the new strategy, see Yang Ling, "Agriculture: Foundation of the National Economy," *Peking Review*, October 18, 1960.

7. On the Chinese position concerning the "law of value," see "Socialist Construction and Class Struggle in the Field of Economics," *Hong Qi*, no. 2 (1970): 7 abridged in *Da Gong Bao*, Hong Kong, February 19-25, 1970. On a more recent view of Chinese economic principles, including commodity production, see Wu Chang, "Study Some Political Economy," op. cit.

8. For a review of work incentive policies during this period, see Hoffmann, *Work Incentive Practices*, Chapter 5. For the industrial setting, see Carl Riskin, "Workers' Incentives in Chinese Industry," in U.S. Congress, Joint Economic Committee, *China: A Reassessment of the Economy* (Washington: Government Printing Office, 1975), pp. 199-224.

9. See Hoffmann, op. cit., Chapters 2-4 and his *The Chinese Worker* (Albany, N.Y.: State University of New York Press, 1974), Chapter 4 for the patterns of incentives.

10. Hoffmann, *Work Incentive Practices*, pp. 17-27.

11. Ibid., pp. 31-34; State Council, "Notification on the Issuance of a Program of Wage Scales for the Workers of State Organs," translated in U.S. Joint Publications Research Service (hereafter JPRS), no. 35,455, (May 11, 1966): 1-55; Barry Richman, "Ideology and Management: The Chinese Oscillate," *Columbia Journal of World Business*, January-February 1971, pp. 23-32; and "Ideology and Management: Communism and Compromise," Ibid., May-June 1971, pp. 45-58.

12. Hoffmann, op. cit., Chapter 3.

13. Ibid., pp. 58-68.

14. Ibid., pp. 68-74.

15. Stephen Andors, "Factory Management and Political Ambiguity, 1961-63," *China Quarterly*, July/September 1974, pp. 435-76 and "Only by Regularly Taking Part in Labor will Cadres Be Able to Maintain Close Ties with the Masses," *Jen-min jih-pao*, August 30, 1964 in JPRS, no. 27, 303 (November 10, 1964): 20-22.

16. Hoffmann, *The Chinese Worker*, pp. 62-67, 102-03, 183.

17. See "What Kind of Question Is That About 'Tangible Means of Control'?" *Jen-min jih-pao*, July 19, 1975, p. 3 in FBIS, no. 147 (July 30, 1975): E1-E2.

18. Hoffmann, *The Chinese Worker*, p. 155.

19. Ibid., p. 157 and information obtained by the author in China in July 1973. See also Chung Shih, "The Dictatorship of the Proletariat and Bourgeois Rights," *Hung Chi'i*, no. 9 (1975) in FBIS, no. 177 (September 11, 1975): E1-E4 for the official position on bourgeois right and the implications for material incentive as well as the clarion call for mass campaigns against ideological backsliding. *Renmin jibao*, July 19, 1975, p. 3, deals with the problem of material incentive.

20. See State Council, "Notification on the Issuance of a Program of Wage Scales"; Hoffmann, *The Chinese Worker*, pp. 98-104; New York *Times*, July 27, 1975, p. 12; and FBIS, no. 144 (July 25, 1975), Tokyo radio broadcast, July 22, 1975, p. A5. Visitors to the PRC have told me that top research personnel receive about ¥350-¥375, which is slightly higher than the maximum for senior professors in universities such as Tsinghua, Peking, and Futan.

21. Data obtained by the author in China in July 1973.

22. See Barry Richman, "Ideology and Management: The Chinese Oscillate," *Columbia Journal of World Business*, January-February 1971, pp. 23-32 on perquisites for cadres.

23. See SWB, FE4977, August 9, 1975, pp. BII4-BII7; FBIS, no. 169, August 29, 1975, pp. G2-G3; FBIS, no. 142, July 23, 1975, pp. G3-G4; and FBIS, no. 77, April 21, 1975, pp. K1-K4.

24. See D. Gordon White, "The Politics of *Hsia-hsiang* Youth," *China Quarterly*, July/September 1974, pp. 491-517 for an interesting and useful analysis of sending youth to the countryside. On the socialization of labor allocation, see Hoffmann, *The Chinese Worker*, pp. 65-67.

25. See Martin King Whyte, "The Tachai Brigade and Incentives for the Peasant," *Current Scene*, August 15, 1969, pp. 1-13.

26. For the roles that ideology and organization play in China, see Franz Schurmann, *Ideology and Organization in Communist China* (Berkeley: University of California Press, 1968), second edition, passim.

27. On Dazhai, see, e.g., "The Tachai Road," *Peking Review*, October 4, 1974, pp. 18-25 and "National Conference on Learning from Tachai in Agriculture," *Peking Review*, September 19, 1975, p. 3.

28. See, e.g., "Relying on the Masses to Consolidate Proletarian Dictatorship," *Peking Review*, July 25, 1975, pp. 5-7 and "Get Rid of the Idea of Bourgeois Right, Contribute Toward Combating and Preventing Revisionism," *Kuang-ming Jih-pao*, May 24, 1975 in U.S. Consulate, Hong Kong, *Survey of People's Republic of China Press* (hereafter SPRCP), June 12, 1975, pp. 122-25.

29. See Hoffmann, *Work Incentive Practices*, pp. 35-42 for details of workers' social insurance and Hoffmann, *The Chinese Worker*, Chapter 6 for a general treatment of workers' housing, food, etc.

30. See SWB, FE4939, June 26, 1975, p. BII6, Changchun broadcast on human relationships in production, June 21, 1975.

31. "Leaders and Workers are Like Fish and Water," *China Reconstructs*, January 1974, p. 2 and "Running a Plant by Proletarian Revolutionary Spirit," *Peking Review*, August 1, 1975, pp. 17-18.

32. Hoffmann, *The Chinese Worker*, pp. 98-104.

33. Quoted in *Peking Review*, April 11, 1975, p. 16.

34. For some examples, see *China Reconstructs*, January 1974, pp. 2-4; FBIS, no. 49 (March 12, 1975): H4-H5, Wuhan broadcast, March 10, 1975 and no. 216 (November 17, 1974): K1-K2, Shihchiachuang broadcast, November 6, 1974; and "Cadres Taking Part in Collective Productive Labour," *Peking Review*, April 11, 1975, pp. 15-20.

35. "The Nanniwan May 7 Cadre School," *China Reconstructs*, July 1974, p. 5-7.

36. *China Reconstructs*, January 1974, p. 4 and January 1975, pp. 8-15.

37. *China Reconstructs*, January 1974, p. 5. See also Andors, "Factory Management and Political Ambiguity" for the GLF forms of three-in-one combinations.

38. *China Reconstructs*, January 1974, pp. 5-6 and Charles Bettelheim, *Cultural Revolution and Industrial Organization in China: Changes in Management and the Division of Labor* (New York: Monthly Review, 1974), pp. 21-32.

39. See FBIS, no. 135 (July 12, 1972): C1, Peking broadcast, July 8, 1972, for the role of a three-in-one combination in Anhwei factory; Richman, *Industrial Society in Communist China* (New York: Random House, 1970), pp. 58, 251, 258, and 276; *China Reconstructs*, January 1974, pp. 7-8; and *Peking Review*, June 13, 1975, pp. 17-20.

40. *China Reconstructs*, May 1975, pp. 40-41.

41. *China Reconstructs*, January 1974, pp. 5-6.

42. Ibid., pp. 7-8. See also Hoffmann, *The Chinese Worker*, p. 117.

43. See FBIS, no. 137 (July 16, 1975): 43-44, Kwangsi broadcast on long-term plans, July 15, 1975.

44. Ibid., p. 6; FBIS, no. 102 (May 24, 1974): M1-M2, Lanchow broadcast, May 19, 1974, on trade unions and criticism experiences; FBIS, no. 127 (July 1, 1974): J3-J5, Kunning broadcast, June 29, 1974, on Lin Piao-Confucius criticism by trade union groups; SWB, FE4866, April 1, 1975, pp. BII25-BII26, New China News Agency broadcast, March 20, 1975, on the role of a Shanghai trade union and discussion of theorist groups; SWB, FE4898, May 8, 1975, BII9-BII10 and FE4899, May 9, 1975, BII10-BII11; and Hoffmann, *The Chinese Worker*, Chapter 5.

45. FBIS, no. 141 (July 22, 1975): G3-G4, Shanghai broadcast on selected workers managing, July 18, 1975.

46. FBIS, no. 85 (May 1, 1975): G4-G5, Peking broadcast, April 28, 1975, on workers' technical training; and FBIS, no. 131 (July 8, 1975): G1-G3, Peking broadcast, July 5, 1975, on Shanghai July 21 College.

47. *China Reconstructs*, January 1975, pp. 8-10; *China News Summary*, no. 555 (February 19, 1975) on demands for higher wages and labor unrest; and SWB, FE4836, March 1, 1975, BII32, Wuhan broadcast, February 18, 1975.

48. *China News Summary*, no. 568 (Mary 28, 1975) on proletarian dictatorship in factories and FBIS, no. 129 (July 3, 1975): Hi-H2, Wuhan broadcast, June 30, 1975, on murdered cadre.

49. FBIS, no. 110, (June 6, 1975): G3-G4, Peking broadcast, June 6, 1975, on hobbing machine; no. 120 (June 20, 1975): M2, Sian broadcast, June 19, 1975, on improvement in worker relations; and no. 122 (June 24, 1975): G4, Tsinan broadcast, June 22, 1975, on steel plant boosting production. See also SWB, FE4939, June 26, 1975, BII9-10, Tsinan broadcast, June 22, 1975, on drive for steel production; FBIS, no. 134 (July 11, 1975): G2-G3, Foochow broadcast, July 8, 1975, on Daqing spirit at vinylon plant; and FBIS, no. 143 (July 24, 1975): G2-G3, Hangchow broadcast, July 21, 1975, on workers, cadres, and technicians studying theory.

50. See Edgerton, op. cit., pp. 7-10, for the framework of deviant behavior and more particularly for discussion of explanations of deviance and nondeviant behavior variation.

51. See "Develop the Socialist New Things," *Hung Ch'i*, no. 12 (1974) in FBIS, no. 231 (November 29, 1974): E3-E8 for a view of the dialectical relation between "old" and "new" things.

52. Quoted in ibid., p. E4.

53. Mao Tse-tung, *On the Correct Handling of Contradictions Among the People* (Peking: Foreign Languages Press, 1960), pp. 15-16.

54. Ibid., pp. 1-27. This point, made almost in passing by Mao in this statement of the late 1950s, has become a major strategy since the Cultural Revolution and is today stressed in the campaigns against bourgeois right and for dictatorship of the proletariat. See, e. g., Liang Hua, "Do a Good Job in Ideological Education work," *Hung Ch'i*, no. 7 (July 1, 1975) in SPRCM, no. 831 (July 28, 1975): 11-13. A review of labor disputes including strikes appears in Hoffmann, *The Chinese Worker*, pp. 144-50.

55. In *On the Correct Handling*, p. 59, Mao refers to strikes in 1956 as one type of contradiction among the people. Other officials place similarly discussed strikes in the same ideological context. See, e.g., Edgar Snow, *The Other Side of the River* (New York: Random House, 1961), p. 240. In line with this position, the right to strike is set forth in the new Constitution of the People's Republic of China (adopted January 17, 1975 by the Fourth National People's Congress), Article 28, Chapter 3. See *Peking Review*, January 24, 1975, p. 17.

56. Schurmann, *Ideology and Organization*, p. 315. See pp. 315ff. for an insightful analysis of the Chinese control system.

57. Hoffmann, *Work Incentive Practices*, pp. 22-24 and 49-51.

58. Schurmann, op. cit., pp. 91, 137-38, and 182-83.

59. Martin King Whyte, "Corrective Labor Camps in China," *Asian Survey*, March 1973, pp. 255-56. See also Jerome Alan Cohen, *The Criminal Process in the People's Republic of China 1949-1963* (Cambridge: Harvard University Press, 1968), pp. 249-51.

60. Cohen, *The Criminal Process*, p. 589.

61. Hoffmann, *The Chinese Worker*, pp. 146-47.

62. See Edgerton, op. cit., pp. 1-3 and 7-10.

63. *China News Summary*, no. 555, (February 19, 1975).

64. SWB, FE4971, August 2, 1975, pp. BII8-BII9.

65. See Hoffmann, *The Chinese Worker*, pp. 119-21 and 137.

66. SWB, FE4967, July 29, 1975, p. BII2.

67. SWB, FE5006, September 13, 1975, p. BII16-BII17.

68. New York *Times*, July 29, August 12 and 19, and October 10, 1975; *What's Happening on the Chinese Mainland* (Taipei), September 15, 1975; *China News Summary*, no. 577 (August 6, 1975) and no. 578 (August 13, 1975); SWB, FE4967, July 29, 1974, pp. BII2-BII3; SWB, FE4989, August 23, 1975, pp. BII4-BII5; and FBIS, no. 179 (September 15, 1975): G6-G7.

69. New York *Times*, July 29, 1975, p. 4.

70. SWB, FE4967, July 29, 1975, p. BII5.

71. New York *Times*, August 19, 1975, p. 3.

72. See Charles Bettelheim, op. cit., for an exposition, based on extended visits to Chinese factories, of the process of developing collectivist work styles in Chinese factories.

This glossary is designed to supplement the text. In the text, English language translations of important Chinese terms and phrases are accompanied by their *pinyin* romanizations given in parentheses. Readers may locate the Chinese character and Wade-Giles equivalents for textual terms and phrases by referring to the center column of the glossary where *pinyin* romanizations are ordered alphabetically. The character equivalents are presented in the left-hand column, first in simplified form and then, where appropriate, in standard form. Wade-Giles equivalents are presented in the right-hand column.

Chinese Characters	*Pinyin* Romanizations	Wade-Giles Romanizations
扒	ba	pa
暴风骤雨 （暴風驟雨）	Baofeng zhouyu	Pao-feng chou-yü
你甲	baojia	pao-chia
保卫科 （保衛科）	baowei ke	pao-wei k'o
本身	benshen	pen-shen
本质 （本質）	benzhi	pen-chih
避过这个运动却避不了用无体直的另一个运动（避過這個運動卻避不了用無體直的另一個運動）	biguo zheige yundong que bibuliao yong wu ti zhi di ling yi ge yundong	pi-kuo che-ko yün-tung ch'üeh pi-pu-liao yung wu t'i chih ti ling i-ko yün-tung
毕业 （畢業）	biye	pi-yeh

208

pinyin	Wade-Giles	汉字
bianfang qu jumin zheng	pien-fang ch'ü chu-min cheng	边防区居民证（边防区居民证）
bianfang tongxing zheng	pien-fang t'ung-hsing cheng	边防区通行证（边防区通行证）
biaoxian de kuakua·qi tan	piao-hsien te k'ua-k'ua ch'i t'an	表现得待（誇）得其误（誤）
bu ji cai li wu li di man gan xingwei	pu-chi ts'ai li wu li ti man kan hsing-wei	不计（针）财（财）理物理 的曼（蛮）干行为（為）
bu wen bu li bu guan bu guanxin	pu wen pu li pu kuan pu kuan-hsin	不匀（問）不理不管不关心
bupiao	pu-p'iao	布票
cheng gong ban shi	ch'eng kung pan shih	承公办（辦）事
cheng yi	ch'eng i	诚（誠）意
chengshi jumin zheng	ch'eng-shih chu-min cheng	城市居民证
chikui zui duo	ch'ih-k'ui tsui to	吃亏（虧）最多

Chinese Characters	Pinyin Romanizations	Wade-Giles Romanizations
创业史 (劉業史)	*Chuang ye shi*	*Ch'uang yeh shih*
打一批孤一批多（勞）改	da yi pi, zhua yi pi lao gai	ta i p'i, chua i p'i lao kai
地總（總）	Di Zong	Ti Tsung
地下工丁（獻）	dixia gongchang	ti-hsia kung-ch'ang
丁玲	Ding Ling	Ting Ling
动机（動機）	dongji	tung-chi
对读书目的没认正確的有伯你公儿（對讀書目的忍識正確的有伯你公之我）	dui dushu mudi renshi zhengque di you baifen zhi ji	tui tu-shu mu-ti jen-shih cheng-ch'üeh ti yu pai-fen chih chi
发（發）	fa	fa
翻旧帳（翻舊帳）	fan jiu zhang	fan chiu chang

210

副食品票	fushipin piao	fu-shih-p'in p'iao
搞上缴	gao shang jiao	kao shang chiao
革命的现实主义(藏)和革命的浪漫主义(藏)的结合	geming di xianshi zhuyi he geming di langman zhuyi di jiehe	ke-ming ti hsien-shih chu-i ho ke-ming ti lang-man chu-i ti chieh-ho
个(個)人成份	geren chengfen	ko-jen ch'eng-fen
个人名利动儿(個人名利動機)	geren mingli dongji	ko-jen ming-li tung-chi
个(個)人名利思想	geren mingli sixiang	ko-jen ming-li ssu-hsiang
工业(業)品票	gongyepin piao	kung-yeh-p'in p'iao
雇员(僱員)	guyuan	ku-yuan
果(菓)	guo	kuo
过关(過關)	guo guan	kuo kuan

Chinese Characters	Pinyin Romanizations	Wade-Giles Romanizations
过得了这个这动过不了另一个这动 (通得了这個運動過不了另一個運動)	guodeliao zheige yundong guobuliao ling yi ge yundong	kuo-te-liao che-ko yün-tung kuo-pu-liao ling i ko yün-tung
好子	hao	hao
浩然	Hao Ran	Hao Jan
黑人黑户	hei ren hei hu	hei jen hei hu
红(紅)旗	*Hong Qi*	*Hung Ch'i*
戶籍	huji	hu-chi
戶籍簿	huji bu	hu-chi pu
戶籍科	huji ke	hu-chi k'o
戶长 (戶長)	huzhang	hu-chang

212

Wade-Giles	Pinyin	Characters
hua-ch'iao kou-mai p'iao	huaqiao goumai piao	华侨购买票（华侨购买票）
hua-ch'iao shang-tien	huaqiao shangdian	华侨药店（华侨药店）
Huang-pu ts'un ti san nien	*Huangpu cun di san nian*	皇甫村的三年
huang-ts'e	huangce	黄册
chi	ji	几（几）
chi-pieh	jibie	级（级别）
chi-kuan	jiguan	籍贯
chi-t'i hu-chi	jiti huji	集体（体）户籍
chia-t'ing ch'u-shen	jiating chushen	家庭出身
chia-t'ing yung-liang chi-hua	jiating yongliang jihua	家庭用粮计（计划）（划）
chia-chang	jiazhang	家长（长）

213

Chinese Characters	*Pinyin* Romanizations	Wade-Giles Romanizations
检举说怪话 (检举说怪话)	jianju shuo guai hua	chien-chü shuo kuai hua
街道青年	jiedao qingnian	chieh-tao ch'ing-nien
金光大道	*Jin guang da dao*	*Chin kuang ta tao*
精神劲头	jingshen jitou	ching-shen chi-t'o
具有积极意义也可能具有消极意义 (具有积极意义也可能具有消极意义)	ju you jiji yiyi, ye keneng ju you xiaoji yiyi	chü yu chi-chi i-i, yeh k'o-neng chü yu hsiao-chi i-i
居民证 (証)	jumin zheng	chü-min cheng
老师 (师) 傅	lao shifu	lao shih-fu
老运动员 (老运动员)	lao yundong yuan	lao yün-tung yüan

214

	Laodong bao	*Lao-tung pao*
劳动报 (劳动報)		
理	li	li
理性认识 (理性認識)	li xing renshi	li hsing jen-shih
利欲熏心又冒险(險)去干	li yu xun xin you maoxian qu gan	li yü hsün hsin yu mao-hsien ch'ü kan
理论 (論)	lilun	li-lun
良民证 (證)	liangmin zheng	liang-min cheng
粮票	liangpiao	liang-p'iao
粮食部	liangshi bu	liang-shih pu
粮食管理所	liangshi guanli so	liang-shih kuan-li so
临(臨)时户口	linshi hukou	lin-shih hu-k'ou
柳青	Liu Qing	Liu Ch'ing
茅盾	Mao Dun	Mao Tun

Chinese Characters	*Pinyin* Romanizations	Wade-Giles Romanizations
美人计(計)	meiren ji	mei-jen chi
名	ming	ming
面(面)	mu	mou
问心的道德体 (體)验(驗)	neixin di dao de tiyan	nei-hsin ti tao-te t'i-yen
你这样做到什么有甚么意思 (你这样做到你有甚么意思)	ni zheiyang zuo dao di you shenmo yisi	ni che-yang tso tao ti yu shen-mo i-ssu
您不信世人做事情由于诚(誠) 或或不存私心的吗(嗎)	nin bu xin shiren zuo shi xi youyu chengyi huo bu cun sixin de ma?	nin pu hsin shih-jen tso shih hsi yu-yü ch'eng-i huo pu ts'un ssu-hsin ti ma?
起带头作用 (是带领作用)	qi daitou zuoyong	ch'i tai-t'ou tso-yung

ch'ien	qian	浅（淺）
ch'ien-i cheng	qianyi zheng	迁移证（遷移證）
ch'ing you k'o yüan	qing you ke yuan	情有可原
Ch'ing-nien pao	*Qingnian bao*	青年报（報）
ch'ün-chung hsüeh-hsiao	qunzhong xuexiao	群众学校（群衆學校）
jen pu wei chi t'ien chu ti mieh	ren bu wei ji tian zhu di mie	人不为己天诛地灭（人不爲己天誅地滅）
jen-chüeh	renjue	人爵
Jen-min jih-pao	*Renmin ribao*	人民日报（報）
jen-shih	renshi	认示（認識）
jen-shih shang ti tao-te tung-chi	renshi shang di daode dongji	认识上的道德动机（認識上的道德動機）
jih-yung-p'in p'iao	riyongpin piao	日用品票

Chinese Characters	Pinyin Romanizations	Wade-Giles Romanizations
肉票	roupiao	jou-p'iao
社会（會）青年	shehui qingnian	she-hui ch'ing-nien
社会主义现实主义（社会主我我现实主我）	shehui zhuyi xianshi zhuyi	she-hui chu-i hsien-shih chu-i
深	shen	shen
身份证（證）	shenfen zheng	shen-fen cheng
什么（麼）都出现（現）	shenmo dou chuxian	shen-mo tou ch'u-hsien
是不是比普通人得意	shi bu shi bi putong ren deyi?	shih pu shih pi p'u-t'ung jen te-i?
狮咁甘大个鼻（獅咁甘大的鼻）	shi gan da ge bi	shih kan ta ko pi

shih-yu p'iao	shiyou piao	食油票
shui-p'ing pi she-yüan kao	shuiping bi sheyuan gao	水平比社員（冒）高
shui-yu p'iao	shuiyou piao	水油票
ssu	si	思
ssu hui fu jan	si hui fu ran	死灰复燃
ssu-hsiang	sixiang	思想
ssu-hsiang p'in-chih	sixiang pinzhi	思想品质
ssu-hsiang wu-ch'i	sixiang wuqi	思想武器
T'ai-yang chao tsai Sang-kan ho shang	*Taiyang zhao zai Sanggan he shang*	太阳照在桑乾河上
t'ien-chüeh	tianjue	天爵
t'ien-chün	tianjun	天君

Chinese Characters	*Pinyin* Romanizations	Wade-Giles Romanizations
统购统销 （统购统销）	tonggou tongxiao	t'ung-kou t'ung-hsiao
铜墙铁壁 （铜墙铁壁）	*Tongqiang tiebi*	*T'ung-ch'iang t'ieh-pi*
同学（學）	tongxue	t'ung-hsüeh
拖拖拉拉慢吞吞	tuotuo la-la man tuntun	t'o-t'o la-la man t'un-t'un
文化程度	wenhua chengdu	wen-hua ch'eng-tu
下乡（鄉）	xiaxiang	hsia-hsiang
县（縣）	xian	hsien
现（現）管分子	xian guan fenzi	hsien kuan fen-tzu
香烟购（購）买（買）票	xiangyan goumai piao	hsiang-yen kou-mai p'iao

响应号召 (響應號召)	xiangying haozhao	hsiang-ying hao-chao
新闻(聞)日报(報)	*Xinwen ribao*	*Hsin-wen jih-pao*
行	xing	hsing
艳阳天 (豔陽天)	*Yanyang tian*	*Yen-yang t'ien*
意	yi	i
义(我)	yi	i
一棍子打死	yi gunzi da si	i kun-tzu ta ssu
意者心之所发(發)	yi zhe xin zhi suo fa	i che hsin chih so fa
一本通书(書)暗到老	yiben tongshu di dao lao	i-pen t'ung-shu ti tao lao
意思	yisi	i-ssu
意义(義)	yiyi	i-i
意志	yizhi	i-chih

Chinese Characters	Pinyin Romanizations	Wade-Giles Romanizations
因	yin	yin
因此运动就是一个接一个搁下去 （因此運動就是一個接一個搁下去）	yin ci yundong jiu yao yige jie yige gaoxiaqu	yin tz'u yün-tung chiu yao i-ko chieh i-ko kao-hsia-ch'ü
营（营）私舞弊	ying si wu bi	ying ssu wu pi
有意义（我）的	you yiyi di	yu i-i ti
元	yuan	yüan
缘份	yuanfen	yüan-fen
运动 （運動）	yundong	yün-tung
运（運）用	yunyong	yün-yung
再也不能复（復）用了	zai ye buneng fuyong le	tsai yeh pu-neng fu-yung le

che-ko tzu yu shen-mo i-ssu?	这个字有什么意思 (这个字有什么麻意思。)	zhiege zi you shenmo yisi?
cheng-ch'üeh ti tu-shu tung-chi	正确的读书动机 (正确的读书动机)	zhenque di dushu dongji
chih	志	zhi
chih shih hsin chih so chih i chih ch'ü ti	志是心之所之一直去底	zhi shi xin zhi suo zhi yi zhi qu di
chih chih fa tung shih i	知之发动是意， (知之是动是意。)	zhi zhi fa dong shi yi
Chou Li-po	周立波	Zhou Libo
Chou Yang	周扬	Zhou Yang
tzu ming pu fan	自命不凡	zi ming bu fan
tzu-fa hu	自发（3发）乎	zifa hu
tsou tzu fa	走自发（3发）	zou zi fa
tsu ho tso-yung	阻碍作用	zu he zuoyong
tso san kung	作散工	zuo san gong

AMY AUERBACHER WILSON has been Lecturer in Sociology at Douglass College, Rutgers University, since 1973. She has published materials on Chinese society dealing with youth and women and is currently doing research on major mass organizations in China. Ms. Wilson received an A.B. from Douglass College and an M.A. from Princeton University. She is completing a Ph.D. at Princeton University, specializing in Sociology and East Asian Studies.

SIDNEY LEONARD GREENBLATT is Assistant Professor of Sociology at Drew University, Madison, New Jersey. Professor Greenblatt is editor of *Chinese Sociology and Anthropology*, a quarterly journal of translation published by International Arts and Sciences Press, White Plains, New York. He is also editor and author of *The People of Taihang: An Anthology of Family Histories* (1976), "Organizational Elites: Peking University, 1949-1964" in Robert Scalapino, ed., *Elites in the People's Republic of China* (1972), reviews in Political Science Quarterly, and papers delivered at various conferences in the social sciences and the China field. Professor Greenblatt holds a B.A. from Harper College of the State University of New York and an M.A. and East Asian Institute Certificate from Columbia University.

RICHARD WHITTINGHAM WILSON is Professor of Political Science and Director of International Programs at Rutgers University. Dr. Wilson has published widely in the area of political socialization. In addition to writing numerous articles, he is author of *Learning to be Chinese* (1970) and *The Moral State* (1974). Dr. Wilson received his A.B., M.A., and Ph.D. from Princeton University.

GORDON BENNETT is Associate Professor of Government at the University of Texas at Austin. His main research and writing on China has been on the subjects of mass campaigns, elite studies, and the politics of financial and commercial issues. His most important works are *Red Guard: The Political Biography of Dai Hsiao* (with Ronald Montaperto, 1971) and *Yundong: Mass Campaigns in Chinese Communist Leadership* (1976). He has lived in Taiwan and Hong Kong for a total of three years, studying the Chinese language and interviewing refugees. He visited the People's Republic of China in June 1976 as a member of the Liaoning Earthquake Study Team of the National Academy of Sciences.

ALFRED H. BLOOM is Assistant Professor of Psychology and Linguistics and Director of the Linguistics Program at Swarthmore College, Swarthmore,

Pennsylvania. He received his Ph.D. in Social Psychology from Harvard University in 1974. Dr. Bloom has written in the areas of political psychology, social psychology, and psycholinguistics. His articles have appeared in *The Handbook of Political Psychology, The Journal of Social Psychology* and the *Papers of the Peace Science Society (International)*.

CHARLES HOFFMANN is Professor of Economics at the State University of New York at Stony Brook. Before coming to Stony Brook in 1963, he was a member of the Economics Department at Queens College of the City University of New York. Dr. Hoffmann's most recent books are *Work Incentive Practices and Policies in the People's Republic of China, 1953-1965* (1967), *The Depression of the Nineties* (1970), and *The Chinese Worker* (1974). His articles and reviews have appeared in *The China Quarterly, Industrial Relations, Asian Survey, Journal of Economic Issues, Journal of Economic History, Current Scene, Journal of Economic Literature,* and the *Annals.* Dr. Hoffmann holds a B.A. from Queens College and an M.A. and Ph.D. from Columbia University.

JOE C. HUANG has done research on contemporary Chinese literature in the last ten years and has published articles in a number of journals, including *The China Quarterly, Far Eastern Economic Review,* and *Saturday Review.* Dr. Huang, author of *Heroes and Villians in Communist China: The Contemporary Chinese Novel as a Reflection of Life*, is now working on a book about post-1949 Chinese theater.

VICTOR H. LI is Shelton Professor of International Legal Studies and Director of the Center for East Asian Studies at Stanford University. His writings deal with the Chinese legal system and Chinese attitudes toward international law and foreign trade. Dr. Li holds a B.A. and J.D. from Columbia University and an LL.M. and S.J.D. from Harvard University.

DONALD J. MUNRO is Professor of Philosophy at the University of Michigan, where he has taught since 1964. Dr. Munro has published widely in the areas of classical Chinese philosophy, Chinese Marxism, and contemporary Chinese educational theory and practice. His publications include *The Concept of Man in Early China* (1969) and *The Concept of Man in Contemporary China* (forthcoming). Dr. Munro received his A.B. degree from Harvard College and his Ph.D. from Columbia University.

LYNN T. WHITE, III is an Assistant Professor in the Departments of Politics and East Asian Studies, and in the Woodrow Wilson School of Public and International Affairs, at Princeton University. He has worked at the University of California's Center for Chinese Studies, at the Center for Southeast Asian Studies of Kyoto University, and at Universities Service Centre in Hong Kong. He has written articles for the *American Political Science Review*, the *Journal of Asian Studies*, and other journals and collections. He specializes in the local affairs of the city of Shanghai, and his book on that subject is in press.

FACTIONAL AND COALITION POLITICS IN CHINA:
The Cultural Revolution and Its Aftermath
Y. C. Chang

A SURVEY OF CHINESE-AMERICAN MANPOWER
AND EMPLOYMENT
Betty Lee Sung

MASS MEDIA IN BLACK AFRICA: Philosophy and
Control
Dennis L. Wilcox

EDUCATION AND THE MASS MEDIA IN THE SOVIET
UNION AND EASTERN EUROPE
edited by
Bohdan Harasymiw

POLITICAL SOCIALIZATION IN EASTERN EUROPE:
A Comparative Framework
edited by
Ivan Volgyes

THE MAOIST EDUCATIONAL REVOLUTION
Theodore Hsi-en Chen